Lean Six Sigma

4th Edition

T0243547

by Martin Brenig-Jones and Jo Dowdall

for dummies®
A Wiley Brand

Lean Six Sigma For Dummies®, 4th Edition

Published by: **John Wiley & Sons, Inc.**, 111 River Street, Hoboken, NJ 07030-5774, www.wiley.com

Copyright © 2022 by John Wiley & Sons, Inc., Hoboken, New Jersey

Published simultaneously in Canada

For general information on our other products and services, please contact our Customer Care Department within the U.S. at 877-762-2974, outside the U.S. at 317-572-3993, or fax 317-572-4002. For technical support, please visit https://hub.wiley.com/community/support/dummies.

Wiley publishes in a variety of print and electronic formats and by print-on-demand. Some material included with standard print versions of this book may not be included in e-books or in print-on-demand. If this book refers to media such as a CD or DVD that is not included in the version you purchased, you may download this material at http://booksupport.wiley.com. For more information about Wiley products, visit www.wiley.com.

Library of Congress Control Number: 2021946527

ISBN 978-1-119-79671-8 (pbk); ISBN 978-1-119-79672-5 (ebk); ISBN 978-1-119-79673-2 (ebk)

SKY10030667_102021

Contents at a Glance

Table of Contents

Introduction

Lean Six Sigma provides a rigorous and structured approach to help manage and improve quality and performance, and to solve potentially complex problems. It helps you use the right tools, in the right place and in the right way, not just in process improvement projects but also in your day-to-day work. Lean Six Sigma really is about getting key principles and concepts into the DNA and lifeblood of your organization so that it becomes a natural part of how you do things.

This book is for practitioners using Lean Six Sigma as well as those who are seeking to "lead and live" Lean Six Sigma in their organizations.

We began to blend Lean and Six Sigma together more than 20 years ago, welcoming a pragmatic rather than purist approach. We discovered how essential it has been to consider people and Change Management when improving processes too — leading to higher levels of acceptance and more effective change.

In this 4th Edition of *Lean Six Sigma For Dummies*, we have added a few more ingredients into the cocktail. You can find out how Agile approaches (and an Agile mindset) can accelerate results. We also discuss how Design Thinking approaches, tools, and techniques for creativity can encourage different thinking about the way the work gets done. This stuff really works.

About This Book

This book makes Lean Six Sigma easy to understand and apply. We wrote it because we know that Lean Six Sigma can help organizations of all shapes and sizes, both private and public, improve their performance in meeting their customers' requirements. We know this because we have seen it!

We also wanted to demonstrate a pragmatic approach and the genuine synergy achieved through the combination of Lean and Six Sigma. For some reason unknown to us, a few people still feel they can use only Lean or Six Sigma, but not both. How wrong they are! In this book, you can discover how to create genuine synergy by applying the principles of Lean and Six Sigma together in your day-to-day operations and activities. And not just that: Change Management, Agile, Design Thinking and Design for Six Sigma are included too. In the true spirit of Continuous Improvement, we are always looking to enhance the approach, adapt the toolkit, and learn as we go.

Foolish Assumptions

In Lean Six Sigma, avoiding the tendency to jump to conclusions and make assumptions about things is crucial. Lean Six Sigma really is about managing by fact. Despite that, we've made some assumptions about why you may have bought this book:

>> You're contemplating applying Lean Six Sigma in your business or organization, and you need to understand what you're getting yourself into.

>> Your business is implementing Lean Six Sigma and you need to get up to speed. Perhaps you've been lined up to participate in the program in some way.

>> Your business has already implemented either Lean or Six Sigma and you're intrigued by what you might be missing.

>> You're considering a career or job change and feel that your CV or resume will look much better if you can somehow incorporate Lean or Six Sigma into it.

>> You're looking to boost the results and progress of your Lean Six Sigma program and are considering how approaches like Change Management, Agile, and Design Thinking can help.

>> You're a student in business, operations or industrial engineering, for example, and you realize that Lean Six Sigma could help shape your future.

We also assume that you realize that Lean Six Sigma demands a rigorous and structured approach to understanding how your work gets done and how well it gets done, and how to go about the improvement of your processes.

Icons Used In This Book

Throughout the book, you'll see small symbols called *icons* in the margins; these highlight special types of information. We use these to help you better understand and apply the material. Look out for the following icons:

Keep your eyes on the target to find tips and tricks we share to help you make the most of Lean Six Sigma.

TIP

Bear these important points in mind as you get to grips with Lean Six Sigma.

REMEMBER

Throughout this book, we share true stories of how different companies have implemented Lean Six Sigma to improve their processes.

EXAMPLE

This icon highlights potential pitfalls to avoid.

WARNING

Beyond This Book

In addition to the material in the print or e-book you're reading right now, this book also comes with some access-anywhere goodies on the web. To view the free Cheat Sheet, go to www.dummies.com and type "Lean Six Sigma For Dummies Cheat Sheet" in the search box.

Where to Go From Here

In theory, when you read you begin with ABC, and when you sing you begin with doh-ray-me (thank you Julie Andrews). But with a *For Dummies* book, you can begin where you like. Each part and, indeed, each chapter is self-contained, which means you can start with whichever parts or chapters interest you the most.

That said, if you're new to the topic, starting at the beginning makes sense. Either way, lots of cross-referencing throughout the book helps you to see how things fit together and put them in the right context.

1

Understanding Lean Six Sigma

Grasp the basics of Lean and Six Sigma.

Comprehend exactly what "sigma" means and why the term is important in Lean Six Sigma.

Get a clear picture of the synergy created by merging Lean and Six Sigma, and understand the key principles underpinning the approach.

Examine the process improvement method known as DMAIC: Define, Measure, Analyze, Improve, and Control.

Get ready to begin by defining the problems you want to solve using Lean Six Sigma.

Chapter 1

Defining Lean Six Sigma

Throughout this book, we cover the tools and techniques available to help you achieve real, sustainable improvement in your organization. In this chapter, we aim to move you down a path of different thinking that gets your improvement taste buds tingling. We look at the main principles behind Lean and Six Sigma and what today's "Lean Six Sigma" is made up of. We'll also introduce some of the main concepts and terminology to help you on your way.

Introducing Lean Thinking

Lean thinking focuses on enhancing value for the customer by improving and smoothing the process flow (covered in Chapter 11) and eliminating waste (discussed in Chapter 10). Lean thinking has evolved since Henry Ford's first production line, and much of the development has been led by Toyota through the Toyota Production System (TPS). Toyota built on Ford's production ideas, moving from high volume, low variety, to high variety, low volume.

Although Lean thinking is usually seen as being a manufacturing concept and application, many of the tools and techniques were originally developed in service organizations. These include, for example, spaghetti diagrams, and the visual system used by supermarkets to replenish shelves. Indeed, it was a supermarket that helped shape the thinking behind the Toyota Production System. During a tour to General Motors and Ford, Kiichiro Toyoda and Taiichi Ohno visited Piggly

Wiggly, an American supermarket, and noticed *Just in Time* and *kanban* being applied. This innovation enabled Piggly Wiggly customers to "buy what they need at any time" and avoided the store holding excess stock.

TIP

Kanban is a Japanese word meaning "card you can see." At the Piggly Wiggly, it was a card that provided the signal to order more stock. You'll see kanbans turning up again in Chapter 16 when we look at how Agile principles and approaches can be used to accelerate Lean Six Sigma projects.

Lean is called "Lean" not because things are stripped to the bone. Lean isn't a recipe for your organization to slash its costs, although it will likely lead to reduced costs and better value for the customer. We trace the concept of the word "Lean" back to 1987, when John Krafcik (who later led Google's self driving car project) was working as a researcher for MIT as part of the International Motor Vehicle Program. Krafcik needed a label for the TPS phenomenon that described what the system did. On a white board, he wrote the performance attributes of the Toyota system compared with traditional mass production. TPS:

>> Needed less human effort to design products and services.

>> Required less investment for a given amount of production capacity.

>> Created products with fewer delivered defects.

>> Used fewer suppliers.

>> Went from concept to launch, order to delivery and problem to repair in less time and with less human effort.

>> Needed less inventory at every process step.

>> Caused fewer employee injuries.

Krafcik commented:

It needs less of everything to create a given amount of value, so let's call it Lean.

And just like that, Lean was born.

Bringing on the basics of Lean

Figure 1-1 shows the Toyota Production System, highlighting various tools and Japanese Lean thinking terms that we use throughout this book. In this chapter we provide some brief descriptions to introduce the Lean basics and the TPS.

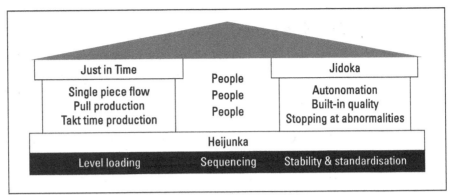

FIGURE 1-1:
The TPS house.

Toyota's Taiichi Ohno describes the TPS approach very effectively:

> *All we are doing is looking at a timeline from the moment the customer gives us an order to the point when we collect the cash. And we are reducing that timeline by removing the non-value adding wastes.*

The TPS approach really is about understanding how the work gets done, finding ways of doing it better, smoother and faster, and closing the time gap between the start and end points of our processes. And it applies to any process. Whether you're working in the public or private sector, in service, transactional or manufacturing processes really doesn't matter.

Think about your own processes for a moment. Do you feel that some unnecessary steps or activities seem to waste time and effort?

We must point out, however, that simply adopting the tools and techniques of the TPS isn't enough to sustain improvement and embed the principles and thinking into your organization. Toyota chairperson Fujio Cho provides a clue as to what's also needed:

> *The key to the Toyota way is not any of the individual elements but all the elements together as a system. It must be practiced every day in a very consistent manner — not in spurts. We place the highest value on taking action and implementation. By improvement based on action, one can rise to the higher level of practice and knowledge.*

Perhaps this is why Toyota didn't mind sharing the secrets of their success. It might be easy to replicate certain practices and adopt certain concepts, but it is not easy to replicate a true culture of Continuous Improvement.

Building people first

"First we build people," stated Toyota chairperson Fujio Cho. "Then we build cars." Figure 1-1 shows that people are at the heart of TPS. The system focuses on developing exceptional people and teams that follow the company's philosophy to gain exceptional results. Consider the following:

>> Toyota creates a strong and stable culture wherein values and beliefs are widely shared and lived out over many years.

>> Toyota works constantly to reinforce that culture.

>> Toyota involves cross-functional teams to solve problems.

>> Toyota keeps teaching individuals how to work together.

Being Lean means involving people in the process, equipping them to be able, and feel able, to challenge and improve their processes and the way they work. Never waste the creative potential of people!

Looking at the lingo

You can see from Figure 1-1 that Lean thinking involves a certain amount of jargon — some of it Japanese. This section defines the various terms to help you get Lean thinking as soon as possible:

>> **Standardization** seeks to reduce variation in the way the work is carried out, so that everyone operates the process in the "one best way." This highlights the importance of following a *standard operating process* or procedure. In the spirit of Continuous Improvement, of course the "one best way" of carrying out the process will keep changing, as people in the process identify better ways of doing the work. You need to ensure the new "one best way" is understood and fully deployed.

>> **Heijunka** encompasses the idea of smoothing processing and production by considering leveling and sequencing:

- **Leveling** involves smoothing the volume of production in the production period, in order to reduce the ups and downs and peaks and troughs that can make planning difficult. Among other things, leveling seeks to prevent "end-of-period" peaks, where production is initially slow at the beginning of the month, but then quickens in the last days of a sale or accounting period, for example.

- **Sequencing** may well involve mixing the types of work processed. So, for example, when setting up new loans in a bank, the type of loan being processed is mixed to better match customer demand, and help ensure applications are actioned in date order. So often, people are driven by internal efficiency targets, whereby they process the "simple tasks" first to get them out of the way and "hit their numbers," leaving the more difficult cases to be processed later on. This means tasks are not processed in date order, and people are reluctant to get down and tackle a pile of difficult cases at the end of the production period, making things even worse for the customer and the business.

» **Jidoka** concerns prevention; it links closely with techniques such as the Failure Mode Effects Analysis (FMEA), which are covered in Chapter 13. Jidoka has two main elements, and both seek to prevent work continuing when something goes wrong:

- **Autonomation** allows machines or processes to operate autonomously, by shutting down if something goes wrong. This concept is also known as automation with human intelligence. The "no" in auto*no*mation is often underlined to highlight the fact that no defects are allowed to pass to a follow-on process. An early example hails from 1902, when Sakichi Toyoda, the founder of the Toyota group, invented an automated loom that stopped whenever a thread broke. A simple example today is a printer stopping processing copy when the ink runs out.

  Without this concept, automation has the potential to allow a large number of defects to be created very quickly, especially if processing is in batches (see "Single piece flow" below).

- **Stop at every abnormality** is the second element of Jidoka. The employee can stop an automated or manual line if they spot an error. At Toyota, every employee is empowered to "stop the line," perhaps following the identification of a special cause on a control chart (see Chapter 8).

  Forcing everything to stop and immediately focus on a problem can seem painful at first, but doing so is an effective way to quickly get at the root cause of issues. Again, this can be especially important if you're processing in batches.

» **Just in Time (JIT)** provides the other pillar of the TPS house. JIT involves providing the customer with what's needed, at the right time, in the right location and in the right quantity. The concept applies to both internal and external customers. JIT comprises three main elements:

- **Single piece flow** means allowing single units of product to flow through the process step by step. When processing in batches, batches (or bundles) of individual cases are processed at each step and are passed along the process only after an entire batch has been completed. Delays are increased when the batches travel around the organization, both in terms of the transport time and the length of time they sit waiting to be actioned. At any given time, most of the units or work items in a batch are sitting idle, waiting to be processed. This represents excess inventory and can be costly. What's more, errors can neither be picked up nor addressed quickly; if they occur, they often occur in volume. And, of course, this also delays identifying the root cause. With single piece flow, we can get to the root cause analysis faster, which helps prevent a common error recurring throughout the process.

In a single piece flow system each person performs an operation and makes a quick quality check before moving their output to the next person in the following process. Naturally this concept also applies to automated operations where inline checks can be carried out. If a defect is detected, Jidoka is enacted: the process is stopped, and immediate action is taken to correct the situation, taking countermeasures to prevent reoccurrence. This concept is a real change of thinking that moves us away from processing in batches.

- **Pull production** is the second element of JIT. Each process takes what it needs from the preceding process only when it needs it and in the exact quantity. The customer pulls the supply and helps avoid being swamped by items that aren't needed at a particular time.

  Pull production reduces the need for potentially costly storage space. All too often, overproduction in one process, perhaps to meet local efficiency targets, results in problems downstream. This increases work in progress, and creates bottlenecks. Overproduction is one of the "eight wastes" covered in Chapter 10.

- **Takt time** is the third element of JIT, providing an important additional measure. It tells you how quickly to action things, given the volume of customer demand. *Takt* is German for "rate." It helps to think about a metronome that musicians use to keep to a consistent tempo, so the takt time is the frequency at which a product or service must be completed in order to meet customer needs.

Taking the strain out of constraints

Much of the focus in Lean thinking is on understanding and improving the flow of processes and eliminating non-value-added activities. Eliyahu Goldratt's *theory of constraints* (explained more fully in Chapter 11) provides a way to address and tackle bottlenecks that slow the process flow. By addressing what is getting in the way, you can enable a smooth flow, and deliver value to the customer.

Considering the customer

The customer, not your organization, specifies value. Value is what your customer is willing to pay for. To satisfy your customer, your organization has to provide the right products and services, at the right time, at the right price and at the right quality. To do this, and to do so consistently, you need to identify and understand how your processes work, improve and smooth the flow, eliminate unnecessary steps in the process, and reduce or prevent waste such as rework.

Imagine the processes involved in your own organization, beginning with a customer order (market demand) and ending with cash in the bank (invoice or bill paid). Ask yourself the following questions:

>> How many steps are involved?

>> Do you need all the steps?

>> Are you sure?

>> How can you reduce the number of steps and the time involved from start to finish?

Perusing the principles of Lean thinking

Lean thinking has five key principles:

>> Understand the customer and their perception of value.

>> Identify and understand the value stream for each process and the waste within it.

>> Enable the value to flow.

>> Let the customer pull the value through the processes, according to their needs.

>> Continuously pursue perfection (Continuous Improvement).

You'll see that the principles are universal, as they apply to any type of process in any type of organization. They are also timeless, as they're as relevant now as they ever were. In Chapter 2, we show how the principles combine with the key principles of Six Sigma to form *Lean Six Sigma*.

Sussing Six Sigma

Six Sigma is a systematic and robust approach to improvement, which focuses on the customer and other key stakeholders. Six Sigma seeks to improve processes so that they deliver consistent, reliable outputs. It was developed in the 1980s within

Motorola and was widely used by General Electric. When Jack Welch, former General Electric CEO, introduced Six Sigma, he said:

We are going to shift the paradigm from fixing products to fixing and developing processes, so they produce nothing but perfection or close to it.

Considering the key elements of Six Sigma

Some simple principles underpin Six Sigma:

» **Understand the CTQs of your customers and stakeholders.** To deliver the best customer experience, you need to know who your customers are and what they want — their requirements and expectations. *CTQ* is short for Critical To Quality, and CTQs are the performance requirements that matter most to your customers. To understand these you need to listen to and understand the *voice of the customer* (VOC). Chapter 4 contains more information on these important elements.

» **Understand your organization's processes and ensure they reflect your customers' CTQs.** You need to know how your processes work and what they're trying to achieve. A clear objective for each process should exist, focused on the customer requirements (the CTQs).

» **Manage by fact and reduce variation.** Measurement and management by fact enables more effective decision-making. By understanding variation, you can work out when and when not to take action.

» **Involve and equip the people in the process.** To be truly effective you need to equip the people in your organization to be able, and to feel able, to challenge and improve their processes and the way they work.

» **Undertake improvement activity in a systematic way.** Working systematically helps you avoid jumping to conclusions and solutions. Six Sigma uses a process called DMAIC (Define, Measure, Analyze, Improve and Control) to improve existing processes. We cover DMAIC in Chapter 2. In designing new processes, we use DMADV (which is covered in Chapter 14).

You'll recognize some similarities with the principles of Lean outlined earlier in the chapter, and some new concepts. Let's look at those concepts in a little more detail, focusing on measurement and variation in particular. Some of the content might seem a little heavy — we want you to have a clear explanation of the concepts — but remember that pragmatism is a theme of this book.

Getting to grips with variation

The *standard deviation* is a measure that reveals the amount of variation. It is represented as the lower-case Greek letter σ (sigma) and describes the average dispersal of the individual data points from their overall average. Why is this helpful? The smaller the standard deviation value is, the less variation there is. Conversely, the larger the value, the more variation. By understanding the amount and type of variation in our results, we can get closer to understanding the "behavior" of the process (or the thing we are measuring) and what this means for customers.

Introducing a simple example

Suppose you want to understand the cycle time (lead time) of a process in your organization in days. You could collect a representative sample of data (more on sampling in Chapter 7), and from that sample, calculate the average (or mean) number of days. Calculating the average difference between each cycle time in your data set and the overall average cycle time will give you the standard deviation. The standard deviation is always expressed as the same unit as the "thing" you are measuring; in this case we're talking about days.

Figure 1-2 shows the time taken to process the orders. The cycle time varies from as short as one day to as long as seven days. Each of the data points represents a customer's experience of the process. As well as seeing how much performance varies, you can also see the "shape" of the data. This data looks normally distributed. In a normal distribution, the shape is symmetrical around the mean, and the data has a 50-percent chance of falling either side of it. Sometimes this shape is referred to as a *bell curve* or a *Gaussian distribution.* Many things that are measured fall into this shape — for example, the heights of people, the size of snowflakes, and IQ scores.

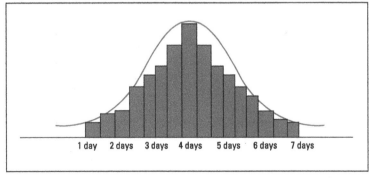

FIGURE 1-2:
Histogram showing the time taken to process orders.

© *Martin Brenig-Jones and Jo Dowdall*

When the data is normally distributed, we can understand the likely percentage of the population within plus one or minus one standard deviation from the average (or mean), plus two or minus two standard deviations from the average, and so on. Assuming your sample is representative, you can see how your data provides a good picture of the process cycle time. You find that approximately two-thirds of them are between 3 days and 5 days, about 95 percent are in the range of 2 days to 6 days, and about 99.73 percent are between 1 day and 7 days. This is illustrated in Figure 1-3.

The formula used to calculate the standard deviation is shown in Figure 1-4. It looks a little scary at first glance, but as with all formulas, when you start to break it down it becomes more accessible.

x in the formula represents your individual data points

x_i represents each x from x_1 up to x_n

n represents the number of data points in your data set

$\bar{x}$ represents the average (mean) of your data points

Σ represents the "sum of"

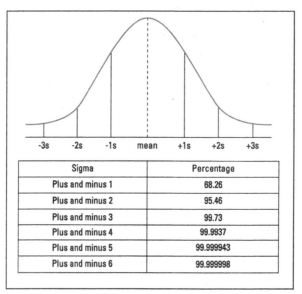

Sigma	Percentage
Plus and minus 1	68.26
Plus and minus 2	95.46
Plus and minus 3	99.73
Plus and minus 4	99.9937
Plus and minus 5	99.999943
Plus and minus 6	99.999998

FIGURE 1-3: Standard deviation.

© Martin Brenig-Jones and Jo Dowdall

As with most things in life, tackling the formula in stages makes it easier, so let's have a go.

Start by adding up all of the data points you have. For example, if the data points are 5, 6, 7, 8 and 9 (we'll demonstrate with some simple ones), the sum is 35. The number of data points we have is 5, so the value of n in the formula is 5. We can then work out the mean (average or $\bar{x}$) of those data points, and the mean ($\bar{x}$) is 7 (because $\frac{35}{5} = 7$). Are you with us so far? Great!

Next we need to work out the $x_i - \bar{x}$ part. This means subtracting the $\bar{x}$ value (7) from each of our data points. $5 - 7 = -2$, $6 - 7 = -1$, $7 - 7 = 0$, and so on. All is going well, but we now have some negative values in the mix, and we need to get rid of them. This is done by squaring the numbers we've just worked out. So $-2 * -2 = 4$, $-1 * -1 = 1$, $0 * 0 = 0$, and so on. Next, add together all of the answers we just got. If you're still with us and have done that bit, you should get 10. So now we have real numbers to work with, and the numbers that we put into the formula are $\frac{10}{5}$ (Yes, we did all that work to get to 10 divided by 5.) 10 divided by 5 is 2. We then, finally, take the square root of 2 to get the standard deviation value of 1.41. Hooray!

Note that there are two versions of the standard deviation formula included in Figure 1-4. The first is used when we have a sample of data, and the second is used when we have the entire population. The data set we used to work through the example above was very small! If we were using the formula for a sample, instead of using n we'd use $n - 1$. So we'd end up with $\frac{10}{4}$, which is 2.5. The square root of 2.5 is 1.58.

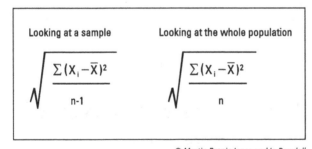

FIGURE 1-4: Standard deviation formula.

In practice, when the sample size is more than 30, there's little difference between using n or $n - 1$. When we refer to a "population," this could relate to people or things that have already been processed, like, for example, a population of completed and dispatched policy documents.

TIP

Now for some good news: You can use a scientific calculator, *Excel*, or any number of online calculators to work out the standard deviation of your data, without having to worry about this formula.

The Process Sigma values are calculated by looking at our process performance against the customer requirements, which we cover in the next section.

Considering customer requirements

So far so good, but without understanding the customer requirements, it's not possible to tell whether cycle time performance is good or bad.

Let's say the customer expects delivery in five days or less. In Lean Six Sigma speak, key customer requirements are called *CTQs, (Critical To Quality)*. We discuss CTQs in Chapter 2 and describe them in more detail in Chapter 4, but essentially they express the customers' requirements in a way that is measurable. CTQs are a vital element in Lean Six Sigma and provide the basis of your process measurement set. In our example, the CTQ is five days or less, but the average performance in Figure 1-2 is four days. Remember that this is the average; your customers experience the *whole range* of your performance.

Too many organizations use averages as a convenient way of making their performance sound better than it really is.

In the example provided, all the orders that take more than five days are *defects* for the customer in Six Sigma language. Orders that take five days or less meet the CTQ. We show this situation in Figure 1-5. We could express the performance as the percentage or proportion of orders processed within five days or we can work out the *Process Sigma value*. The Process Sigma value is calculated by looking at your performance against the customer requirement, the CTQ, and taking into account the number of defects involved where you fail to meet it (that is, all those cases that took more than five days).

We explain the Process Sigma calculation in the next section.

Calculating Process Sigma values

Here are three good reasons for calculating Process Sigma:

» It makes you consider customers' performance needs. How long are they prepared to wait for their order to be processed?

» It makes it easier to compare the performance of different processes. If different metrics are used for each process, comparison is tricky, and it's difficult to prioritize improvements. Process Sigma is a standard quality metric that can be used to measure any process.

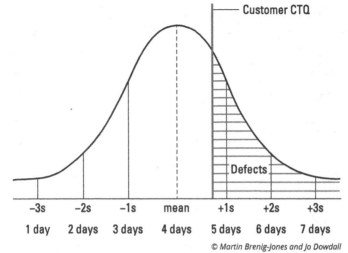

FIGURE 1-5: Highlighting defects.

» It supports decision-making on what performance needs to be, rather than using an arbitrary target. For example, 99.9 percent success sounds impressive, but it would mean 100 plane crashes worldwide every day, and one hour without electricity every month.

The Process Sigma value represents the population of cases that meet the CTQs right first time. Sigma values are expressed as *defects per million opportunities* (DPMO) to emphasize the need for world-class performance.

Not all organizations using Six Sigma calculate Process Sigma values. Some organizations just use the number of defects or the percentage of orders meeting CTQs to show their performance. Either way, if benchmarking is to be meaningful, the calculations must be made in a consistent manner.

Figure 1-6 includes *yield* figures — the right first time (or 'first pass yield') percentage. You can see that Six Sigma performance equates to only 3.4 DPMO.

Calculating the DPMO for your process measures quality using *defects* rather than *defectives*. This is an important distinction that requires more explanation.

Let's say your customer has several CTQs relating to an order — for example not just the speed (cycle time) but also accuracy and completeness. Each CTQ represents a defect opportunity. Thus, more than one defect may occur in the transaction. You could have a situation whereby the speed CTQ was met, but the accuracy and completeness CTQs were missed. The outcome would be one *defective* delivery (as a result of these two *defects*).

Yield	Sigma	Defects per 1,000,000	Defects per 100,000	Defects per 10,000	Defects per 1,000	Defects per 100
99.99966%	6.0	3.4	0.34	0.034	0.0034	0.00034
99.9995%	5.9	5	0.5	0.05	0.005	0.0005
99.9992%	5.8	8	0.8	0.08	0.008	0.0008
99.9990%	5.7	10	1	0.1	0.01	0.001
99.9980%	5.6	20	2	0.2	0.02	0.002
99.9970%	5.5	.30	3	0.3	0.03	0.003
99.9960%	5.4	40	4	0.4	0.04	0.004
99.9930%	5.3	70	7	0.7	0.07	0.007
99.9900%	5.2	100	10	1.0	0.1	0.01
99.9850%	5.1	150	15	1.5	0.15	0.015
99.9770%	5.0	230	23	2.3	0.23	0.023
99.670%	4.9	330	33	3.3	0.33	0.033
99.9520&	4.8	480	48	4.8	0.48	0.048
99.9320%	4.7	680	68	6.8	0.68	0.068
99.9040%	4.6	960	96	9.6	0.96	0.096
99.8650%	4.5	1,350	135	13.5	1.35	0.135
99.8140%	4.4	1,860	186	18.6	1.86	0.186
99.7450%	4.3	2,550	255	25.5	2.55	0.255
99.6540%	4.2	3,460	346	34.6	3.46	0.346
99.5340%	4.1	4,660	466	46.6	4.66	0.466
99.3790%	4.0	6,210	621	62.1	6.21	0.621
99.1810%	3.9	8,190	819	81.9	8.19	0.819
98.930%	3.8	10,700	1,070	107	10.7	1.07
98.610%	3.7	13.900	1.390	139	13.9	1.39
98.220%	3.6	17,800	1,780	178	17.8	1.78
97.730%	3.5	22,700	2,270	227	22.7	2.27
97.130%	3.4	28,700	2,870	287	28.7	2.87
96.410%	3.3	35,900	3,590	359	35.9	3.59
95.540%	3.2	44,600	4,460	446	44.6	4.46
94.520%	3.1	54,800	5,480	548	54.8	5.48
93.320%	3.0	66,800	6,680	668	66.8	6.68
91.920%	2.9	80,800	8,080	808	80.8	8.08
90.320%	2.8	96,800	9,680	968	96.8	9.68
88.50%	2.7	115,000	11,500	1,150	115	11.5
86.50%	2.6	135,000	13,500	1,350	135	13.5
84.20%	2.5	158,000	15,800	1,580	158	15.8
81.60%	2.4	184,000	18,400	1,840	184	18.4
78.80%	2.3	212,000	21,200	2,120	212	21.2
75.80%	2.2	242,000	24,200	2,420	242	24.2
72.60%	2.1	274,000	27,400	2,740	274	27.4
69.20%	2.0	308,000	30,800	3,080	308	30.8
65.60%	1.9	344,000	34,400	3,440	344	34.4
61.80%	1.8	382,000	38,200	3,820	382	38.2
58.00%	1.7	420,000	42,000	4,200	420	42
54.00%	1.6	460,000	46,000	4,600	460	46
50%	1.5	500,000	50,000	5,000	500	50
46%	1.4	540,000	54,000	5,400	540	54
43%	1.3	570,000	57,000	5,700	570	57
39%	1.2	610,000	61,000	6,100	610	61
35%	1.1	650,000	65,000	6,500	650	65
31%	1.0	690,000	69,000	6,900	690	69
28%	0.9	720,000	72,000	7,200	720	72
25%	0.8	750,000	75,000	7,500	750	75
22%	0.7	780,000	78,000	7,800	780	78
19%	0.6	810,000	81,000	8,100	810	81
16%	0.5	840,000	84,000	8,400	840	84
14%	0.4	860,000	86,000	8,600	860	86
12%	0.3	880,000	88,000	8,800	880	88
10%	0.2	900,000	90,000	9,000	900	90
8%	0.1	920,000	92,000	9,200	920	92

FIGURE 1-6: Abridged Process Sigma conversion table.

© Martin Brenig-Jones and Jo Dowdall

In calculating sigma values for your processes, you need to understand the following key terms:

» **Unit:** The item produced or processed.

» **Defect:** Any event that does not meet the CTQ.

» **Defect opportunity:** Any event that provides a chance of not meeting a customer CTQ. The number of defect opportunities will equal the number of CTQs.

» **Defective:** A unit with one or more defects.

You can work out your Process Sigma performance against the CTQs as shown in Figure 1-7. We have a sample of 500 processed units. The customer has three CTQs, so we have three defect opportunities. The CTQs are related to speed, accuracy and completeness. We find 57 defects. With software, you can determine a precise Process Sigma value, but with the abridged table in Figure 1-6, find the sigma value that's closest to your DPMO number of 38000. As you can see, this is 3.3.

FIGURE 1-7:
Calculating
Process Sigma
values.

⚬ Number of units processed	N=500
⚬ Total number of defects made (include defects made and later fixed)	D=57
⚬ Number of defect opportunities per unit (equate to CTQs)	O=3
⚬ Calculate # defects per million opportunities	$\text{DPMO} = 1{,}000{,}000 \times \dfrac{D}{(N \times O)}$
	$= 1{,}000{,}000 \times \dfrac{57}{(500) \times (3)}$
	$= 38000$
⚬ Look up process sigma in sigma conversation table (see Figure 1-6)	$\text{Sigma} = 3.3$

© Martin Brenig-Jones and Jo Dowdall

There is a small quirk to be aware of here. A Process Sigma and standard deviation are not quite the same thing. This results from Motorola adjusting the sigma conversion tables to reflect the variation they observed in their processes over the long term, after studying it for several years. The adjustment is referred to as a "1.5 sigma shift," reflecting the extent of the shift in performance. Although this adjustment related to Motorola's processes, everyone adopting Six Sigma has also adopted the adjusted sigma scale.

When we talk about Six Sigma performance before the adjustment, we're talking about performance data within plus or minus six standard deviations of the average, which embrace 99.999998 per cent of the data. This is the percentage of cases that are right first time in terms of meeting the requirements of the customer. It equates to 0.002 DPMO! Even with the adjustment, we're still looking at a truly demanding standard, with 99.999666 per cent of cases right first time in meeting the CTQs.

Bringing Lean and Six Sigma together

A natural synergy exists between Lean and Six Sigma, and your organization needs both. Bringing the two together provides a sound set of principles and a broad set of tools and techniques that can enhance effectiveness and delivery efficiency. We'll explore this further in Chapter 2.

Adding More to the Mix

Lean Six Sigma has evolved significantly since its inception. Today's Lean Six Sigma is more than a combination of Lean and Six Sigma: It includes Change Management, Project Management, Agility, Design Thinking, and more. In the spirit of Continuous Improvement, it's fitting to include "the best of the best" frameworks, tools, techniques and approaches in this edition of *Lean Six Sigma For Dummies*. These firmly establish the ongoing relevance and value of Lean Six Sigma.

But bear in mind the importance of a pragmatic approach. The "new" elements haven't been included because they sound impressive; they've been included because they work. As with Lean and Six Sigma, we'll outline some basics here and delve into detail in future chapters.

Managing change

Lean Six Sigma practitioners should make good use of frameworks, tools, and techniques to manage change, as people's acceptance and engagement is vital if any change or improvement is going to succeed. Bringing Change Management into Lean Six Sigma can help you to do the following:

>> Establish and communicate a clear need for change and sense of purpose.

>> Build engagement with stakeholders.

- ❯❯ Develop a vision and a plan that gives people a clear picture of "what's in it for me."

- ❯❯ Handle resistance and conflict while supporting the team to make change happen.

- ❯❯ Embed change by addressing aspects of behavior that could reinforce or hinder it.

- ❯❯ Monitor progress.

- ❯❯ Communicate effectively to build acceptance and appetite for change.

Chapter 6 provides further detail on managing people and change.

Applying Agility

Agile has evolved from being something software developers did to becoming recognized as a way of boosting the performance of projects in general. Applying Agile concepts and an Agile mindset to Lean Six Sigma helps to speed up the delivery of improvement results and bring focus and cohesion to a team.

These aspects of Agile are of particular relevance and value:

- ❯❯ Focusing on delivering the benefits in a timely way. For example, not releasing all of the changes or deliverables on one hit but doing so in increments, so customers feel the benefits quicker and can provide feedback on what's working and what's not. Letting go of perfection is necessary here. In the words of Mark Twain, "Continuous improvement is better than delayed perfection."

- ❯❯ Embracing a culture of experimentation: being prepared to test and try things out and learn from them. You recognize that not everything will work and are comfortable with failure.

- ❯❯ Using aspects from the Scrum approach (see Chapter 16) to deliver the Lean Six Sigma work in timely, focused "sprints" of activity rather than letting projects drag on over long periods of time.

- ❯❯ Visualizing the "to do" list of a Lean Six Sigma project by using the kanban approach.

- ❯❯ Creating an atmosphere of "psychological safety" where team members feel safe, comfortable, and confident to make their contribution.

Agility is a powerful enabler when it comes to Lean Six Sigma. Chapter 16 looks at Agile in more detail.

Employing innovation

We live in an age of innovation, where customers' needs and expectations change rapidly and technological advances can make nearly anything possible. Innovation (whether disruptive — the type that creates a dramatic shift away from what's gone before — or more incremental) can help shape effective responses to changes and opportunities, and create new concepts or processes to excite customers.

The basics of Robotic Process Automation are featured in Chapter 13 of this book. There are also some tools for creative thinking and ideas generation that support "thinking differently" (see Chapter 12).

As with all of the new ingredients in today's Lean Six Sigma mix, there are entire books devoted to this subject. A fantastic summary of the mindset required to drive innovation is provided in the *Design Thinking Playbook* (authored by Lewrick, Link, and Leifer and published by Wiley). Lean Six Sigma practitioners can benefit greatly from these, and we'll delve a little deeper into Design Thinking in Chapter 15.

>> Being driven by curiosity, and looking at things from different angles

>> Focusing on the people and their needs

>> Accepting complexity in the systems our work exists in

>> Visualizing and showing to aid understanding

>> Experimenting and iterating in order to learn, solve problems, and improve

>> Seeking to grow and expand capabilities

>> Developing an awareness of the process

>> Collaborating across departments and organizations

>> Reflecting on thinking, activities, and attitudes because they shape actions and assumptions

Practicing Project Management

Project Management is about getting things done and getting them done in a structured way. Tools and techniques for Project Management can help Lean Six Sigma practitioners to do the following:

>> Establish a project timeline.

>> Plan the work by breaking it down into tasks, including task owners, required resources, due dates, and so on.

- » Work effectively with a team (remembering the acronym Together Everyone Achieves More).

- » Monitor progress against the plan.

- » Manage the scope of the work to avoid the dreaded *scope creep* (the tendency of a project to grow into something bigger and more difficult to manage).

- » Report the benefits achieved.

- » Apply *governance* to the project, such as, for example, in identifying and managing risks and holding tollgate reviews.

- » Identifying and sharing lessons learned.

As you get to know more about Lean Six Sigma, you'll notice there are a few overlaps between Project Management and Lean Six Sigma. The tools and methods of Project Management can certainly help when it comes to managing Lean Six Sigma improvements, and indeed some of them are included in the Lean Six Sigma / DMAIC toolkit (such as planning, managing stakeholders, and establishing a project sponsor).

TIP

Just as "too many cooks spoil the broth," too many tools might spoil the improvement effort. Trying to use every single aspect of these approaches as well as all the tools in the book is likely to slow you down and overcomplicate things. And it might leave stakeholders with a bad taste in their mouths. Rather than incorporate everything, use only the ingredients that you know will enrich the desired result. As you become more experienced, it gets easier to recognize what could help your situation.

Chapter **2**

Understanding the Principles of Lean Six Sigma

I n this chapter we look at the synergy produced by combining the approaches of Lean and Six Sigma to form Lean Six Sigma — along with the best of the approaches outlined in Chapter 1. The merged approach provides a comprehensive set of principles, and supporting tools and techniques, to enable genuine improvements in both efficiency and effectiveness for organizations.

Considering the Key Principles of Lean Six Sigma

Lean Six Sigma takes the features of Lean and of Six Sigma and integrates them to form a magnificent seven set of principles. The principles of each approach aren't dissimilar (check out Chapter 1 to read more about the individual components), and the merged set produces no surprises. The seven principles of Lean Six Sigma are described in the following sections.

Focus on the customer

The elements of your service or offering that customers consider most important are known as CTQs (Critical to Quality requirements) in Lean Six Sigma. (See Chapter 4 for more on CTQs.) Written in a way that ensures they're measurable, the CTQs provide the basis for determining the measures you need to help you understand how well you perform against these critical requirements. As you improve your performance in meeting the CTQs, you're also likely to win and retain further business and increase your market share.

Identify and understand how the work gets done

The *value stream* describes all of the steps in your process — for example, from receipt of a customer order to the issue of a product or the delivery of a service, through to payment. By drawing a map of the value stream, you can highlight the non-value-added steps and areas of waste and ensure the process focuses on meeting the CTQs and adding value. To undertake this process properly, you must "go to the Gemba." The Japanese word *Gemba* means the place where the work gets done — where the action is — which is where management begins. You could try Process Stapling (outlined in Chapter 5), which involves spending time in the workplace to see how the work really gets done, not how you think it gets done. This helps you to understand the problems that you want to tackle and determine a more effective solution for your day-to-day activities.

Manage, improve and smooth the process flow

Among the things to look out for when carrying out a Process Stapling exercise (or going to the Gemba) are clues that highlight bottlenecks or interruptions to the flow of work through the process. Are there delays at certain points? Are there high levels of work in progress? We'll look more closely into bottlenecks in Chapter 11.

Processing work in batches doesn't help items flow smoothly through the process. If possible, use single piece flow (processing one item at a time), moving away from batches, or at least reducing batch size. The concept of pull, not push (see Chapter 1), links to your understanding the process and improving flow. And it can be an essential element in avoiding bottlenecks. Overproduction or pushing things through too early is a waste.

Remove non-value-adding steps and waste

Focusing on the customer and the concept of value-add is important because typically, still only 10 to 15 percent of the cycle time (or lead time) of a process is spent on value-adding activities. This may be surprising but should grab your attention and help you realize the potential waste at play in your own organization. The concept of value-added process steps is covered in Chapter 10, along with information on the eight types of waste to be on the lookout for.

Manage by fact and reduce variation

Managing by fact, using accurate data, helps you avoid jumping to conclusions and solutions. You need the facts! And that means measuring the right things in the right way. Data collection is a process and needs to be managed accordingly. In Chapter 1, we looked at the significance of variation. Quality guru W. Edwards Deming stated that "uncontrolled variation is the enemy of quality." In other words, it's in everyone's best interest to achieve a consistent, reliable, and predictable level of performance. This can be achieved by understanding and addressing the amount of variation, the type of variation, and the sources of variation. Using control charts (Chapter 8 has more on these) enables you to interpret the data correctly and understand the process variation. You then know when to take action and when not to.

Involve and equip the people in the process

To be effective, you need to involve the people in the process, equipping and empowering them to both *feel* able and *be* able to challenge and improve the way the work gets done. Involving people is what has to be done if organizations are to be truly effective, but, like so many of the Lean Six Sigma principles, it requires different thinking if it's to happen. (See Chapter 6 for more about the power of the people.) Continuous Improvement is a mindset — some call it a "growth mindset" — that embraces challenges and seeks opportunities to learn and understands that it's worth putting in the effort to get the results. Leaders play an important role in creating this type of spirit in their organizations so that everyone can contribute.

Undertake improvement activity in a systematic way

The systematic approach used is known as DMAIC: Define, Measure, Analyze, Improve and Control. One of the criticisms sometimes aimed at "stand-alone" Lean is that improvement action tends not to be taken in a systematic and standard way. In Six Sigma, DMAIC is used to improve existing processes, but the framework is equally applicable to Lean and, of course, Lean Six Sigma. Where a new process needs to be designed, the DMADV method is used. Chapters 14 and 15 describe DMADV and the Design Thinking approach.

Less is usually more. Tackle problems in bite-sized chunks and never jump to conclusions or solutions.

The focus in the following section is on improving existing processes with DMAIC using the appropriate tools and techniques from the Lean Six Sigma toolkit. But these tools, and the seven principles identified earlier in this chapter, also provide a framework to improve the day-to-day management and operation of processes. We look at this aspect of Lean Six Sigma, which we refer to as "Everyday Operational Excellence," in Chapter 18.

Improving Existing Processes: Introducing DMAIC

DMAIC (Define, Measure, Analyze, Improve, and Control) provides the framework to improve existing processes in a systematic way. DMAIC projects begin with the identification of a problem, and in the Define phase you describe what you think needs improving. Without data this might be based on your best guess of things, so in the Measure phase you use facts and data to understand how your processes work and perform so that you can pinpoint the problem more effectively.

Now you can Analyze the situation by using facts and data to determine the root cause(s) of the problem that's inhibiting your performance. With the root cause identified, you can now move to the Improve phase, identifying potential solutions, selecting the most suitable, and testing or piloting to validate your approach, using data where appropriate. You're then ready to implement and monitor the solution in the Control phase.

The Control phase is especially important. You need to implement your solution, checking that your customers feel the difference in performance. You'll need to use data to determine the extent of the improvement and to help you hold the gains. After all that work, you don't want the problem you've solved to recur. With the right ongoing measures in place, you should also be able to prompt new opportunities.

The following sections provide a little more detail about the five DMAIC phases. Figure 2-1 shows how the phases link together, though the process is not necessarily linear. It could be that in the Define phase, for example, the problem that you are planning to tackle can't be adequately quantified. In the Measure phase, you'll be collecting data that enables you to go back to Define and update your description of the problem.

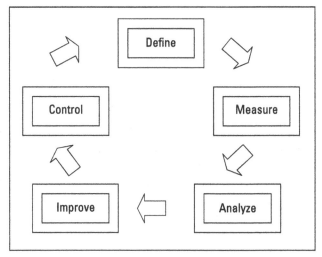

FIGURE 2-1:
The five phases of DMAIC.

Defining your project

When you start an improvement project, ensuring that you and your team understand why you're undertaking the project and what you want to achieve is an essential ingredient for success. With a DMAIC project, you start with a problem that needs to be solved. Before you can solve the problem, you need to define it. One of the key outputs from the Define phase is a completed *improvement charter*.

The improvement charter is an agreed document defining the purpose and goals for an improvement team. It can help address some of the elements that typically go wrong in projects by providing a helpful framework to gain commitment and understanding from the team. Keep your charter simple and try to contain the document to one or two sides of A4 in line with the example shown in Figure 2-2.

The improvement charter contains the following key elements:

>> **A high-level business case** providing an explanation of why undertaking the project is important.

>> **A problem statement** defining the issue to be resolved.

>> **A goal statement** describing the objective of the project.

Improvement Charter

Project title: Date commenced:

Why *High level business case describing why this project is important and how it links to our business plans*

What *The problem and goal statements, the scope, and the CTQ and defect definitions for the relevant customers and processes*

Problem statement	Goal statement
In frame	Out of frame
CTQs	Defect definition

Who *The process owner, Champion, team leader, and team members. Who are they and what are their roles, responsibilities, and time commitments? What involvement is expected of the Champion? How often should they meet?*

Name	Roles & Responsibilites	Time commitment

When *High level timeframes for the phases. This could be mapped to the eight steps.*

	Date	Date	Date	Date	Date	Date
Define						
Measure						
Analyse						
Improve						
Control						

FIGURE 2-2:
A sample improvement charter.

© Martin Brenig-Jones and Jo Dowdall

>> **The project scope** defining the parameters and identifying any constraints.

>> **The CTQs** specifying the problem from the customer's perspective. Unless you already have the CTQs, these may not be known until the Measure phase.

>> **Roles** identifying the people involved in and around the project, expectations of them and their responsibilities. The improvement charter forms a contract between the members of the improvement team, and the champion or sponsor.

>> **Milestones** summarizing the key steps and provisional dates for achieving the goal.

The improvement charter needs to be seen as a "living document" and be updated throughout the various DMAIC phases, especially as your understanding of the problem you're tackling becomes clearer.

Outlining the problem

Creating the problem statement can be trickier than it sounds. A well done statement provides an effective starting point ("a problem well stated is a problem half solved" said John Dewey), but it should not include the cause of the problem, or the potential solution. Remember, the DMAIC framework will take us there, and at this stage, if you really do already know the cause of the problem and the solution to address it (with data to back you up), then you don't need DMAIC. You just need to get on and do it!

Here's an example of a problem statement:

> *Sales of online products have dropped over the last three months, from $272k to $181k, and our forecast is down by 25%.*

You'll notice that some baseline information has been included to help underline the extent of the problem. This makes the problem statement more effective, as it's far easier to communicate the problem and to start to influence stakeholders with a factual problem statement like this than it is to say something vague like, "I think sales are dropping."

The *5Ws and 1H tool* can help to add structure and detail to problem statements. This tool is brilliantly simple and extremely versatile. "5Ws and 1H" stands for What, Why, When, How, Where and Who — six questions that, when answered with facts, provide all the information needed to define the problem:

WHAT is the problem?

WHY is it beneficial to address this problem now?

WHEN does it happen / when did it start?

HOW does it show itself to be a problem? (For example, rework, customer complaints, feedback from a regulator.)

WHERE does it happen?

WHO is affected by it?

WARNING

Don't fall into the trap of explaining the cause of the problem here, or what you think might be the solution. The DMAIC approach will lead you to the right conclusions. As they say, let DMAIC do DeMAgIC!

Framing the scope

One of the most important things to have in place when starting a project is a clear scope. Without a clear scope, it can be very difficult to manage the improvement (how will you know when you've finished?), and it can also be difficult for project stakeholders to understand what will be affected by the project, the effort involved, the timescales, and the results that can be expected. Managing expectations is vital.

The tool used, which is shown in Figure 2-3, is very simple:

1. Draw a picture frame onto a flipchart, large sheet of paper, or online collaboration tool. Label the area inside the frame as "In." Label the area outside of the frame as "Out." Label the frame itself as "Up for discussion."

2. Brainstorm various issues and write them on sticky notes. These could be related to customers or market segments in or out of scope, products, services, geographical regions, people affected, systems involved, and so on. The 5Ws and 1H mentioned in the preceding section might be useful here.

3. Place the sticky notes in what appears to be the most appropriate position.

4. Review and discuss all of the items with stakeholders.

5. Following the review and decisions made, seek to move all of the "Up for discussion" items either In or Out.

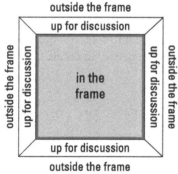

FIGURE 2-3: Framing the scope of your improvement project.

© Martin Brenig-Jones and Jo Dowdall

WARNING

It can be very easy to grow the scope of an improvement project. As you learn more about the process and its issues, you might be tempted to take on further aspects of the problem. You might also have stakeholders who want you to "solve everything" in one go. Our advice is always to manage and control the scope of the project and take everything in bite-size chunks.

Throughout your project, developing a storyboard summary of the key decisions and outputs helps you review progress and share what you've learned. A storyboard builds up as you work your way through your project by capturing the key outputs and findings from the DMAIC phases. A storyboard would include, for example, your improvement charter and process map (see Chapter 5) as well as other tools you'll use in your DMAIC journey and the conclusions they help you to reach. The storyboard also helps your communication activities. Developing and reviewing a communication plan is an essential activity. You really need to keep your team and the people affected by your project informed about the progress you're making. Communication begins on day one of your project.

Measuring how the work is done

After you've defined the problem, at least based on your current understanding, you need to clarify how, and how well, the work gets done. To understand the current situation of your process, knowing what it looks like is the best starting point. You need to know what's currently happening, step by step, and how the process supports the delivery of the customer's CTQ requirements.

Knowing the current performance of your process is essential because this knowledge becomes your baseline. Measure what's important to the customer, and remember also to measure from the perspective of the customer. Gathering this information can help focus your improvement efforts in the areas that matter most and prevent you from going off in the wrong direction. Using graphs and charts (which we cover in Chapter 8) can help you make better sense of the data, as they provide a visual picture that demonstrates performance and can show you, among other things, the variation within the process. You can also calculate the Process Sigma using the method described in Chapter 1.

TIP

If you asked your customers to measure the process, would they measure it in the same way that you do? Use the CTQs as the basis for getting the right process measures in place. Understanding how well you meet the CTQs is an essential piece of management information. Chapter 7 provides more detail on getting the right measures.

Lean Six Sigma projects can take longer than you might like because the right data isn't in place in the day-to-day operation. So often, organizations have data coming out of their ears — but not the *right* data. You need to develop the right measures and start collecting the data you do need.

Analyzing your process

In the Measure phase, you discovered what's really happening in your process. Now you need to identify why it's happening, and determine the root cause(s).

You need to manage by fact, though, so you must verify and validate your ideas about possible suspects. Jumping to conclusions is all too easy.

Carrying out the Analyze phase properly helps you determine the right solution(s) when you get to the Improve phase. Clearly, the extent of analysis required varies depending on the scope and nature of the problem you're tackling, and, indeed, what your Measure activities have identified. Essentially, though, you're analyzing the process and the data that the process produces.

Checking the possible causes of your problem using concrete data to verify your ideas is crucial. You may find the "usual suspects" aren't guilty at all! Identifying and removing the root causes of a problem prevents it happening again.

Improving your process

Now you've identified the root cause of the problem, you can begin to generate improvement ideas to help solve it. Improve, however, involves three distinct phases:

1. **Generate ideas about possible solutions.**

   The solution may be evident from the work done in the previous two steps. Make sure that your proposed solutions address the problem and its cause.

2. **Select the most appropriate solution.**

   Take account of the results from any testing or piloting, and the criteria you've identified as important, such as customer priorities, cost, speed, or ease of implementation. Ensure your solution addresses the problem and that customers will see a difference if you adopt it.

3. **Plan and test the solution.**

   This step seeks to ensure the smooth implementation of your chosen solution. Focus on prevention here can help you to avoid implementing a solution that causes problems elsewhere. Carrying out a pilot or a test is likely to be helpful.

Coming up with a control plan

After the Improve phase, you need to implement the solution in a way that ensures you make the gains you expected and hold onto them. If you're to continue your efforts in reducing variation and cutting out waste, the changes being made to the process need to be consistently deployed and followed.

If the improvement team is handing over the "new" process to the process team, the handover needs to ensure that everyone understands who's responsible for what and when. Misunderstandings are all too easy, and a clear cut-off point must exist signaling the end of the improvement team's role. A control plan should be developed to ensure that the gain is secured and the new process effectively deployed.

The *control plan* helps to ensure that the process is carried out consistently. It also identifies key points in the process where measurement data is needed, plus highlights what action is required depending on the results. Ensuring you have the right ongoing measures in place is extremely important. Chapter 18 includes information on key Control phase tools, including the Process Management Chart.

Reviewing Your DMAIC Phases

Informal reviews of the progress of your improvement project on a weekly or even daily basis may be very sensible. These reviews involve the improvement team and the champion or sponsor. You could consider using aspects of the Agile scrum process outlined in Chapter 16.

As a minimum, you should conduct a formal tollgate review at the end of each DMAIC phase. A *tollgate review* checks that you have completed the current phase properly and reviews the team's various outputs from it. The improvement team leader and the sponsor or champion of the improvement activity should conduct this review. In effect, you're passing through a tollgate.

Before moving from one phase to another, stepping back, assessing progress and asking some key questions is crucial. For example:

>> How are things going? For instance, is the team working well together?

>> Are we on course?

>> What have we discovered?

>> What went well? Why?

>> What conclusions can we draw?

The tollgates also provide an opportunity to update your improvement charter and storyboard. Doing so pulls together some of the key elements of your project; for example, a picture of the process and a control chart showing performance. The tollgate also enables you to take stock of the benefits accruing and the financial details; for example, reductions in errors, improvements in processing time and customer satisfaction. In determining the benefits and financial details, ensure you record the assumptions behind your estimates or calculations, as you may need to explain these to others in the organization.

At the end of the Analyze phase, the tollgate review is of particular importance. It provides an opportunity to review the scope of your project; that is, how much improvement you're seeking to achieve from it.

Before the project began, you may well have best-guessed a business case that justifies starting the work. By the end of this phase, you should be able to *quantify the opportunity* — to really understand the extent of non-value-adding activities and waste, and the potential for improvement. On completion of the Measure phase, you're able to understand the current situation and level of performance. Following the Analyze phase, your level of understanding will have increased significantly and you'll understand the root cause of the problem:

>> You know why performance is at the level it is.

>> You understand the costs involved in the process, both overall and at the individual step level.

>> You have identified the waste and the non-value-adding steps, including the extent of rework, and understood their impact on your ability to meet the CTQs.

In quantifying the opportunity, you first need to calculate the saving if all this waste and non-value-adding work were eliminated, making sure you document your assumptions. You may feel the opportunity is too small to bother about, or so large it justifies either widening the scope of the project or developing a phased approach, by breaking the task into several smaller projects, for example. Either way, review and agree your project goals now, sensibly estimating what's possible for your project.

The benefits are reviewed again closely following your completion of the Improve phase. You're looking to confirm the deliverables from the project, and secure authority for the solution to be fully implemented. As with quantify the opportunity, the post-Improve review also provides an opportunity to look at the project more generally, and key questions include the following:

>> Are we on course?

>> What have we discovered? And forgotten?

>> What went well? Why?

>> Can we apply the solution elsewhere?

>> What conclusions can we draw?

Confirming the benefits you expect to achieve is the main focus of this second benefits review; for example, in reduced rework or improved processing speeds. In completing the phase, you should feel confident that the chosen solution addresses the root cause of the identified problem, and ensures you meet the project goals. Management by fact is a key principle of Lean Six Sigma, so you should have appropriate measurement data and feel confident that your solution will deliver.

Quite a range of differing benefits may occur, including:

>> Reduced errors and waste

>> Faster cycle time

>> Improved customer satisfaction

>> Reduced cost

In assessing how well these benefits match the project objectives, bear in mind that quantifying the softer benefits of enhanced customer satisfaction may be difficult. And in projecting when the benefits are likely to emerge, don't lose sight of the fact that a time gap will probably exist between the cause and effect, especially where customer satisfaction feedback and information is concerned.

As well as looking at the benefits, this review also confirms any costs associated with the solution and its implementation. The piloting or testing activity carried out in the Improve phase (see "Improving your process" earlier in this chapter) should have helped you pull this information together, provided you treated it as though it were a full-scale implementation. Internal guidelines will probably be available to help you assess and present the benefits and costs, but ensure you've documented the assumptions behind your benefits assessment.

A third and final benefit review follows the Control phase, enabling you to confirm the actual costs and benefits and whether any unexpected debits or credits have occurred. And you should know the answers to these questions:

>> Do our customers feel an improvement has occurred? How do we know?

>> Can we take any of the ideas or "best practices" and apply them elsewhere in the business?

This review is the formal post-implementation phase involving the project sponsor or champion. In some organizations, you may find a wider team of managers forming a "project board" or "steering committee," which provides overall guidance for improvement teams and helps prevent duplication of effort with different teams tackling the same or similar problems. This review is likely to involve your team presenting their storyboard, as described in the "Defining your project" section earlier in this chapter.

TIP

Taking time for these reviews and tollgates is an important element in developing a culture that manages by fact. Maintaining an up-to-date storyboard as you work your way through the DMAIC phases helps you prepare for the reviews and share discoveries. The storyboard is created by the team and should present the important elements of its work — the key outputs from the DMAIC process.

Taking a Pragmatic Approach

Six Sigma and DMAIC have been criticized by some for being too complex, and for projects taking too long. Be pragmatic. Projects need to take as long as is appropriate and often only a few simple tools and techniques are needed to secure quick and successful improvements.

Some say that "pure" Lean doesn't always ensure a systematic and controlled approach to achieving and holding on to improvement gains. This is where the Control phase of DMAIC is so important. For relatively straightforward problems, *rapid improvement events* can be used, and they can be run in one-week sessions. The implementation of the improvement may take a further month or so, and some pre-event planning and data collection is necessary.

These events bring together the powerful concepts of *Continuous Improvement*, or *Kaizen*, to involve people in continuously seeking to improve performance within the framework of DMAIC. That improvement comes from focusing on how the work gets done and how well. Kaizen is the Japanese word for Continuous Improvement, where "Kai" means "change" and "zen" means "good." Put together, Kaizen means "change for the better."

Rapid improvement events can also be run as a series of half or one-day workshops, over a period of five or six weeks, or less. They follow the DMAIC framework, and particular emphasis is placed on the Define and Control phases. So, for example, the first workshop focuses on getting a clear definition of the problem to be tackled (Define), and so on. The aim is to tackle a closely scoped bite-sized problem using the expertise of the people actually involved in that process to solve it. They'll need someone with Lean Six Sigma experience as a facilitator, because they may need help using some of the tools and techniques required (for example, Value Stream Maps — see Chapter 5). So often, the people doing the job know what's needed to put things right. You may well find that the solution is already known by the team, but historically they haven't been listened to. Implementation of the solution can thus be actioned quickly, much of it during the actual event. Rapid improvement events can provide the people doing the job with the opportunity to use their skills and knowledge.

In terms of time, the short duration of rapid improvement events compares to perhaps four months part time in a traditional DMAIC project, though the actual team hours may be similar.

WAX ON, WAX OFF: LEAN SIX SIGMA AND MARTIAL ARTS

The different levels of training in Lean Six Sigma are often referred to in terms of the colored belts acquired in martial arts. Think about the qualities of a martial arts Black Belt: highly trained, experienced, disciplined, decisive, controlled and responsive, and you can see how well this metaphor translates into the world of making change happen in organizations. (Thankfully, no bricks need to be broken in half by hand.)

Some organizations develop a pool of **Yellow Belts**, who typically receive two days of practical training to a basic level on the most commonly used tools in Lean Six Sigma projects. They work either as project team members or carry out mini-projects themselves in their local work environment under the guidance of a Black Belt.

Green Belts are trained on the basic tools and lead fairly straightforward projects. The extent of training varies somewhat. In the USA, for example, it's typically 10 days, whereas in the UK, some organizations break the training along the following lines:

- Foundation Green Belt level (four to six days of training) covers Lean tools, process mapping techniques and measurement, as well as a firm grounding in the DMAIC methodology and the basic set of statistical tools.

- Advanced Green Belts (an additional six days of training) receive further instruction on more analytical statistical tools and start to use statistical software. This helps ensure the training is delivered "just in time," since early projects can be relatively simple, often involving an assessment of how the work gets done, enabling the identification and elimination of non-value-added steps, without the need for detailed statistical analysis.

Green Belts typically devote the equivalent of about a day a week (20 per cent of their time) to Lean Six Sigma projects, usually mentored by a Black Belt.

(continued)

(continued)

An expert Lean Six Sigma practitioner is trained to **Black Belt** level, which means attending several modules of training over a period of months. Most Black Belt courses involve around 20 days of full-time training as well as working on projects in practice under the guidance of a Master Black Belt. The role of the Black Belt is to lead complex projects and give expert help with the tools and techniques to the project teams.

Black Belts are often from different operational functions across the company, coming into the Black Belt team from customer service, finance, marketing or HR, for example. The Black Belt role is usually full time, often for a term of two to three years, after which they return to operations. In effect, they become internal consultants working on improving the way the organization works, changing the organizational systems and processes for the better.

The **Master Black Belt (MBB)** receives the highest level of training and becomes a full-time professional Lean Six Sigma expert. The MBB will have extensive project management experience and should be fully familiar with the importance of the soft skills needed to manage change. An experienced MBB is likely to want to take on this role as a long-term career path, becoming a trainer, coach or deployment advisor, and working with senior executives to ensure the overall Lean Six Sigma program is aligned to the strategic direction of the business. MBBs tend to move around from one major business to another after typically three or four years in one organization. MBBs are likely to have been a Black Belt for at least two years before moving into this role.

Where people are provided with an introduction to the topic — an Awareness program — the term **White Belt** has been adopted. No certification process is involved, and these programs vary in length from an hour or two through to a full day.

In addition to the classic belts, we have seen some new colors and levels appearing out in the sigmaverse. For example, some organizations have developed **Orange Belts** with a skillset between Yellow Belt and Green Belt level, and a Lemon Belt exists between white and yellow. A new **Business Black Belt** qualification has emerged, developed by Catalyst Consulting, in recognition of the fact that not all organizations require the degree of statistical analysis that the traditional Black Belt is trained for. Business Black Belts are equipped with the tools and skills required to become a "transformation maestro or maestra."

Certification processes are operated in many organizations to ensure a set standard is reached through exams and project assessments. Certification processes are established in many countries, such as the British Quality Foundation and the American Society of Quality. Many large corporate businesses set up their own internal certification processes, with recognition given at high-profile company events to newly graduated belts.

2

Lean Six Sigma Foundations

Identify the customers of your process and understand their requirements in specific and measurable terms.

Look at your processes and identify what *really* happens, step by step.

Understand the impact that managing people and change can have on the success of Lean Six Sigma in your organization, and discover some practical tools to support you.

Chapter **3**

Identifying Your Process Customers

All organizations have a whole range of different customers — internal and external, large and small. Each organization's processes should be designed and managed in a way that meets its customers' various needs. In this chapter we help you understand who customers are and what their requirements are. In Lean Six Sigma, our definition of a customer is anyone who receives the output of a process. So it makes sense to start by thinking about processes.

Understanding the Process Basics

A process is a series of steps and actions that produce an output in the form of a product or service. Ideally, each process should add value in the eyes of the customer.

All work is a process, and a process is a blend of PEMME:

» **People:** Those working in or around the process. Do you have the right number of people in the right place, at the right time and possessing the right skills for the job? And do they feel supported and motivated?

>> **Equipment:** The various items needed for the work. Items can be as simple as a stapler or as complicated as a lathe used in manufacturing. Consider whether you have the right equipment, located in an appropriate and convenient place, and being properly maintained and serviced.

>> **Method:** How the work gets done — the process steps, procedures, tasks and activities involved.

>> **Materials:** The things necessary to do the work — for example, the raw materials needed to make a product or the information needed to provide a service.

>> **Environment:** The working area — perhaps a room or surface needs to be dust-free, or room temperature must be within defined parameters.

Focusing on PEMME helps you think differently when considering what a process actually is. (All the elements of PEMME also combine to influence the results from your processes in relation to variation — as covered in Chapter 8.)

Pinpointing the elements of a process

The concept of processes and PEMME applies to everything you do, from getting up in the morning, to making a cup of tea, to placing an online order. All of these activities can be broken down into a series of steps. The process model shown in Figure 3-1 has PEMME at its heart (the "process"), but it also builds on PEMME and helps you think about the wider requirements of the process. To meet your customers' requirements (the CTQs (Critical to Quality) covered in Chapters 2 and 4), the process elements must be addressed.

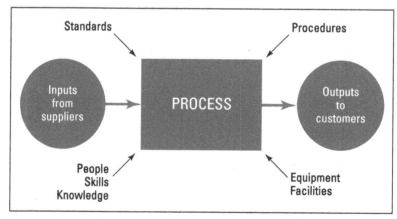

© Martin Brenig-Jones and Jo Dowdall

FIGURE 3-1:
Using a process
model.

Ensuring that the CTQs are understood and agreed on is the first requirement of a process. More often than not, a lack of quality or rework is the direct result of not understanding or defining the customer's requirements properly. Even for apparently simple things, a little extra time spent in translating the voice of the customer and clarifying requirements can help save time and potential upset later on. Once the customer's requirements have been agreed, determining your own requirements from suppliers is the next step. Now you're the customer, so spend time with your suppliers to ensure your needs are properly understood and agreed.

Make sure you have the right number of people working in the process, and that they have the necessary knowledge and skills. If they don't, appropriate training needs to be delivered.

You'll need to document the process (or procedures) too. Documented processes (whether in the form of words, pictures, or videos) should describe precisely how the work gets done — the method — and must be developed, agreed, appropriately documented, and kept up to date, especially in a culture of Continuous Improvement, where enhancements are regularly being made to the process. Importantly, they should be simple to follow and understand.

Properly describing relevant standards is also sensible. They may well form part of the method, applying, for example, to regulatory requirements or service-level agreements that need to be followed. Like procedures, the standards should be documented in an easily accessible manner. Similarly, if budget constraints or authority limits on certain actions apply, management must ensure the people in the process know the details.

Equipment and facilities are needed to operate the process, and need to be capable of meeting or exceeding the customer requirements. These must be appropriate from day one, located in the right place and correctly maintained thereafter. Also ensure the environment is appropriate for the activity. The facilities link to the environment element of PEMME and could include having the right workspace, for example.

Identifying internal and external customers

All of your processes are likely to involve other people. There will be people involved in the different steps of the process. They may be members of your team or department, but could also be in other departments or functions. There will also be people who provide the inputs you need to start the work — for example, information, perhaps a schedule of available products, or an approved order. These are your suppliers. There will be people who receive the outputs of your process. These are your customers. Suppliers and customers could be internal (from inside your organization) or external (from outside your organization), or both!

Knowing who the internal customers and suppliers are, and how they fit into the picture, is important because together they form the end-to-end process, the value stream that ultimately provides the external customer with the service or product they're looking for.

Consider Figure 3-2. Department A produces output for Department B, which produces output for Department C, which provides the answer to an external customer enquiry. Each of these departments is involved in the process and needs to understand the objectives of the "big process" or overall system.

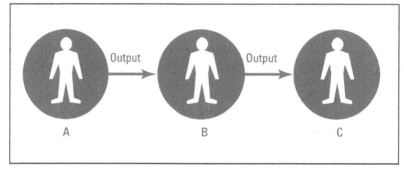

FIGURE 3-2: Identifying your internal customers.

All too often, departments work in a vacuum, doing their own thing without regard for its impact on the end-to-end process. They may have their own targets, measures and priorities, for example. Possibly, the end-to-end process or value stream isn't even known; each team or department involved works as though their step in the process is independent of any others. In reality, the end-to-end process is a series of interdependent steps, and the overall system is made up of a series of processes.

Internal customers and suppliers must understand their relationship and how their different roles contribute to "the bigger picture." If they don't, the external customers will receive poor service or product — the very people who should be viewed as the most important because they're paying the organization for the services or products they provide.

Even if you're not directly dealing with the external customer, you're quite likely to be dealing with someone who is. So, understanding the bigger picture is important, and meeting the requirements of your internal customers could well be the key to successfully meeting the external customers' CTQs. Quality Function Deployment (QFD) is helpful here. QFD establishes a clear link between each process requirement and the end customer, making it easier for each employee to see the role that they play in meeting customer requirements. We cover QFD in Chapter 14.

Getting a High-Level Picture

To really understand how the work gets done, and to identify just who the internal and external customers are, you need to draw a picture of the process. These pictures are known as *process* or *Value Stream Maps* (covered in detail in Chapter 5). Avoid going into fine detail at this stage, as too much information can be distracting. Keep it simple and "high level."

Resist the temptation of capturing what "should" happen and capture what actually "does" happen. You might be surprised about the differences between the two. It's important to create a safe environment where people feel comfortable talking about what actually happens (warts and all) without fear of punishment. If you don't discuss the "warts," you could miss the opportunity to tackle them.

It is possible to map processes at several levels. Right at the top of an organization are some very high-level processes that describe what the organization does, such as "business development." These Level 1 processes break down into a number of sub-processes that describe how that work is undertaken. Level 2 and 3 processes gradually increase the amount of detail. You could then develop Level 4 or 5 processes that cover the step-by-step procedural tasks and elements.

Our example in Figure 3-3 has "business development" at Level 1 and shows the various sub-processes down to Level 3.

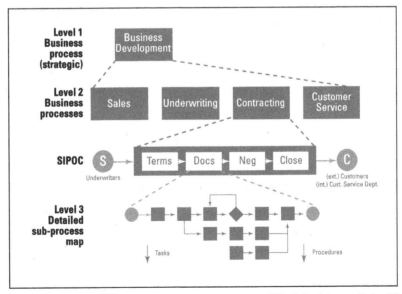

FIGURE 3-3:
Process levels.

© Martin Brenig-Jones and Jo Dowdall

Drawing a high-level process map

Welcome to the Invasion of the SIPOCs! SIPOCs might sound like creatures from a sci-fi movie, but they're far friendlier and more useful than that. A SIPOC is a high-level process map that provides a framework to help you understand your process and its customers and suppliers better. It encourages you to think about what needs to be measured in the process to help understand performance and opportunities for improvement (covered in Chapters 7 and 8). Figure 3-4 shows the SIPOC model. SIPOC stands for:

>> **Suppliers:** The people, departments or organizations that provide you with the "inputs" needed to operate the process. When they send you an enquiry or order form, the external customer is also included as a supplier in your process as they are providing an input! Suppliers also include regulatory bodies providing information, and companies providing you with equipment or raw materials.

>> **Inputs:** Forms or information, equipment or raw materials, or even the people you need to carry out the work. For people, the supplier may be the human resources department or an employment agency.

>> **Process:** In the SIPOC diagram, the P presents a picture of the process steps at a relatively high level, usually Levels 2 or 3, as shown in Figure 3-3.

>> **Outputs:** A list of the things that your process provides to the internal and external customers. Your outputs will become inputs to their processes.

>> **Customers:** The different internal and external customers who'll receive your various process outputs.

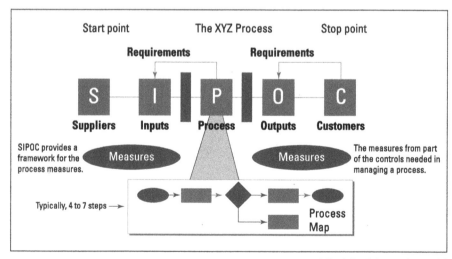

FIGURE 3-4: The SIPOC model.

© Martin Brenig-Jones and Jo Dowdall

The SIPOC model identifies your customers and the outputs they need, presents a high-level process map, usually comprising four to seven steps, identifies your suppliers and confirms your input requirements from them.

REMEMBER

The customer can also be a supplier, particularly of information needed by you.

Some people refer to the SIPOC as a COPIS, because when they create the diagram, they start with the customer on the right-hand side of the model before listing the outputs that go to them.

In previous editions of this *Dummies* book, we have demonstrated the SIPOC technique using the COPIS method, starting with the customer and working backwards. In this version, we'll show you how we start with the process and work outwards from the center. In truth, there are lots of different ways you can create your SIPOC. One reason for starting with the process is that we find it easier to identify all of the outputs and the customers who received them once we have defined what the process steps are. You might like to practice different methods and find the one that works best for you.

The best way to create your SIPOC diagram is to gather your team around a large sheet of paper or online collaboration tool and follow these steps. After starting with the process, it doesn't really matter whether you work to the left (inputs) or right (outputs) as long as you capture them. (Figure 3-5 provides an example of how it might look).

1. **Set out all the steps in the process.**

   Use sticky notes (or virtual sticky notes) to construct a high-level picture of the process. Typically it involves four to seven steps. Don't go beyond this; otherwise, you'll be dealing with too much detail too soon. (Chapter 5 covers process and Value Stream Mapping in detail.)

   In Figure 3-5, the start and stop points are represented with the oval shapes, the process steps with the rectangular boxes, and points in the process involving questions with the diamond shapes. Diamonds are decision points, such as, for example, showing the need to do something different if you're dealing with product A or product B, or where different authority levels may come into operation in underwriting a loan, perhaps based on the loan value. Diamonds tend to be not so relevant in the SIPOC diagram, though there will be times when you need to use them. In Figure 3-4, we include one purely for reference. Figure 3-5 simply uses the square boxes.

2. **List all the inputs that go into the process.**

   Include order forms and information, materials, criteria, and so forth. As shown in Figure 3-5, you could use arrows to show which inputs relate to which process steps.

3. **Identify where all the different inputs come from.**

   Under S for Suppliers, list the sources of all of your inputs. Again, use arrows to clarify who's supplying what. Remember that some of your customers might be suppliers, as they may be providing an input such as a request or an order.

4. **List all the outputs that come from the process.**

   As well as the "main" outputs (like the products produced by your process), there may be others, such as records created, documents filed, and waste to be disposed of. At this stage (remember we are dealing with "warts and all" here), there may also be some undesirable outputs like rework or scrap.

5. **List all of the customers who receive outputs.**

   Include both internal and external customers, such as, for example, managers who receive reports or information. Consider third parties such as regulatory bodies, where relevant. Drawing arrows showing who receives which outputs can be helpful.

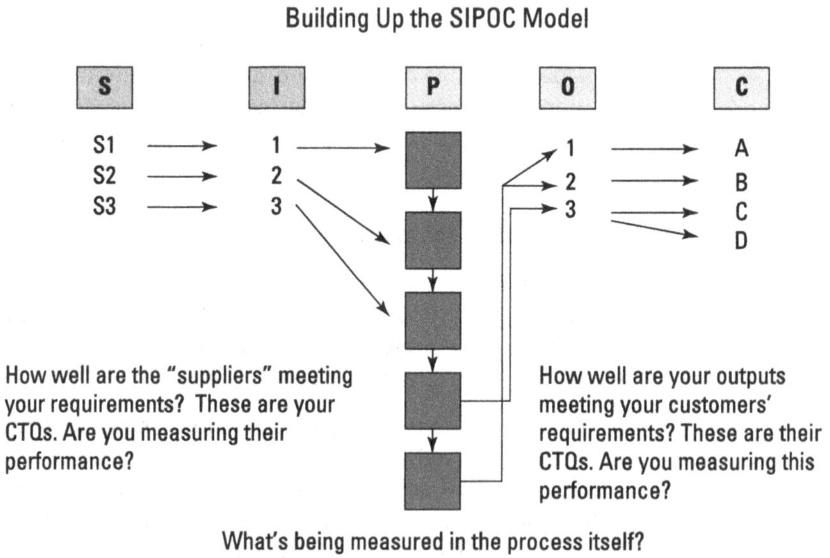

Building Up the SIPOC Model

FIGURE 3-5: Building up the SIPOC model.

How well are the "suppliers" meeting your requirements? These are your CTQs. Are you measuring their performance?

How well are your outputs meeting your customers' requirements? These are their CTQs. Are you measuring this performance?

What's being measured in the process itself?

© Martin Brenig-Jones and Jo Dowdall

SIPOCs provide a helpful checklist, identifying who your customers are and the outputs that go to them. They highlight areas where greater clarity is needed, especially in relation to requirements and outputs. They also help you focus on what needs to be measured, like, for example, how well are you delivering the outputs to your customers, and how well are your suppliers meeting your requirements of them? (Measurement is covered in more detail in Chapters 7 and 8, with Chapter 8 focusing on how you present your data and understand your results.)

Creating a SIPOC process map provides an opportunity to begin thinking about the various elements involved in your process, whether you have all the information you need and if segmenting your customers is necessary.

Segmenting customers

In developing your SIPOC process map, you need to identify your customers and the outputs that go to them. Possibly, you classify or segment your customers in some way, for example by size or geographical location.

Think carefully about these different customer segments. Do they actually have different CTQs? Will the process outputs be the same for each segment, or will these vary to some degree?

We look at segmentation in a little more detail in Chapter 4, but ensure your SIPOC map and the thinking that accompanies it takes appropriate account of your different customer segments.

Chapter **4**

Understanding Your Customers' Needs

I n focusing on our customers, we're looking to provide value for them. Amongst other things, this means the right products and services, at the right time, the right price and the right quality. And, of course, in the right place. That's a lot to get right!

Throughout this book we make several references to the "voice of the customer" (VOC) and to CTQs (Critical to Quality requirements). The voice of the customer helps you understand customer requirements. This expression describes information coming from the customer, perhaps through market research or face-to-face discussion, which enables you to determine your customers' CTQs and what value means to them. The CTQs are vital elements in Lean Six Sigma, providing you with the basis to assess how well you're performing in meeting your customers' requirements. This chapter looks at how to obtain the VOC and develop the CTQs.

Considering Kano

In striving to understand customers' requirements and their perception of value, it's useful to understand the Kano model, as shown in Figure 4-1.

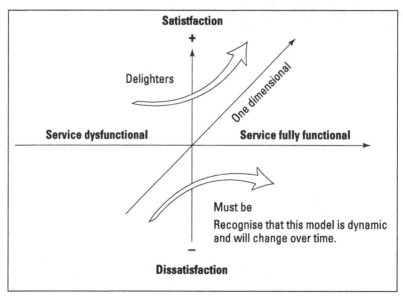

FIGURE 4-1:
Can you Kano?
You must know
the must-be
requirements.

Developed by Professor Kano at the University of Tokyo, the model looks at customer requirements and helps you understand how your customers will perceive the service and products you provide. The Kano model includes three main categories:

>> **Must-bes:** These are sometimes referred to as the unspoken customer requirements. To the customer, they're so obviously required that they don't expect to have to spell them out. Meeting these requirements will not increase customer satisfaction; they're the absolute minimum the customer is expecting. But the customer will be very dissatisfied if they're not met — so miss them at your peril. The must-be requirements are also sometimes referred to as *dissatisfiers*.

>> **One-dimensionals:** The more of these requirements that are met, the higher the level of customer satisfaction. The requirements might relate to product features or elements of service delivery, or both. One-dimensionals are sometimes referred to as *satisfiers*.

>> **Delighters:** Here, the customer is surprised and delighted by something you've done, and their satisfaction increases. Note that the other things need to be done right if the delighters are to have the desired effect. If the must-bes aren't right, the delighters will fail to deliver the wow factor.

Do remember, though, that over time things will change. A one-dimensional satisfier will become a must-be and delighters will become one-dimensionals.

Let's put all of this information into a context. What are your must-be requirements when your car is serviced? Your must-be requirements might be that the service has been carried out correctly. Some years ago that would have been all you could have expected and hoped for. But delighters started to appear. The car was cleaned inside and out! The garage offered to collect and return the car or provide a courtesy car while yours was being serviced. Other garages offered a while-you-wait service with complimentary coffee and biscuits. A recent breakthrough that has had a real impact on customer satisfaction has been the addition of a "virtual" walk through the service. Mechanics now routinely film the service and the findings and send this to the customer to reassure them that any issues identified during the service are genuine.

Very quickly, delighters became one-dimensionals. And, for some customers, they became must-be requirements! The model is dynamic. However, bear in mind that other customers will also exist who only want a basic, no-frills service. They'll see no value in the extras they're paying for, albeit in the hidden costs linked to the service charge. Understanding your different customer segments is vital if you're to deliver value and meet their CTQs (as we discuss in Chapter 2).

Obtaining the Voice of the Customer

We find out what our customers want by talking with, listening to and observing them. You can source the customer's voice in lots of places, such as market research results, focus group discussions, survey results, hits on your organization's website and customer complaints. The trick is to translate what the customer says into a measurable requirement — the Critical to Quality (CTQ) customer requirement. You gather input from your customers in order to understand their needs, identify the key issues and translate them into terms that mean something to your organization and that you can measure.

WARNING

Listening to the voice of the customer (VOC) is about determining your customer requirements, not determining solutions to meet those requirements — it isn't about jumping to conclusions about what they mean, either!

Doing things properly usually involves a number of conversations with your customer, the Process Owner and all the other people involved in the process. The *Process Owner* is the person responsible for the process, for example a manager or director; they need to ensure the process is designed and managed to meet the CTQs so they must understand what the customer is saying.

TIP

On occasion, the customer may not be totally clear about their requirements. Reflect back your interpretations to ensure they're correct.

Taking an outside-in view

Many organizations assume they know what their customers want — but this isn't always the case. Even when you try to be objective, the fact that you know your products and services so well, and understand your workplace's jargon, means seeing things from your customers' perspective is actually quite difficult.

Customers aren't all the same. They come in all sorts of different shapes and sizes, and your customers may have different requirements, even for the "same" product or service. Identifying the different customer segments that your organization deals with, and recognizing that each segment may have different CTQs, is essential. For example, a small company may be happy to receive your products on a monthly basis, whereas a larger business may need daily deliveries of those same products.

Seeing customer segments

Grouping your customers into segments helps you see your customers' different requirements. By segmenting them, you can develop the right products and services for each group, and create specific measures that help you understand your performance in meeting their differing requirements. To help you segment your customers, list some categories that describe both your current customers and the people or organizations that you consider to be potential customers. You might also look at past customers in this way too.

Consider the following potential segmentation categories in relation to your customers:

>> Industry

>> Size

>> Spend

>> Geographical location

>> End use

>> Product characteristics

>> Buying characteristics

>> Price/cost sensitivity

>> Age

>> Gender

>> Socioeconomic factors

- » Frequency of purchase/use

- » Impact/opinion leader

- » Loyalty

- » Channel

- » Technology

Naturally, you need to determine the categories that are relevant to your own organization, but this list provides a good starting point. If appropriate, you can also create umbrella customer segments to include, for example, frequency of purchase and spend.

Prioritizing your customers

Every customer is important, but some customers use your services more frequently or are more critical to your business than others. You may need to devote more time and resources to these particular customers.

TIP

Italian economist Vilfredo Pareto developed the idea of the 80:20 rule, when he described how 80 percent of the wealth of his country was in the hands of 20 percent of the population. Your organization may well have a "vital few" customers, perhaps 20 percent who provide you with 80 percent of your margin. If that's the case, those customers are very important to the ongoing success of your business and understanding their requirements and their perceptions of your performance in some detail is crucial.

You could prioritize by customer segment, but you need to understand the most appropriate way to prioritize customers for your organization. For many organizations, the priority may be revenue, but more sensibly it should be profit. As your understanding of your customers increases, you'll find it easier to determine your organization's priorities.

Truly focusing on customers, as opposed to simply saying you are, requires real investment in understanding your customers' needs. Knowing who your customers are, how they're segmented and which ones are your priority is a vital prerequisite to your research and data gathering.

Your customers may be both internal and external. Thinking in terms of processes helps you identify where you need to focus and highlights who your internal customers are. The SIPOC tool explained in Chapter 3 will help you to do this.

Researching the Requirements

Researching your customers follows a natural progression. You may start with little or no information about customers, but will end up with a collection of quantified, prioritized customer needs and expectations. You might also gain information about how your competitors succeed in meeting their — and your! — customers' needs.

Start by investigating what information you already have and then determine the gaps in your customer information.

You then need to develop a customer research plan that moves you from where you are right now to where you need or want to be, so you can close the gaps.

Use Table 4-1 to help you determine the sequencing of your research plan.

Table 4-1 helps you think about the information you currently have, and the information you need to get and how to go about getting it.

TABLE 4-1   **Researching the Requirements**

Input	Research Method	Output: What You Get
No information	Interview/focus group What is important?	Customer wants and needs (general ideas, unprioritized, not clarified, all qualitative)
Known preliminary customer wants and needs	Interview/focus group Which are most important?	Customer wants and needs (clarified, more specific, preliminary prioritization) Customer input to list of competitors, best-in-class
Qualitative, prioritized customer wants and needs	Survey Face-to-face Written mail Telephone Electronic	Quantified prioritized customer wants and needs Competitor comparative information

If you have little or no information to begin with, the first step is interviewing some representative customers, perhaps in a focus group, to help you understand what's important to them about the service or product you're offering. You should be able to capture some general ideas about their wants and needs; though these are unlikely to be totally clear, and you probably won't be able to prioritize them yet. This first step helps you determine your customers' preliminary needs and enables you to now undertake some more detailed interviews or focus groups.

The second row in Table 4-1 shows how more detailed analysis should lead you to a clearer picture of customer requirements, and at least a preliminary prioritization of them. This stage also gives you the opportunity to ask the customers about their experience of your competitors.

With this clear picture, you can move to the third row in the table. Your interviews and focus groups will have been run with a relatively small number of customers. This approach is described as *qualitative* research. You now need to test their views and opinions by conducting research with a larger number of customers. This approach is described as *quantitative* research, involving a survey.

Quantitative research is important because it enables you to feel confident that you have a true picture of customer wants and needs. The results from the qualitative research may have been skewed in some way if you had inadvertently included unrepresentative customers. For example, you may have carried out research on a product aimed at the high end of the market, but interviewed customers from a different market segment by mistake. The same issue can occur where customers fail to respond to your survey. Is there a particular reason why they haven't, but others have? This situation is known as "non-response bias" and can be just as troublesome.

As you plan your research, be aware of the following issues:

>> The customer may offer you a "solution" rather than express their real needs. Ask the customer "Why do you want this?" until you truly understand the real need.

>> Different customers may perceive the same product or service differently. For example, a shirt that shows off the designer's logo may command a premium price over a similar article without the logo, but only for some customers.

>> Remember that how your customers say they'll use a product or service isn't always the same as how they actually use it!

EXAMPLE

For a long time, Heinz ketchup was notoriously difficult to get out of the bottle. Users would have to shake or pat the bottle and wait a long time for the ketchup to run out onto their food. In the 1970s, there was even an ad campaign that used the line "Good things are worth waiting for." The designer Paul Brown noted that customers would often store their ketchup bottles up-side down to make them easier to pour from, but that this could result in too much ketchup running out of the bottle. He designed a valve that allowed users to squeeze the ketchup from an upside-down style bottle and made our lives easier! Heinz could then use the line "Ready when you are" to promote ketchup.

>> External customers generally express *effectiveness needs* — needs that relate to the value they receive from the product or service. Internal customers, on the other hand, tend to express *efficiency needs* — needs that relate to the amount of resources allocated to or consumed in meeting customers' needs.

Interviewing your customers

Customer interviews are helpful as a research technique. The aims of customer interviews are to *understand* a specific customer's needs and requirements, values and points of view on service issues, product/service attributes and performance indicators/measures. Customer interviews are useful and enable you to explore issues with them during your customer research.

The advantages of customer interviews are:

>> Flexibility: You can obtain more detailed explanations by probing and clarifying.

>> Greater complexity: You can administer highly complex questionnaires/surveys and can explain questions to interviewees.

>> Ability to reach all customer types: You can interview populations that are difficult or impossible to reach by other methods.

>> High response rate: The degree to which the information collection process reaches all targets is higher.

>> Assurance that instructions are followed: Because the interview is taking place in person, you can ensure that all steps are followed.

The disadvantages of customer interviews are:

>> They could be costly to administer.

>> They're the least reliable form of data collection because the interviewer may influence the responses to the questionnaire.

>> Less anonymity is possible.

>> Carrying out and transcribing the interviews is time consuming.

>> Generating supportable quantitative evidence can be difficult.

>> Results can be difficult to analyze.

>> The sample size may not be sufficient to draw supportable conclusions.

>> Use of different interviewers asking questions in a particular way may result in bias (see the "Avoiding Bias" section later in this chapter).

>> Positive response bias may occur, whereby people give higher ratings in personal interviews.

TIP

Ask open questions to get the interviewee talking, rather than asking a series of closed questions that simply elicit a yes or no response. The key is to listen to what the customer is saying — their responses often provide the answers to some of the specific issues you need information on.

Focusing on focus groups

Focus groups are interviews, usually involving between six to ten people at the same time in the same group. Typically, they run for two to three or four hours. Focus groups are a powerful means to capture views and opinions, to evaluate services or test new ideas, or (in the context of this chapter) to clarify and prioritize customer requirements.

Essentially, a focus group is a carefully planned discussion designed to obtain perceptions concerning a defined area of interest in a non-threatening environment. Listening to the members of the focus group is key!

The focus group participants should share characteristics that relate to the focus group topic; all being in the same customer segment, for example. To avoid bias, running more than one focus group is sensible; run three as a minimum.

Focus groups are used:

>> To clarify and define customer needs.

>> To gain insights into the prioritization of needs.

>> To test concepts and receive feedback.

>> As a next step after customer interviews or a preliminary step in a survey process.

The participants will be asked to thoroughly discuss very few topics, and often only three or four questions will be posed during the focus group. These will be very general questions, such as "What do you find important in service delivery, generally?" or "What is it that makes you feel you have received good or bad service?"

Focus groups aim to get the participants talking and you listening, ideally recording the discussion for subsequent analysis.

Considering customer surveys

You can run customer surveys in a number of ways, in person, on paper or electronically. They enable you to measure the importance or performance of customer needs and requirements. You can check out your focus group findings with a larger group of customers.

The pros and cons of customer surveys are shown in Table 4-2.

TABLE 4-2

Pros and Cons of Customer Surveys

Advantages	Disadvantages
Low cost	Low rate of return
Efficiency of large samples	Non-response bias
Ready access to hard-to-reach respondents	Little control
No interviewer bias (though take care with wording the questions)	Limitations on questions
Potential to use visuals	Potential misunderstanding of questions or rating scale
High reliability and validity	Oversimplification of format
	Slowness — requires development
	Requires pre-testing
	Difficulty of obtaining names

Using observations

Observations are another way of identifying your customers' needs. Observing customers provides an effective way to understand how they use and view your products and services. For example, by observing the purchasing patterns of customers, supermarkets strategically position the products in their store to increase sales. Key products appealing to older customers are positioned on middle shelves so they don't have to bend or stretch to reach them.

EXAMPLE

Toyota allocates some of its engineers to ride as passengers in customers' cars, enabling them to observe their customers' driving first-hand. One result of such observations was the introduction of drink holders in Toyota's cars. The engineers observed children in the back seats holding drinks but having nowhere to put them. The inclusion of drink holders may not have increased sales as such, but they're now a standard requirement for most buyers, and their inclusion in a car as "standard" helps maintain or enhance the general level of customer satisfaction. Drink holders are a good example of Kano in practice, where their introduction was a delighter or wow factor, but their inclusion in cars and vans quickly became a "must-be."

Avoiding Bias

Whichever approach you take to collecting voice of customer (VOC) information, you need to recognize the potential for bias. Possibly you may ask the wrong questions, or ask the wrong customers because you haven't segmented them properly, or simply misinterpret, deliberately or otherwise, what the customer says.

WARNING

You need to really listen to what the customer says — not to what you think they're saying or you'd like them to say! In a focus group, asking very open questions is best. Make sure you listen to the responses. Leading customers through a series of closed questions results in closed answers, which are then open to interpretation and bias.

On questionnaires, the wording of questions is vital. Each question should address a single aspect only. So, for example, you may ask the customer to rate your performance on a scale of one to five, where one is poor and five is super. Suppose you pose this question: "How well do you feel we perform in terms of speed and accuracy?" Then you may receive a response relating to only speed or accuracy, not both.

Beware of asking leading questions. For example, you can ask, "Should caring organizations survey their customers every month?" And the respondent is almost obliged to say "yes" in order to appear caring. A better way to ask this question and avoid bias would be to ask, "How frequently should organizations survey their customers?" The options for answering the question should include "never."

Considering Critical To Quality Customer Requirements

When you've collected the VOC information (see the earlier sections of this chapter), you need to develop the CTQs. Write the CTQs in a measurable form: they provide the basis for your process measurement set. This set will enable you to put the right measures in place to assess your performance (see Chapter 7).

CTQs help you focus on your customer requirements and provide the foundation for your measurement activity. Figure 4-2 provides a framework to help you define your CTQs. Looking at the first example, the CTQ for getting through to the right person first time is straightforward to understand and to measure, but to define the CTQ covering speed you need to go back to the customer and agree what "quickly" means. You might then define a second measurable requirement as "The call is answered within 10 seconds."

Voice of the Customer	Key issues(s)	CTQ
You either put me on hold, or put me through to the wrong department or person	The customer wants to be put through quickly to the right person	• Customer gets through to the correct person the first time
You send me an invoice at different times of the month	Consistent monthly billing	• Customer bill received same day of the month
It takes too long to process my mortgage application and get me the money when it's needed	Speed up loan so I get the money on time	• Customer receives cheque on customer request date

© Martin Brenig-Jones and Jo Dowdall

FIGURE 4-2: Determining the CTQs.

Without this type of data, you won't know how you're performing in meeting the customer requirements, as information that determines where improvement actions are required.

TIP

A CTQ shouldn't prescribe a solution. A CTQ should be measurable and, where appropriate, have upper and lower specification limits and a target value. A CTQ should be a positive statement about what the customer wants rather than a negative statement about what the customer doesn't want.

Say you agree an arrival time window for a customer's boiler to be repaired. The upper specification limit might be midday, the lower specification 8 a.m. and the target time 10 a.m., for example. So you aim to be there for 10 a.m. plus or minus two hours, but, of course, you also aim to repair the boiler and restore heat for the customer!

The affinity diagram (see Chapter 9) provides a useful format for sorting VOC information into themes. These themes can then be broken down into more detailed elements, as a CTQ tree, as shown in Figure 4-3.

First level	Second level	
Friendly staff	Willing to answer question Shows respect	
Knowledgeable staff	Knows the loan process	You will probably need to go down to more levels. And remember the CTQs need to be measureable
	Knows the market	
	Understands my situations	
Speed	Money when I need it	
	Application fast to fill out	
Accurate	Don't make mistakes	
	Give me the right rate	

© Martin Brenig-Jones and Jo Dowdall

The example in Figure 4-3 is from a bank that has taken the various customer statements and comments from a survey and sorted them into themes. The high-level themes are shown in the first level; the second level shows some of the comments within the theme. These comments break down into another level of detail (rather like the branches on a tree) to ensure the requirements are properly understood — thus a CTQ tree.

When you develop CTQs, you can usually group customer requirements under common sets of headings. We do this, and show a selection of examples and potential measures, in Table 4-3. Note the list is not exhaustive, as you may come up with other categories that are applicable to your process.

This common list allows you to structure the process of gathering requirements and reduces the risk of you missing a CTQ.

TABLE 4-3   **Some Common CTQs**

CTQ grouping	Examples	Measures
Speed	Bills paid on time (in and out)	Elapsed times and deviation from target
	Deliveries made on time	Turn-around times
	Time to answer calls	Call answer rate
	Turn-around time on IT project delivery	Call abandon rate
Accuracy	Orders containing the correct information	Number of defects in orders, deliveries, products or software
	Computer system that works	Number of calls to helpdesk
		Number of bugs reported by users testing a new computer system or a program change
Capacity	Needs to cope with the right volume of orders/number of simultaneous enquiries	Number of items per order
		Number of clients
		Number of concurrent users
		Number of orders per day
Data/ information	Easy access to order details and status	User can access order details and status within five minutes of request while mobile
	Software developer needs to understand how a software module works before changing it	Time spent converting data and cleansing data
		Percentage of software modules not meeting development standards
Safety	No customers or staff injured on company premises	Score on monthly safety audit, so, for example, number of injuries, near misses, and time between these incidents
Compliance	Industry applicable regulation, e.g. data protection, product safety, etc.	Complies
Money	Cost savings or cost avoidance	Cost of supplies
		Costs of poor quality
		Volume and/or cost of scrap
Environment	Recycling policy	Percentage of offices with recycling containers in daily use
	Biodegradable packaging	
	Emissions	Volume or percentage of waste recycled by type

Establishing the Real CTQs

Interpreting a customer's needs to form appropriate and realistic CTQs that can be measured presents a challenge. Often, customers jump to preconceived solutions and prescribe those solutions as part of their requirements. If you take these customers' requirements literally, several problems can occur, including missing their *real* requirements. The product or service you provide them with may then not be quite right. In turn, misunderstanding could then lead to you delivering more expensive or less efficient solutions than the particular CTQs require.

The secret to finding the real CTQs is to keep challenging the customer by asking "Why?" until the real need becomes clear. The Five Whys technique is outlined in more detail in Chapter 9. Below are two, real-life examples:

>> An internal customer said, "We need one integrated SAP system handling all orders instead of splitting orders between our different European divisions." But *why* do we need this?

The internal customer responded: "Because customers think we are unprofessional." But *why* do customers think that? The internal customer's answer explained that customers get more than one order acknowledgement if the order is split between divisions.

This answer gives us the real CTQ: "Customers require single order acknowledgement for all orders." You may find several solutions to meet this requirement without going to the expense of a single integrated SAP system.

>> An internal customer asks for a web-based order enquiry system. But *why* do they need this? They respond that enquiries currently take ages.

But why do enquiries take so long? The current process involves having to go to four different screens to get the information needed. By asking why speed is important, we discover that the customer is left waiting on the phone, but expects the answer within 30 seconds.

The real CTQ becomes: "Customers' order enquiries by telephone should be satisfied within 30 seconds." As with the first example, there could be several solutions to meeting the CTQ — the web-based idea may not be the most appropriate or economical.

Prioritizing the requirements

Clarifying your customers' CTQs (which we describe in the previous section) is vital, but you also need to find out which of the CTQs are especially important.

You can prioritize your CTQs in a number of ways. You can simply ask your customers to weight their own CTQs, or you can use a simple tool such as *paired comparisons.*

The paired comparisons technique provides a way to determine priorities and weight the importance of criteria. Using the paired comparisons tool forces you to make choices by looking at each pair from a list of options — in this case, a list of CTQs. Instead of asking your customers to identify their top choice, you ask them to select their preference from each pair.

For example, if you have five CTQs, you ask: "Do you prioritize A or B? A or C? A or D? A or E?" After A, you compare B and C, B and D, and B and E and so on.

You can use this technique face-to-face or by working virtually using a "voting grid" like that shown in Figure 4-4, where participants circle their choices for each comparison. In the example, ten preferences will be expressed. Imagine that A comes out with 4 votes, C gets 3, E has 2, but B receives only 1, and D none at all. It's clear that the most important CTQs are A and C, with E reasonably important in the middle, whereas B and D are of little consequence by comparison. In these circumstances you now know how especially important it is to get A and C right for the customer.

Item	Description				
A		A/B	A/C	A/D	A/E
B			B/C	B/D	B/E
C				C/D	C/E
D					D/E
E					

© Martin Brenig-Jones and Jo Dowdall

FIGURE 4-4: Paired comparisons: Do you prefer this or that?

Measuring performance using customer-focused measures

Talking about being customer-focused is much easier than actually *being* customer-focused. Using *outside-in* thinking and measures to assess your CTQ performance is one way to help you think differently and focus on the customer.

Determining your CTQs provides a basis for your measures. In Chapter 7 we look at measurement and data collection in some detail, but here we take a brief look at some of the different thinking you need in order to focus on your customers.

Think about what your customer sees and experiences in terms of your organization's products, services, and performance in meeting customers' requirements. Consider for example whether being a customer of your organization is easy.

TIP

Try to drag yourself outside your organization and take a look in — this is outside-in thinking. Think about what your customers see and experience and consider whether they're happy.

Understanding what your customers measure is helpful. Ask yourself whether your customers measure the same things as you — and then think about how their data compare with yours. Consider why differences may be evident. Then think about what your customers do with the output from your processes: where it fits in their processes. Here's a classic example:

Airlines make money when their planes are in the air. When a plane is out of commission, perhaps for servicing, the airline makes no money — the company needs the plane up and flying again as quickly as possible.

EXAMPLE

Staff in General Electric's (GE) aircraft engines division discovered the value of outside-in thinking when they realized their customers were measuring GE's performance a little differently from the way the organization did. GE would receive an engine into their servicing process — and their clock would start. When the service was complete, their clock stopped and they reported that this service had taken "X" hours to complete.

What they were forgetting was the fact that their customers were counting the time from when the engine came off the plane to the time when it was put back on — the *wing-to-wing time*. The phrase and the thinking caught on. Then-chief executive officer, Jack Welch, deployed this concept throughout the GE operations and divisions, worldwide.

Think about how your measures measure up. Is there scope for wing-to-wing thinking in your processes?

IN THIS CHAPTER

» Going to the Gemba and using
Process Stapling

» Drawing a spaghetti diagram to see
how the work gets done

» Creating a detailed map of the
process

Chapter **5**

Understanding the Process

W. Edwards Deming said, "If you can't describe what you are doing as a process, you don't know what you're doing." Having an up-to-date picture of what you are doing (the process) makes DMAIC (Define, Measure, Analyze, Improve and Control) improvement projects far easier to undertake (dive into Chapter 2 for more on doing DMAIC).

The Measure phase of DMAIC is about understanding how and how well the work gets done. We look at the "how well" aspect in Part 3; our focus here is to understand how the work currently gets done. Only when you understand how the process works *now* can you see the opportunities for improvement in your process and manage performance better.

Finding Out How the Work Gets Done

Process mapping is the main focus of this chapter. We look at two types: the deployment flowchart and the Value Stream Map. These maps build on the high-level SIPOC diagram explained in Chapter 3, and provide really helpful pictures of how the work gets done.

Before you draw any kind of process map, visit the workplace and see for yourself what's really happening. The Japanese refer to this observation as "going to the Gemba."

You're likely to find surprises waiting for you in the Gemba. Very often you'll find the process is being carried out differently to how you thought it was happening, especially when more than one team is involved. We cover techniques such as *Process Stapling* and *spaghetti diagrams* in this chapter. These techniques help you to see the reality of your workplace and enable you to identify unnecessary steps and eliminate waste. (We wade through waste in detail in Chapter 10.)

Practicing Process Stapling

Process Stapling offers a simple way to really understand the process and the chain of events. It means following the process, not from the perspective of the person operating the process, but from the perspective of the *thing* going through the process. For example, if it's the process for taking a customer order, you would walk through the entire process, step by step, as though you were the order.

No matter where the order goes, you go too. By following the order you start to see what really happens, who does what and why, how, where and when they do it. You might also see that the order "sat idle" for large chunks of time, which not only means that no value is being added, but also highlights a lack of "flow."

TIP

Carrying out a Process Stapling exercise with a small team of people can be an ideal first step. Sometimes, there can be advantages in beginning the exercise from the end of the process and working backwards. People will be less familiar with this "reverse flow," helping them think more carefully about things.

Before you go to the Gemba or do Process Stapling it's good practice to inform the team operating the process what you're doing and why you're there. When you're at the Gemba be respectful, listen, observe and learn.

The sidebar "Process Stapling in action" demonstrates the power of this technique. You begin to understand all the steps in the process and how much time and movement is involved in carrying out the work. Process Stapling helps you identify a number of improvement opportunities, even if you don't use the exercise to create a spaghetti diagram or process map.

You might, for example, spot opportunities for tidying up the workplace, making it easier and safer to find things. (We shine a light on neatness in Chapter 13.) The Process Stapling exercise helps you spot the frustrations in the process, such as inconsistencies and "why-on-earth-do-we-do-this?" activities. You can then see the steps that add value and those that don't. (We unveil value in Chapter 10 as well.)

It's not uncommon for only 10–15 percent of the time taken in a process to be spent on value-adding activities. Capturing or visualizing this can generate some powerful "a-ha!" moments.

WARNING

When introducing the idea of Process Stapling, you may find some people telling you that this is what they already do. But what they actually do is get a group of people in a room and use sticky notes to help draw up the process. They're missing the point! The picture they draw will be what they think is happening. Process Stapling enables you to see what's *really* happening.

TIP

Try taking photos of each step in the process (with the permission of the people involved). Apart from providing an ideal record of what you've seen, photos enable you to make an effective presentation to management of what you've found. Be prepared for them to be surprised. You can have fun taking the pictures especially if you act the role of the thing going through the process.

As your understanding of the process increases, you're likely to find real value in working with your customers to extend the Process Stapling concept to incorporate their activities with yours. In this way, you can work out how your process and its output link to your customer's process, what your customer's process looks like and how your customer uses your process outputs.

Extending Process Stapling provides great insight into how you can generate improvements in your process that really add value to your customers' experiences and make an impact that delights them. The technique can also lead to joint improvement activity with a DMAIC project being carried out in concert with your customer.

PROCESS STAPLING IN ACTION

This example reflects our experience of Process Stapling in at least one of our client organizations. Ann receives a customer order — she needs to input some information to the system, print out an internal form, add some additional information to it and then send it to Brian.

You now need to "staple" this form to yourself and take it over to Brian (imagine attaching it to your clothing, for example). Brian is some distance away. Immediately, you have a sense of how much transport is involved.

When you get to Brian, you find that his first action is to correct all of Ann's mistakes. You ask Ann whether she's aware that she'd got things wrong. She's not happy about this, as she thinks she'd been doing what Brian needed, and had always done it this way. Ann tells you that Brian has never mentioned anything about her mistakes. You find that Brian never bothers to tell Ann about the errors, which had been caused by misunderstanding, because he finds it easier to correct the mistakes himself.

After Brian corrects the errors, he sends the papers to Clare. You're dismayed to find that Clare sits next to Ann — shame the papers didn't go straight to Clare in the first place!

Clare tells you that this step is a complete waste of time. She's told her manager this, but her manager says the step is an important element of Clare's work. Clare just checks that the system is updated, that certain information is in the right box on the form and that Brian has put his signature on the form. She finds this task boring and has never yet found a case that needs correction, so she simply puts these items to one side, lets the work build up and then clears them all on a Friday afternoon before going home.

Drawing spaghetti diagrams

A spaghetti diagram provides a visual representation of the movement involved in a process including the flow of information and the people carrying out the work.

In Figure 5-1 we show a pretty confused series of movements in a garage as an example. We've seen similar situations in hospitals, offices, and staff restaurants. You can apply the technique to any working area or your home. You could even use a screen shot of an order entry application, for example, as the "map" and then trace the path of the computer cursor as the agent fills out a form. Spaghetti diagrams aren't restricted to operations that are physically spread out.

Think about the movements you make and the distance you travel when undertaking tasks such as picking up your printing or making a cup of tea.

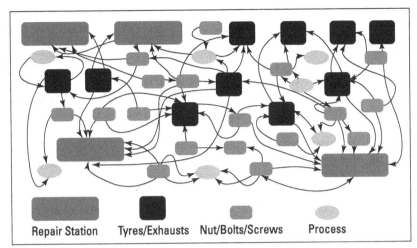

FIGURE 5-1:
A spaghetti
diagram.

Repair Station   Tyres/Exhausts   Nut/Bolts/Screws   Process

© Martin Brenig-Jones and Jo Dowdall

The spaghetti diagram may throw up some real surprises about how much movement happens in your organization, including how often things go back and forth. This technique helps you identify waste and provides a visual catalyst to stimulate change in your workplace.

TIP

The different shades used in Figure 5-1 have no special significance, but you do need to distinguish between the movement of people, materials and information. When you create a spaghetti diagram, you may want to use a current office plan, for example showing where the furniture, equipment and power points are located. Make sure the plan is current and that it includes all additional items, including those boxes in the corner that seem to have appeared from nowhere.

In developing a spaghetti diagram you can measure how far and why people are moving. You may be able to make some simple changes to your office layout to reduce the distance moved, or even to avoid it completely. You could even use a long ball of string or a pedometer to help you develop a more accurate diagram and better understand the movement involved. Recording the total distance travelled on the baseline of the diagram and then doing the same for the new and improved method is good practice. You then have a measure of the extent of improvement made.

EXAMPLE

The owner of an Italian restaurant in London tried spaghetti mapping (seriously!). As a result of analyzing how the counter was being used, they were able to reduce its size and fit another table, for more customers, into the floor space. *Che grande!*

When you use Process Stapling and spaghetti diagrams together, you may see the opportunity for a significant reduction in wasted movement and in other non-value-adding steps too. So, in the Process Stapling example described in the nearby sidebar, is Brian's step necessary? If it were, would sitting Ann, Brian and Clare more closely together make sense?

Unnecessary travelling and movement waste so much time. Sitting the relevant people and equipment together is often a relatively simple way of reducing waste and processing time. We look at waste in more detail in Chapter 10.

Creating a spaghetti diagram for the work you can't see, as well as the work you can see is beneficial — arguably more so. Where the item being processed is intangible (for example, in the form of a request that's being processed electronically), mapping the different systems or servers being used in the process highlights waste that might otherwise be invisible and go unchallenged.

Painting a Picture of the Process

When trying to understand your processes and how the work gets done, the phrase "a picture paints a thousand words" is certainly true. In this section we look at two specific options for painting that picture of your process — a deployment flowchart and a Value Stream Map. These are both forms of process maps, and we use the term "process mapping" in this section to describe their development.

TIP

When you paint the picture of your process, keep in mind why you're doing it. Developing the picture helps you understand how the work gets done and the degree of complexity in the process. Your picture can highlight the internal and external customer and supplier relationships or *interfaces,* and help you determine the input and in-process measures you need (see Chapter 7 for more on these).

You're not painting this particular picture as the specification for a computer system change, so keep things simple. This picture is for you and will help you manage and improve the process. You're drawing a "current state" picture to see how things are done *now.*

A "future state" map will show how the process could be undertaken to achieve a higher level of performance at some future point. When you've drawn and implemented your picture of a future state map, it becomes the current state map! With Continuous Improvement in mind, you now need to develop a new future state picture.

Your process picture can provide a useful framework that prompts a whole range of questions:

>> Who are the customers that have expectations of the process?

>> Why is the process done? What is its purpose? Does everyone involved understand the purpose?

>> What are the value-added and non-value-added steps?

>> How can you carry out essential non-value-added steps using minimal resources?

>> What are the critical success factors — that is, the things you must do well?

>> Why is the process done when it is done?

>> Why are tasks in the process carried out in that order? Are all the steps involved in the process necessary? Do all the steps add value for the customer?

>> Why is the process carried out by a particular person or people?

>> What measurement is in place to assess performance and identify possible improvement opportunities? Think in particular of how you might identify and measure those parts of the process that are repetitive and important to ensuring the process conforms to requirements.

>> What is the cycle time (the time it takes to complete the process for one unit of work)? Why is the cycle time longer than the processing time?

>> What are the barriers that prevent the supplier from producing a quality output?

>> If decisions need to be made as part of the process, are the criteria that will be used to make the decisions understood by everyone involved? Are the decisions communicated adequately? Are the authority limits appropriate?

>> How do you and others deal with problems that occur in the process?

>> What are the most common mistakes that occur in the process? What impact do these mistakes have on customers?

>> Where have improvements already been tried in the process? What were the outcomes?

Whichever questions you ask, don't forget to keep asking "Why?"

Keeping things simple

Process mapping can use lots of different symbols, or *conventions*; try to use as few as possible. To create a deployment flowchart, which we talk about in the next section, just two or three conventions are usually enough: the circle, the square box and the diamond, as shown in Figure 5-2:

>> The circle indicates the start and stop points in your process.

>> The square box signifies a step or action.

>> The diamond poses a question, where the answer determines which route the process follows next.

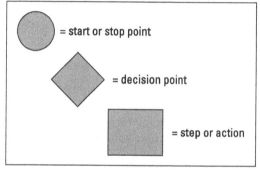

© Martin Brenig-Jones and Jo Dowdall

FIGURE 5-2:
Keeping it simple
with process
mapping
symbols.

Take a bank underwriting a loan application as an example. The process steps may be different depending on the amount of money being requested as a loan. In the case of underwriting the request, it may be that large cases need to go to a senior underwriter or require key documents from the client, whereas a small loan might be processed at a more junior level or need less documentation. So, the diamond indicates a decision point with a question about the size of the loan, as shown in Figure 5-3.

Developing a deployment flowchart

The deployment flowchart builds on the high-level SIPOC diagram described in Chapter 3, and goes into a little more detail. This flowchart identifies who's involved in the process and what they do, including the different members of a team who are involved in different stages of the process, and also other teams and departments, the internal customers and suppliers.

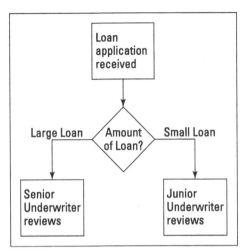

FIGURE 5-3: Which route do we follow?

Spotting moments of truth is easier when using a deployment flowchart. *Moments of truth* are touch points with the customer (when a customer comes into contact with a company), which we consider in the later section "Identifying moments of truth."

TIP

Before you begin working on a deployment flowchart, make sure you have an objective for the process that reflects the CTQs (we cover Critical To Quality elements in Chapter 4). And make sure you can answer the question, "Why are you doing this process?"

Involve the people who work in the process when you develop a deployment flowchart. Because different perceptions exist of how the process works, use a sticky note (physical or virtual) for each step in the process so that you can move things around simply. You may well discover that the process is more complex than you think it is, which is why carrying out a Process Stapling exercise first can be so useful.

Process mapping can be done face-to-face, with brown paper and sticky notes. It can also be done virtually using an online collaboration tool. There are some great ones to try including Mural and Miro.

EXAMPLE

In the sidebar "Process Stapling in action" earlier in this chapter, we introduce Ann, Brian and Clare. If you haven't read this sidebar, have a quick flick through it because we use the same example, beginning with Figure 5-4, when we develop our map. Each time a different person or another area in the workplace is involved, the work moves to a different lane. Telling the story of Ann, Brian, and Clare helps to bring the work to life here, but it's preferable to include roles or teams rather than the names of individuals in your charts.

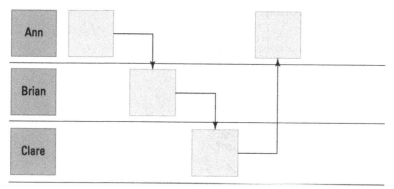

FIGURE 5-4:
The deployment
flowchart.

These charts usually have lines between the different people/roles and are often referred to as "swim lane" charts.

TIP

In Figure 5-4, we focus on Ann, Brian, and Clare, but including the customer in the picture will help you to identify the moments of truth (see the "Identifying moments of truth" section later in this chapter). Computer systems can also be included in your cast of characters. Seeing the whole picture is vital.

We cover measurement in more detail in Chapters 7 and 8, but here we highlight some of the opportunities to put measurement in place. Understanding what's happening at the interfaces or "handoffs" (where process work changes lane) can be particularly helpful, as most problems occur at these points — for example, when the work passes between Ann and Brian, as shown in Figure 5-5. Measures would help to identify if problems exist, perhaps caused by unclear requirements.

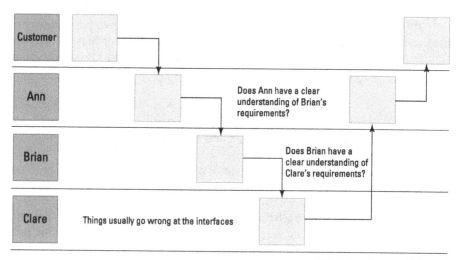

FIGURE 5-5:
Highlighting the
interfaces.

Chapter 7 looks at the need to collect good data and develop a data collection plan and considers the importance of "in-process" measures. Your results here will have a major impact on your performance for the customer, so having a clear understanding of what's happening and how well it's happening is essential. In Figure 5-4, for example, you'd want to know whether Ann's output to Brian and Brian's output to Clare is always correct, and so on. If it isn't, you'd then want to find out what type of errors were occurring so that you could begin improving the situation.

Measuring time can highlight other improvement opportunities, as shown in Figure 5-6. For example, you may ask how long each step takes and why.

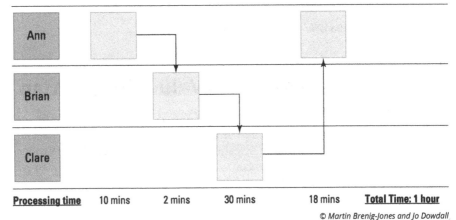

FIGURE 5-6:
Measuring time.

Processing time	10 mins	2 mins	30 mins	18 mins	Total Time: 1 hour

© Martin Brenig-Jones and Jo Dowdall

In Figure 5-6 you're simply measuring *unit time* or processing time — the time it takes to complete this step. While this measurement could prompt some interesting questions, viewing the bigger picture is more helpful as it also includes the *elapsed* or overall time taken. Figure 5-7 shows the cycle time of the process from beginning to end, which includes waiting time between steps.

Building in the overall time helps you identify *dead time* — so-called because from the customer's perspective nothing's happening. In Figure 5-7, step number two is causing a problem. If Brian's step can possibly be removed from the process, and Ann or Clare takes up Brian's work, you may be able to halve the cycle time. Possibly Brian's step is a non-value-adding step (explained in Chapter 9) and isn't needed at all.

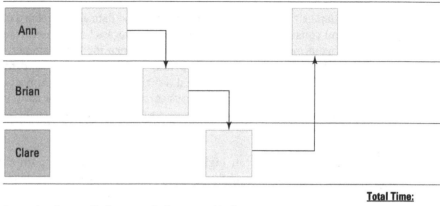

						Total Time:
Processing time	10 mins	2 mins	30 mins	18 mins		1 hour
Cycle time		1 day	2 days	3 days	4 days	4 days

FIGURE 5-7: Total time showing dead time experienced by customers.

Constructing a Value Stream Map

A Value Stream Map could be used as an an addition or an alternative to the deployment flowchart as a way of looking at how work gets done in your organization. The Value Stream Map shows all the tasks, both value-adding and non-value-adding (more on value in Chapter 10), which take your product from concept to launch or from order to delivery, for example. These actions include steps to process information from the customer, and steps to transform the product on its way to the customer.

Toyota's Taiichi Ohno summarized the value stream nicely in 1978 when he said:

> All we are doing is looking at a timeline from the moment the customer gives us an order to the point when we collect the cash. And we are reducing that timeline by removing the Non-Value-Adding wastes.

Value Stream Maps follow a product's path from order to delivery to determine current conditions.

Value Stream Mapping is also used (some would say best used) as a strategic tool to visualize the flow of value across the organization from end to end. Leaders get real benefit when they review this "big picture" together, in its current state, and identify waste and improvement opportunities. They can see the organization as a system rather than as "silos" or separate functions. The team (including leaders and Subject Matter Experts) can then develop an agreed and improved "future state" picture based on Lean Six Sigma principles and concepts. The improvement actions required to move from the current state to the future state might include eliminating waste by, for example, combining three aspects of the operation into one, or instigating a defects reduction program, or automation. These improvements could form a transformation road map that could take 12 months or so to complete, and Lean Six Sigma can likely be used to address many elements of the work.

Note that "automation" is the last thing on the list of potential activities. "Simplify first, then automate" is a mantra we will explore further in Chapter 13. Simply put, there is no point automating steps that don't add value!

EXAMPLE

An organization we worked with in the energy sector mapped their "core" processes and rationalized them from over 70 to 5. They then assigned a Value Stream Manager to each one to maintain accountability for the value stream from end to end. More power to their elbow, as the saying goes!

TIP

Process Stapling is an ideal first step to help you create a Value Stream Map, and you really do need to go to the Gemba to see what's happening. For the low-down on these concepts, check out the "Going to the Gemba" sidebar and the "Practicing Process Stapling" section earlier in this chapter.

The Value Stream Map is similar to the format of a SIPOC diagram, which we talk about in Chapter 3. Ideally, your Value Stream Map includes a picture of where the various activities happen and shows the flow of both materials and information, as shown in Figure 5-8.

FIGURE 5-8:
Part of a Value
Stream Map.

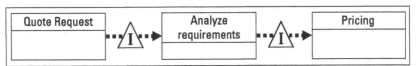

© Martin Brenig-Jones and Jo Dowdall

Figure 5-8 keeps things very simple. It includes some extra information; in this case, a triangle that identifies work in progress (the "i" is for inventory) — work waiting to be actioned. In practice, Value Stream Maps are straightforward, but they'll be a little more detailed than this example (see Figures 5-10 and 5-11) and will use more conventions than you use in a deployment flowchart (which we cover in the "Developing a deployment flowchart" section earlier in this chapter). A selection of the more commonly used conventions is shown in Figure 5-9.

To draw your Value Stream Map, work through the following steps:

1. **Identify the process you want to look at, agreeing and defining the start and stop points.**

   Describing the product or service this process is supporting is also helpful.

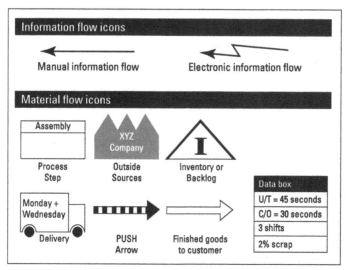

FIGURE 5-9:
Value Stream
Map conventions.

Information flow icons

Manual information flow   Electronic information flow

Material flow icons

Assembly

Process Step

XYZ Company

Outside Sources

I

Inventory or Backlog

Monday + Wednesday

Delivery

PUSH Arrow

Finished goods to customer

Data box

U/T = 45 seconds

C/O = 30 seconds

3 shifts

2% scrap

© Martin Brenig-Jones and Jo Dowdall

2. **Set up a small team to do the analysis.**

   The team should have knowledge of all the steps involved, from supplier input to external customer, so it must include people working in the process.

3. **Go to the Gemba.**

   Go where the action is and watch what actually happens. Value Stream Mapping starts in the workplace.

4. **Working at a reasonably high level, draw a process map of the material/ product flow in the whole value stream.**

   Some people prefer to do this exercise starting at the customer end and working backwards. Write down the steps as you go, rather than trying to remember everything. As well as material and product flow, remember to capture the information flow that causes product or material to move through the process.

5. **Identify the performance data you'd like to know.**

   Useful information often includes processing time (also referred to as unit time), waiting time between process steps, scrap or rework rates, the number of staff/resources, batch sizes, machine uptime, changeover time, inventory, and backlog.

6. **Collect the data you need for each step in the process.**

   Add the data to your map in boxes. For example, in Figure 5-9, you can see a data box capturing a range of information, including unit time (U/T = 45 seconds).

The "C/O = 30 minutes" entry refers to changeover time. This is the time it takes to set up the equipment to move from processing one type of product to another, or to close one system and open another. A focus on reducing changeover time was one of the keys to success for Toyota in gaining market share over many of the Western car manufacturers, where it was referred to as SMED — *single minute exchange of die* (die are the casts and molds in the production system).

EXAMPLE

Where does the "single minute" come in? Working as a consultant in Toyota, Shigeo Shingo believed the company could make huge gains if changeovers could be actioned more quickly. He set a target to reduce any set-up time by 59/60ths. Shingo felt that many companies had policies designed to raise the skill level of their workers but few had implemented strategies to lower the skill level required by the set-up itself.

Changeovers and set-ups aren't relevant only to manufacturing companies and processes — they're just as relevant to service organizations.

7. **Add arrows to show information flows.**

The Value Stream Map shows information flow as well as material flow, separately identifying whether the information is sent manually or electronically (see the different symbols in Figure 5-9). The Value Stream Map shows the information flow in the top half of the map, with the material flow below.

8. **Add an overall timeline to show the average time taken.**

This timeline shows how long the item spends in the whole process. The example in Figure 5-10 identifies the process steps A to I and indicates the processing or unit time and the lead time. The figure shows a process with a unit time of only four hours, but taking 187 days to complete! "Lead time" in a Value Stream Map shows the time it takes to for one unit of work to go through the entire process. It takes into account the number of items of work in the queue (inventory). Inventory identified is in the triangles between the process steps.

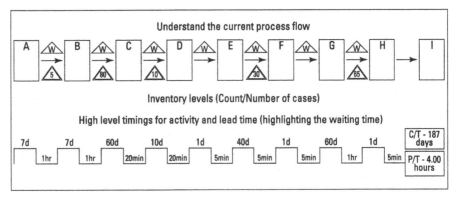

FIGURE 5-10: Identifying the delays.

As an example of a Value Stream Map, consider ABC Company's order process. The process begins with customer service receiving an email or telephone order. The product price is checked using the product price database.

Availability is checked in terms of stock inventory using the stock management system. If inventory cannot be allocated, the order is passed to the manufacturing team through the manufacturing order system and scheduled for production the next day.

The delivery date is determined, the customer is advised and the order entry records are completed through the customer service order management system. The "current state" picture of the value stream will resemble that shown in Figure 5-11.

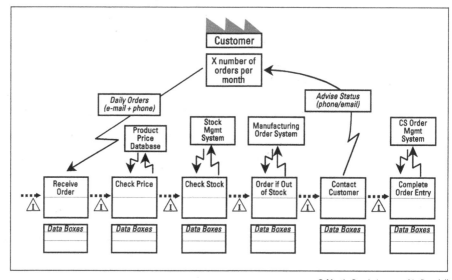

FIGURE 5-11:
The ABC order process as a Value Stream Map.

© Martin Brenig-Jones and Jo Dowdall

WARNING

Using averages is usually fine, but do recognize the danger of averages and remember that the actual times vary either side of the mean — known in the worlds of statistics and mathematics as "variation." We cover variation in detail in Chapter 8.

In the ABC example, the current state map includes some triangles containing the letter "i." These triangles are for the levels of inventory, or work in progress. When you create a Value Stream Map for one of your processes, you need to remember that the map describes the current state of your organization — a snapshot in time. Whether people in the organization feel the inventory isn't usually that high or low isn't relevant; for whatever reason, the inventory is what it is *right now*.

In order to have a complete view of things, you need to incorporate data such as activity time (also known as processing time or unit time), waiting time between steps (also known as lead time) changeover time, inventory, and overall lead time.

The following example of a Value Stream Map in a service organization demonstrates how valuable the addition of data becomes. It enables you to not only see how the work gets done, but also how well it gets done.

The next few pages focus on a bank example, and the creation of the Value Stream Map for the loans application process. This example demonstrates the steps in creating the map and then shows how problem areas within the process can be identified, flagged and prioritized for improvement action.

The loans team had already developed a SIPOC diagram (explained in Chapter 3), but they weren't sure that it was entirely accurate. So the first step in this instance was for them to understand how the work gets done by carrying out a Process Stapling exercise. In doing so, they took note of the work in progress levels (the "i" in the triangles; see Figure 5-9), and they created a current state map step by step, as shown in Figures 5-12 to 5-18.

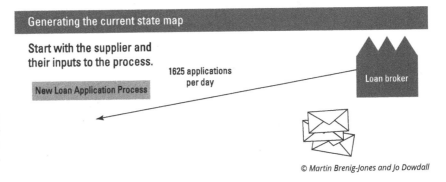

FIGURE 5-12: Building up the Value Stream Map.

© Martin Brenig-Jones and Jo Dowdall

The loan applications are sent into the company by loan brokers acting on behalf of individuals. In Figure 5-13, you can see that 1,625 applications have been received on this particular day.

In many ways, this picture is similar to the SIPOC, but it lacks information about who all the different customers and suppliers are (both internal and external), and the associated inputs and outputs. Having created this picture, it's time to add in some data, as shown in Figure 5-14.

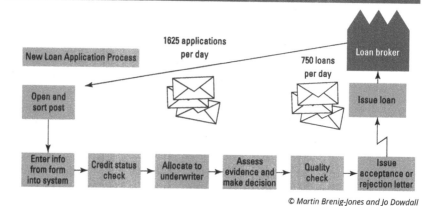

FIGURE 5-13:
Developing the
picture.

© Martin Brenig-Jones and Jo Dowdall

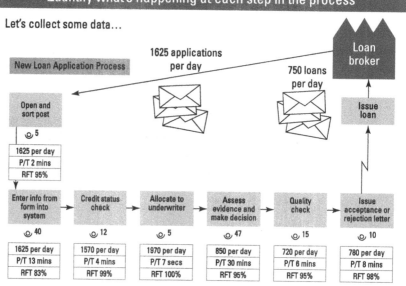

FIGURE 5-14:
Collecting data.

© Martin Brenig-Jones and Jo Dowdall

We're beginning to create a detailed picture of what's happening in this process. The data shows the number of people working on each step, work volumes and the levels of accuracy. Already we can see opportunities for improvement through the reduction of errors.

The circle and half circle symbols and the numbers alongside them indicate the number of people working at that process step. The data boxes hold the information you decide is important. In this case, the bank has included the number of items received each day, the processing time (P/T) and the percentage "right first time" (RFT). You might have wanted other information like, for example, the changeover time or productivity details.

Either way, you can see there's scope for reducing errors, especially in the "enter info from form into system" step, where the error rate is 17 percent. This high error rate would be a problem anywhere in the process, but at such an early stage is likely to lead to delays for the customer, particularly if the errors aren't picked up straight away. And think about the cost too.

By building in the inventory (work in progress information), we're getting clues about the backlogs and bottlenecks, and the dangers inherent in a "push" system are becoming obvious.

In Figure 5-15, the work in progress figures — the numbers alongside the triangle — confirm the delays in the process and help highlight the areas that need addressing. The bottlenecks need to be managed, or you'll find that they manage you and your process.

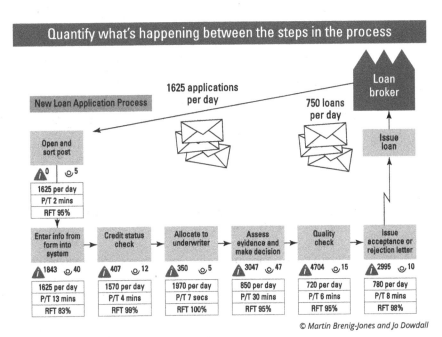

FIGURE 5-15: Looking at the interfaces.

© Martin Brenig-Jones and Jo Dowdall

You can see that with 4,704 items the "quality check" step has a serious backlog, but issues are evident throughout the process, something the addition of a time-line will further confirm.

The timeline shown in Figure 5-16 enables us to focus on the inventory — the reason why there is a difference between the time it takes to complete the process for one unit and the time it takes for a unit to go through the entire production cycle (lead time).

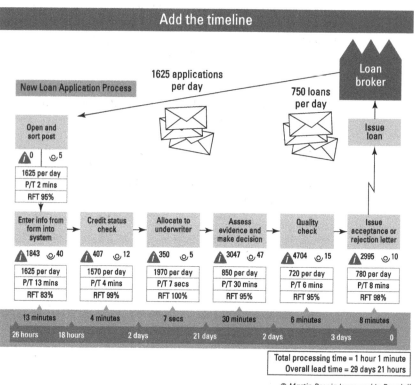

© Martin Brenig-Jones and Jo Dowdall

FIGURE 5-16: So what's the time?

Clear links are evident between measuring time and the theory of constraints, which we cover in Chapter 11.

The timeline information will also help you identify whether the line needs to be better balanced. And, of course, if you then determine takt time (see Chapter 1 for more on this), you can assess the staffing levels needed to deal with the customer volumes.

Clearly, improvement opportunities exist and the next step is to highlight these on the Value Stream Map.

A selection of the opportunities and observations are included in Figure 5-17. This continues the process of bringing the picture to life and creates the basis to discuss the opportunities for improvement action. Apart from tackling the bottlenecks, non-value-adding steps may exist that can be removed, or perhaps people and equipment could be relocated into a more efficiently laid out workspace. Some activities could be combined, too, and, if there are different types of loan application, an option may exist to set up a process team for the relevant product family, using the concept of cell manufacturing.

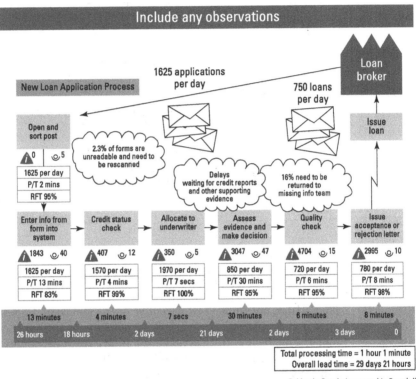

FIGURE 5-17: Process mapping and data may help highlight the opportunities for analysis.

© Martin Brenig-Jones and Jo Dowdall

The improvement ideas or objectives could be added to the map for further review and prioritization and this could help you develop a future state map in line with that shown in Figure 5-18.

Developing a picture of your process, using a deployment flowchart and/or a Value Stream Map will also help you identify the moments of truth.

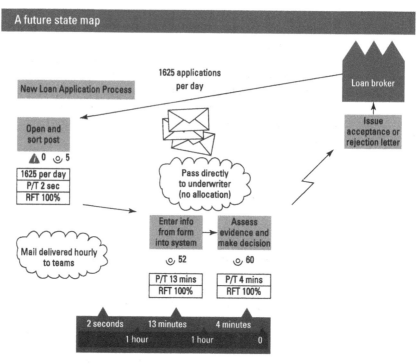

FIGURE 5-18:
A future
state map.

Total processing time = 17 minutes 2 seconds
Total lead time = 2 hours
Takt time = 25200 seconds/1625 = 15 seconds

Identifying moments of truth

Jan Carlzon, one-time Chief Executive of Scandinavian Air Services (SAS), developed and popularized the concept of moments of truth in his book of the same name. A moment of truth occurs every time a customer comes into contact with a company, whether in person, online, on the telephone, by post, when reading company literature or seeing a company advertisement. Each customer touch point provides an opportunity to make or break the organization, since the customer is either pleased or displeased with the outcome. Everyone in your organization is responsible for the outcome of customer touch points and for delivering a great customer experience.

Carlzon informed all SAS staff that the organization needed to improve by 1,000 percent! He asked his staff to improve 1,000 things by 1 percent and then to keep doing it. He wanted them to focus on customer contacts — the moments of truth — such as booking a ticket, checking in or boarding a plane. Carlzon used an example of a passenger pulling down the meal tray. If the tray was dirty, what would the customer think? What might that tell the customer about the maintenance of the plane?

To achieve what your customers want, you need to understand the many moments of truth opportunities that exist and find ways of enhancing the customer's experience. Process Stapling, deployment flowcharts and Value Stream Maps can help you identify both internal and external customer touch points.

Chapter **6**

Managing People and Change

Whatever its size or sector, whatever its location or its unique selling proposition, an organization is about people. And the good news is that people bring potential, a wealth of knowledge, experience and creativity. Enabling and empowering people to fulfill their potential is a key Lean Six Sigma principle. When it comes to understanding how processes work and identifying how they could be improved, who better to involve than the people who operate the process? People potential is so important that failing to unlock it and realize it has been identified as one of the eight "deadly wastes" found in organizations (which we cover in Chapter 10).

U.S. Army General George Patton clearly saw the potential in people when he said, "Never tell people how to do things. Tell them what to do, and they will surprise you with their ingenuity."

Understanding people is key to implementing Lean Six Sigma and making improvements work. Almost always, if a Lean Six Sigma project fails, people issues of one form or another are the cause. In this chapter, we offer guidance and tips for managing the human aspects of change. We're tackling this important issue near the beginning of the book because it's something to be addressed at the very start when using Lean Six Sigma.

TIP

Get started with the "people" side of Lean Six Sigma at the earliest possible opportunity such as, for example, at the beginning of an improvement project, or maybe before the project even starts!

Getting into the Grey Matter

We know that people are full of potential, and their contribution is a key factor in driving improvement. But the very fact that *we are people* can cause problems when it comes to making changes. Neuroscience is increasingly being used as a means to understand the impact of change on people, and insights from this field are now used to inform Change Management approaches and the world of work in general. In *Neuroscience for Organizational Change*, Hilary Scarlett highlights the value of working with the brain to support Change Management. This can reduce negative impacts on mental health and well-being — a key present day concern.

Going back millions of years, when humans had just begun to walk upright and were starting to use tools for the first time, life was very different. We were surrounded by threats to our very existence (diseases, predators, and so on), and we needed to be on our guard. Our brains are wired to protect us in these circumstances — to respond to threats in order to survive. This way in which we are wired affects how we respond to threats in today's world, so we're constantly on the alert for changes, and we're sensitive to the dangers they might represent.

We also struggle with uncertainty associated with change. Uncertainty activates the parts of our brain that deal with fear and pain. We're less able to think clearly when confronted with uncertainty because as anxiety increases, we feel more threatened, and we expect the worst. It's difficult in these circumstances to maintain normal levels of professionalism, productivity, and positivity. No wonder we find it difficult when faced with change, even if that change will ultimately make things better. Luckily, there are some tools to help.

Gaining Acceptance

George Eckes, a well-known writer on this subject, uses a simple but eloquent expression to describe gaining acceptance for change, whether for a whole Lean Six Sigma program or for the changes resulting from part of a Lean Six Sigma project:

$$E = Q \times A$$

E is the effectiveness of the change.

Q is the quality of the solution. The tools of Lean Six Sigma will have proven that the solution works when tested.

A is the acceptance of the change by people — the degree to which they take the change on board and adopt the solution.

An ideal solution may have been identified, but its effectiveness depends on how well it is accepted. If acceptance is low, even the best solution won't deliver the benefits it deserves. Some practitioners believe that the A factor is more important than the Q factor and is the real key to success in Lean Six Sigma. To understand how people perceive things and to win support, you need to score well on both factors. If you're in the early stages of deploying a Lean Six Sigma program, the A factor is likely to start with winning support from senior managers.

Remember $Q \times A$ as a simple shorthand for a highly complicated issue . . . dealing with the human mind.

Sizing Up the Status Quo

Responses to change are shaped by many factors. These may include "initiative fatigue," anxiety (words like "efficiency" and "change" can drive fearful responses), disillusionment, or disinclination, as well as excitement and enthusiasm. There are some simple tools that can help weigh up the current situation.

Using a forcefield diagram

A forcefield diagram, shown in Figure 6-1, is a useful graphical representation of the positive and negative forces influencing a particular project or initiative. This tool will help to put your project into the context of your organization or situation.

» First brainstorm the factors (forces) working for and against the change. Positive forces are those that will work in favor of the change. Negative forces are those that could hinder it.

» Now determine the "strength" of the forces. You could use a score here, or use the size of the arrows to indicate their strength (the longer the arrow, the stronger the force).

» Discuss and agree what can be done to build on positive forces and maximize their potential, and reduce or remove the negative forces.

» Take appropriate actions to support success, and revisit the forcefield diagram frequently.

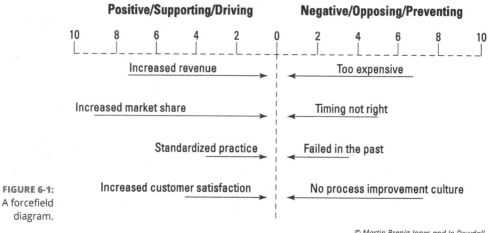

Positive/Supporting/Driving   **Negative/Opposing/Preventing**

10   8   6   4   2   0   2   4   6   8   10

Increased revenue → ← Too expensive

Increased market share → ← Timing not right

Standardized practice → ← Failed in the past

Increased customer satisfaction → ← No process improvement culture

FIGURE 6-1:
A forcefield
diagram.

© Martin Brenig-Jones and Jo Dowdall

Analyzing your stakeholders

Stakeholder analysis is another useful technique for identifying the "interest groups" (stakeholders) in your project and their levels of support.

Use the matrix in Figure 6-2 to show where the stakeholders are now on the positive/negative scale, and also where they should be for the project to be successful. This kind of stakeholder analysis needs to be regularly updated during the life of a project, and is best kept for the team's eyes only. You're dealing with sensitive stuff: how people think and whether they're for or against change.

Stakeholder matrix

Names	Strongly against	Moderately against	Neutral	Moderately supportive	Strongly supportive	Hot/Cold spots	Next steps
A	X		0				
B				X	0		
C					X 0		
D			X	0			

X = where they are   0 = where we need them to be

FIGURE 6-2:
Stakeholder
analysis.

© Martin Brenig-Jones and Jo Dowdall

No matter what change you propose, some people will be very much for it, some completely against, some in-between, and some almost indifferent. And that's pretty much life! Don't be surprised when you find this range of attitudes applying to your project or to the solution that you and your team eventually develop. Finding out early in the project what the for/against situation looks like, both on the surface and beneath it, is a good idea.

A *key stakeholder* is anyone who controls critical resources, who can block the change initiative by direct or indirect means, must approve certain aspects of the change strategy, shapes the thinking of other critical parties, or owns a key work process impacted by the change initiative. So in your Lean Six Sigma team, ask these questions:

>> Who are the key stakeholders?

>> Where do they currently stand on the issues associated with this change initiative?

>> Are they supportive and to what degree?

>> Are they against and to what degree?

>> Are they broadly neutral?

Given their status or influence on your project, where do you need the stakeholders to be? Moving some stakeholders to a higher level of support may be both desirable and possible, so work out how you can do so. Consider what turns them on or off, and think about how you can present the project in a more appealing and effective way for them.

Coping with Change

Several models illustrate the stages that people go through when coping with change in their lives. Many people know the Kübler-Ross model involving the following stages: denial, anger, bargaining, depression and acceptance.

Figure 6-3 illustrates how people typically react to change over time. This figure includes some additional elements based on observations made by change experts since the original model was developed.

When using this model, note that the stages are not "linear," which means some people won't experience all of them, and they won't necessarily experience them in the sequence presented here. Note also that the stages apply to individuals rather than teams. A manager or change agent wishing to employ particular strategies to support the team through change should recognize that each individual within the team will experience the stages at different times and for different durations of time. So a "one size fits all" approach will not be effective.

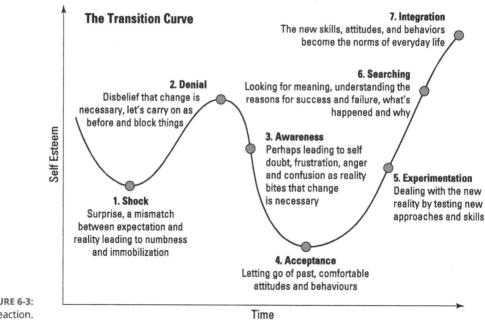

The Transition Curve

2. Denial
Disbelief that change is necessary, let's carry on as before and block things

1. Shock
Surprise, a mismatch between expectation and reality leading to numbness and immobilization

3. Awareness
Perhaps leading to self doubt, frustration, anger and confusion as reality bites that change is necessary

4. Acceptance
Letting go of past, comfortable attitudes and behaviours

5. Experimentation
Dealing with the new reality by testing new approaches and skills

6. Searching
Looking for meaning, understanding the reasons for success and failure, what's happened and why

7. Integration
The new skills, attitudes, and behaviors become the norms of everyday life

Self Esteem

Time

© Martin Brenig-Jones and Jo Dowdall

FIGURE 6-3:
Change reaction.

The Kubler-Ross Transition Curve is a useful reference point because it's helpful to know how people experience change so we can respond and manage change appropriately and effectively.

Kurt Lewin's iceberg model (also referred to as Change as Three Steps or CATS) dates back to the late 1940s but has influenced succeeding models and frameworks associated with change. Here's how it works:

1. **Unfreeze.** In this first phase, we move away from the way things currently are. Of course, depending on the circumstances, this may be easy or not, or desirable or not. Leaders play an important role in unfreezing when organizations are changing, as the need for change should be communicated clearly and well understood. Here they should be working to build the level of acceptance for change and communicating a compelling need.

2. **Change.** Having accepted and understood the need for change, we go into this second phase in an "unfrozen" state where we're ready to let go of old ways. Because we're not frozen into a fixed position, it's possible to change shape. The change phase is not a one-off event but a *process,* as here we begin to get used to new ways of working or being. Leaders contribute in this phase by ensuring that communication is ongoing and support is available, and by providing role models for the "future state." This phase is not always easy, and some trial and error and can be expected.

3. **Refreeze.** In the final phase, those new ways of working become embedded and accepted as the status quo. In the same way that we apply the Control phase in a Lean Six Sigma DMAIC project, the focus is on cementing the change and avoiding slipping back into old habits. Reinforcing positives and recognizing efforts can support sustainability, as can addressing the old and unhelpful habits from the previous state.

Lewin's model shows that it's impossible to change if you're frozen or locked firmly into old habits, and it's difficult to sustain them if they're still being formed and are not yet fully fixed in place.

It is helpful to understand that refreezing is not likely to be permanent. We'll need to change again and again. We probably won't stay frozen in the new state for a long time. (This is the spirit of Continuous Improvement! Things will continue to change, and we'll want to unfreeze and change with them.)

Creating the Vision

In his bestselling book, *Start with Why*, Simon Sinek outlines why "why" is so important to human beings. And it goes back to where we started this chapter: to how our brains are wired.

Sinek uses the Golden Circle shown in Figure 6-4 to illustrate why "typical" approaches to communication don't work as well as they could. Using the typical approach, a message would start with *what* is going to happen, followed by *how* it is going to happen, and finally, *why* it is going to happen.

But Sinek says this method, that moves from the outside in is ineffective. Inspired communicators start from the inside, with *why*, and work outwards. If you were to look down on a diagram of the human brain, you'd see a pretty similar image to the one shown here. The part of the brain that deals with feelings and emotions (the Limbic brain) is right in the middle. It's this part that processes the why and how messages. The part of our brain that helps us deal with the what, by focusing on analytical and rational thought (our neocortex), is on the outside.

So Sinek says that starting with why and moving from the inside out is by far the most effective method of communicating because you're talking directly to the part of the brain that controls behavior.

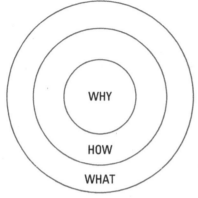
Customers, business leaders and employees all view the future from different perspectives. Imagining a time machine is an ideal way to develop a vision: you can speed ahead and discover for real what it will be like when the change has been completed. What is different? What is there more or less of? Being in the future you can find out how the change has affected people's attitudes and behaviors. What does it feel like now? How does it look from the view of the customer, the leader and the employee?

A time machine is outside the scope of even the most extensive Lean Six Sigma Master Black Belt toolkit, so we use a simple technique called *backwards visioning*. This technique helps you create a picture of the future expressed in behavioral terms — that is, what the culture will be like in the future. The improvement team (the Lean Six Sigma team) imagines that their change has been completed successfully and then considers what they'd expect to see, both internally and externally, which may include the following:

>> Customer satisfaction

>> Behaviors

>> Results

>> Rewards

>> Recognition

By determining the team's perceptions of these issues, you can begin to understand the actions that you may need to take as part of your progress towards the desired state — the future after the change has been made. These actions include the activities and behaviors that you need to reduce and remove and those that you need to introduce and increase.

You may want a more supportive culture, in which people help each other to a greater extent, work better in teams and operate less according to their own private agendas. Creating a vision is about leadership, taking responsibility and working in the best interests of the business.

Writing down a backwards visioning statement provides a helpful framework for developing influencing strategies. For example, a good vision for the future for an airport operator working on reducing queues and increasing security is:

> *Our goal is to transform the security experience of the travelling passenger by: (a) exceeding expectations by eliminating queues, and (b) creating a highly professional environment overseen by security staff who are rigorous, professional, helpful and proactive.*

A clear vision provides clarity about the outcomes of the change effort and helps you to identify at least some of the elements that the change aims to transform. A vision secures commitment and support from anyone involved in delivering this service by helping people understand what you want to change — and why.

Busting Assumptions

"Your assumptions are your windows on the world," wrote Isaac Asimov. "Scrub them off every once in a while, or the light won't come in." *Assumption busting* is a useful tool for challenging why things are done in the way they are. Keep asking "Why are things done this way?" to get beyond the initial, often superficial, responses.

EXAMPLE

A project to speed up land registry applications in the UK provides a good example. Registrations had always been sent to the legal department for review if the property value exceeded a particular amount. It transpired that no logic was involved in this decision as the value of the property made no difference to the complexity of the title — but it did add three months to the completion time!

Assumption busting is done in three simple but very effective steps:

1. **Identify the assumptions** (and don't miss the obvious ones).

2. **Challenge them.** It can't be done? Why not?

3. **Identify how it *can* be done.** Asking "what if?" can be helpful here.

Here are some common false assumptions:

- » It is impossible to do that.
- » The rules will not allow that approach.
- » We will never get it through IT in time (okay, maybe that one is fair!).
- » Department A, B, C (take your pick) will never agree.
- » These all need to go for authorization before being processed.
- » Every project needs to have all 164 project documents produced before being given the go-ahead (even small projects?).
- » We don't have the money, equipment, room or personnel.
- » Central office would never agree to it.
- » You can't teach an old dog new tricks.
- » It's too radical a change.
- » That's beyond our responsibility.
- » The employees will reject it outright.

Work with your team to see if you can bust these assumptions and challenge the status quo.

To deal with the people issues we describe in this chapter and to understand the key elements involved in managing change, we use the elements of change model shown in Figure 6-5, based on work by John Kotter, to help you in the deployment of the overall approach and in local and cross-company projects.

This model can be used as a simple but effective tool to assess how well you're doing in relation to the Change Management elements of individual projects and also of the overall deployment program. You can use the radar-like chart shown in Figure 6-6 to carry out regular assessments of progress.

Scoring 100 percent means perfect, whereas scores nearer the center indicate areas where more work needs to be done. This chart is a great tool to use in your team; everyone can carry out their own assessment initially and then share each other's to see where common themes or differences of opinion exist.

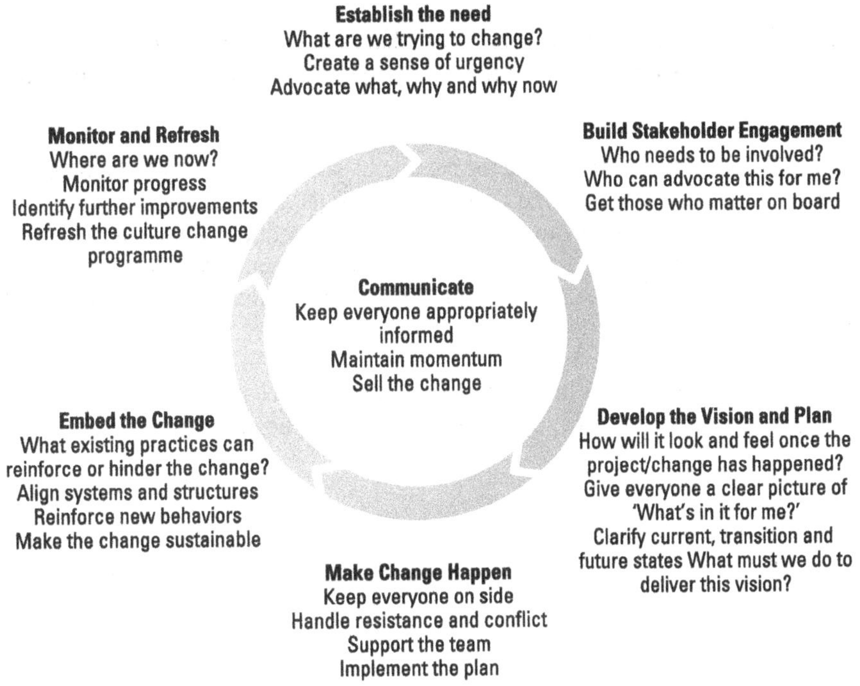

FIGURE 6-5: Elements of change model.

Establish the need
What are we trying to change?
Create a sense of urgency
Advocate what, why and why now

Build Stakeholder Engagement
Who needs to be involved?
Who can advocate this for me?
Get those who matter on board

Monitor and Refresh
Where are we now?
Monitor progress
Identify further improvements
Refresh the culture change
programme

Communicate
Keep everyone appropriately
informed
Maintain momentum
Sell the change

Embed the Change
What existing practices can
reinforce or hinder the change?
Align systems and structures
Reinforce new behaviors
Make the change sustainable

Develop the Vision and Plan
How will it look and feel once the
project/change has happened?
Give everyone a clear picture of
'What's in it for me?'
Clarify current, transition and
future states What must we do to
deliver this vision?

Make Change Happen
Keep everyone on side
Handle resistance and conflict
Support the team
Implement the plan

© Martin Brenig-Jones and Jo Dowdall

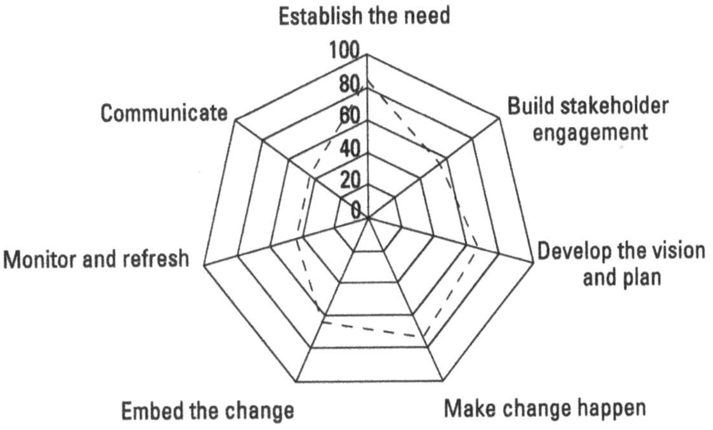

FIGURE 6-6: Chart to assess team progress.

© Martin Brenig-Jones and Jo Dowdall

You'll also find that some organizational characteristics are inherent in a particular culture. For example, some organizations are much faster at using new methods of internal communications than others. Some are good at making a change happen but fall down on embedding that change.

TIP

Consider the use of storyboards to capture and communicate the essence and key elements of a team's improvement activity, ideally incorporating photos and videos.

One common factor central to successful Change Management is effective communication. To ensure that you get the right messages to the right people at the right time, and via an appropriate medium, you need to develop a communication plan as part of your overall deployment plan. Try to think about the different audiences and to see them as both teams and individuals. And remember, we all see and hear things differently.

Change is interwoven into the core of Lean Six Sigma. It's why we do it! So Change Management is an intrinsic part of the approach.

3

Understanding Performance and Analyzing the Process

Use a balanced set of measures to understand how well your process meets customer requirements, and which key variables are driving performance.

Measure effectively using a five-step data collection process.

Develop a sampling approach that will help you to achieve a sound understanding of performance by using comparatively small amounts of representative data.

Decide how to present and interpret your data, and use control charts to identify process variation so that you know when to take action and when not to.

Identify and verify the root causes of process problems using a variety of tools and techniques.

Identify non-value-adding steps and waste in your process.

Improve process flow through a number of concepts including *pull* and the *theory of constraints*.

Chapter **7**

Gathering Data

Managing by fact is one of the key Lean Six Sigma principles. For this you need relevant, accurate and reliable data, that is produced by a measurement system that is consistent. This chapter focuses on developing a data collection process to ensure the data you collect meets these criteria.

You need to view data collection as a process that needs managing and improving just like all your other processes.

Managing by Fact

Whether you manage a process or lead an improvement project, you need accurate data to help you make the right decisions. The following quote summarizes the importance of facts:

Unless one can obtain facts and accurate data about the workplace, there can be no control or improvement. It is the task of the middle management and managers below them to ensure the accuracy of their data which enables the company to know the true facts.

Kaoru Ishikawa, *What is Total Quality Control? The Japanese Way*

The following sections highlight the importance of good data, and will help you develop an effective data collection plan to help you understand, improve, and manage your processes.

Realizing the importance of good data

Good data supports good decision-making. It may prompt you to implement an improvement project by highlighting poor performance against the CTQs (see Chapter 3), or show you opportunities to tackle waste (see Chapter 10). It enables you to understand the current performance levels of a process and provides you with the means to benchmark that performance and prioritize improvement actions.

When you undertake an improvement project, you need to identify and address the causes of the problem you're tackling, in order to prevent the problem from recurring. Good data helps you quantify and verify those possible causes so you can develop effective, appropriate solutions.

You're probably aware of the phrase "garbage in, garbage out," which is often applied to data. You need to ensure you have good data going into your various management information reports and analyses. For that, you must have a sound data collection plan, and we describe the key elements later in this chapter. First, you need to consider what you're measuring.

Reviewing what you currently measure

Many organizations have data coming out of their ears! Unfortunately, that data isn't always the right data. Sometimes organizations measure things because they *can* measure them — but those things aren't necessarily the right things to be measured and the resulting data doesn't help you manage your business and its processes.

Sometimes data isn't accurate, and even if the data is accurate, it may be presented in a way that leads to missed or wrong conclusions. For example, data is often presented as averages or percentages so that you can't understand the range of process performance or the process variation, which is what your customers will be experiencing (which we cover in Chapters 4 and 8). Results may be presented as a page of numbers to encourage comparisons with last week's results or even the results for this week last year, but this is simplistic and again can lead to the wrong conclusions and actions.

Figure 7-1 provides an effective format to help you review your measures. It serves as a reminder to measure the aspects of your processes that matter most to customers.

Output Measures

	Customer Requirements (CTQs)	% in 5 hours	Cycle Time	Number of errors	Error Types
○ Strong Measure					
● Medium Measure	Issue new service requirement advice within 5 hours of receiving customer call	●	○	▲	▲
▲ Weak Measure	No errors in the information recorded			○	●

FIGURE 7-1: Getting the measure of the CTQs.

Deciding what to measure

You already know that choosing what to measure and how to present your data are important. But so too is deciding what *not* to measure. Lean Six Sigma requires you to manage by fact and have good data — but that doesn't mean you need more data than you currently produce. It means you have the *right* data.

Review the data you currently have and decide whether it really is helping you manage your process. Does the data add value? Who uses it? How and why is the data used? The CTQs should provide the basis for your process measures, and you should consider whether your current measures describe how well you are meeting them. Figure 7-1 uses symbols to identify the strength of your performance measures in relation to the CTQs.

If you look at the CTQ for delivery within five hours, you can see that the first measure in the matrix, the percentage issued within five hours, is rated only as a "medium strength." That measure tells you the percentage of cases processed within the CTQ service standard, but it doesn't tell you anything about the individual results, or the range of performance. Some cases will have been completed in one hour and some in ten hours, for example. This important information is provided by the second measure, the "cycle time," where you're recording the results of each case, (or at least a representative sample). With this information, you can understand a lot more. You can determine the average performance, the range of performance, and, of course, you can extract the "percentage within five hours" information because you can see how many cases took five hours or less.

In this chapter and the following chapter, we show how understanding variation, and creating a balance of measures can help you understand and predict performance. The first stage in that process is to review your measures and create a data collection plan that helps ensure you collect the right data in the right way.

Developing a Data Collection Plan

Data collection is a process that needs to be designed, managed and improved, just like any other process. Your data will be only as good as the process that collects it. Data collection involves five steps:-

1. Agree on the measures linked to the process outputs that matter most to customers (the CTQs)

2. Develop operational definitions (discussed later in this chapter) and procedures that help ensure everyone is clear about what's being measured, why it's being measured, and how to make the measurement.

3. Validate the measurement system to make sure the data collected is of good quality.

4. Develop the sampling plan.

5. Manage the data collection process.

Step 1: Agreeing on the measures

In this first step, we begin with the end in mind by considering the output measures. By linking the data to your key outputs, you can be sure that you are measuring the things that matter most to customers. After the output measures have been agreed on, you need to develop some additional measures to help you understand how the inputs into your process and the various activities in the process influence the output results.

TIP

Agreeing on goals and outputs is usually straightforward if you've described the CTQ customer requirements in a clearly measurable way (we explain how to do so in Chapter 4). Use our suggested symbols in Figure 7-1 to check whether you have an appropriate set of measures. You need at least one strong measure for each CTQ.

When you already have a collection of output measures, use Figure 7-1 to review whether your output measures are appropriate. This may be particularly relevant if you've only recently determined the CTQs. You may not have measured this particular aspect of the process before if you've only just identified how important it is to your customers. After using Figure 7-1 in this way, you may consider abandoning some measures and creating other, more appropriate ones.

TIP

Time is often a useful measure. However, if you simply measure whether or not each item meets the service standard, you don't know the range of performance being delivered. For example, you may see that the organization processes 80 percent of orders within the service standard of five hours, but you may not be able to see that some orders take one hour, some take two or three hours, and the 20 percent that fail take ten hours. With a measure of cycle time or lead time, you can understand this aspect of performance fully.

The above is an example of thinking about *data types*. Data that is produced as the result of measuring something on a scale (such as time, length, weight) is called *continuous data*. Data that is produced by counting (how many pages there are in this book or how many orders fail to meet the service standard) is known as *discrete data* (or *attribute data*). You can see from the above example that, in general, we prefer to use continuous data where we can.

In Figure 7-2, we show a process trying to meet the customer's requirements. The feedback from the customer and the process highlights two gaps that need to be closed. First, we have the difference between what the customer wants (the voice of the customer) and how the process is actually performing (the voice of the process). There is a need for some improvement action here. Second, there is a gap between what the organization is measuring (the *average* of 6 days) and the full range of each instance of process performance as experienced by the customer.

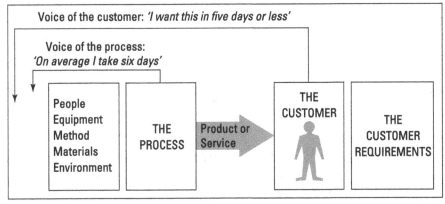

FIGURE 7-2:
Matching the voices of the customer and the process.

© Martin Brenig-Jones and Jo Dowdall

Getting a balance of measures

We started by looking at the output measures. But if all you have is output measures, you will be able to understand what performance looks like, but not what caused it.

To understand what's causing the process outputs to perform like they do, you need a balance of measures in your data collection plan. Not just output measures, but measures from the process inputs and measures from in the process itself. The link between input and in-process variables will influence the process output, as shown in Figure 7-3.

Getting the balance of measures and understanding how they interrelate:

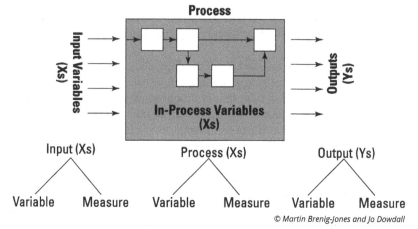

FIGURE 7-3:
The different variables will all need corresponding measures to help you assess performance.

© Martin Brenig-Jones and Jo Dowdall

Some use the terms *leading* and *lagging* to describe this balance of measures. Lagging measures are the output measures (as they describe what has happened), and leading measures are the input and in-process measures (because they can help to predict and influence it).

The concept of *cause and effect* is important in Lean Six Sigma. Xs and Ys are used to illustrate it. In Lean Six Sigma lingo, the output measures are represented by the letter Y, as you can see in Figure 7-4. And the factors in the process or in the inputs to the process that influence Y are termed *variables*. They are represented by the letter X. This is expressed as Y=f(x), or if you were to explain it in words, "Y is a function of X."

Connecting things up

Figure 7-4 provides a reminder of how the CTQs are pulled together and incorporates Figure 7-1 from earlier in this chapter.

Step 2: Creating clear operational definitions

When you know what to measure, you need to develop a sufficiently detailed, clear, unambiguous description of the measure and how it is obtained. This is called an *operational definition*. Operational definitions help everyone in the team to understand the who, what, where, when and how of the measurement process, which in turn helps you produce reliable data. For example, if you measure cycle time, you define when the clock starts and finishes; which clock you use; whether you measure in seconds, minutes or hours; and whether you round up or down so that you can tell others *how* to make the measurement.

Voice of the Customer	Key issue	Measurable CTQ
To meet timescales we need to know about new service requirements ASAP	Speed is key as the service must be completed within agreed timeframes	Issue new service advice within 5 hours of receipt of customer call
We must have the right details and information	Accuracy is vital to avoid wasted activity and lost time	No errors in the information recorded

Output Measures

○ Strong Measure
● Medium Measure
▲ Weak Measure

Customer Requirements (CTQs)	% in 5 hours	Cycle Time	Number of errors	Error Types
Issue new service requirement advice within 5 hours of receiving customer call	●	○	▲	▲
No errors in the information recorded			○	●

What are the input and in-process X variables?

○ Strong Measure
● Medium Measure
▲ Weak Measure

Output Measures			
% in five hours			
Cycle time			
Number of errors			
Type of errors			

FIGURE 7-4: Bringing the CTQs into the mix.

© Martin Brenig-Jones and Jo Dowdall

EXAMPLE

The 1999 launch of NASA's Mars Lander is an infamous example of murky definitions. This $125 million vehicle was designed to investigate whether water had existed on the red planet. Unfortunately, the vehicle disappeared, never to be heard from again. The cause was rather embarrassing: the team that built the spacecraft and managed its launch worked in feet and inches, but the team responsible for landing the craft on Mars worked using the metric measurement system — and no one had thought to convert the data. As a result, the angle of entry into Mars was too sharp and the vehicle burned up.

Step 3: Validating your measurement system

The operational definition tells us *how* to make the measurement but that doesn't prove we *can* make the measurement successfully, which leads us to the third step in the data collection plan.

WARNING

There is no such thing as a perfect measurement system because the values you obtain will not always be the exact "size" of the things you are measuring. So when we see data from our process, the data is actually made up of true process variation and "errors" from the imperfect measuring system.

This could make life very complicated, but the practical way forward is to ensure that the measurement system variation is so small that it is irrelevant and can be ignored. In other words, they would make no difference to our understanding of what we are measuring.

Measurement System Analysis (MSA) is a family of techniques that provides a way of establishing how much of variation in the data we have obtained is due to the measurement system. *Gauge R and R* and *Attribute Agreement Analysis* are the techniques used for assessing the capability of measurement systems that produce continuous and discrete (attribute) data, respectively. Let's start with Gauge R and R.

"Gauge R and R" stands for Gauge Repeatability and Reproducibility. Gauge is just another name for a measuring device such as a ruler or bathroom scale.

>> **Repeatability** is a measure of the variation seen when one operator measures the same thing multiple times using the same measuring device. If you were to use a ruler to measure the width of this book several times, you could easily get a different result each time because of how you hold the book and ruler, how you line up the zero mark on the ruler to the edge of the book, your eyesight, light conditions, and so on. This variation in these measurements is called the repeatability of the measurement system. After all, it's the same book and it doesn't change, so the differences must be due to the measuring system. Note that the measuring system consists of the ruler, the environment, you, and the operational definition that tells you how to make the measurement.

>> **Reproducibility** is a measure of the variation seen when different people use the same device to measure the same thing. To assess reproducibility, you ask someone else to measure the same book with the same measuring device and conditions and see if the results are different on average from those of the first person. The size of the difference is called the reproducibility.

If repeatability or reproducibility are too high, our process data will contain too much measurement system error and therefore be unreliable. To decide whether they are acceptable or whether we need to improve the measurement system, we can do a simple calculation as shown in the following example.

In Figure 7-5, two people — Timekeeper A and Timekeeper B — measure the same batch of products in a random sequence. By averaging the difference of the two readings over the number of products in the batch, we can determine the Gauge R and R.

Measure	Timekeeper A	Timekeeper B	Tolerance
Vet form	45	41	9.30%
Add info. to form	90	89	1.12%
Update records	175	177	1.14%
Print agreement	100	95	5.13%
Issue to customer	66	72	8.70%
Total Time	**476**	**474**	**0.42%**

© Martin Brenig-Jones and Jo Dowdall

FIGURE 7-5: Checking out the measurement system.

In Figure 7-5, Gauge R and R appears to be good for total time at 0.42 percent, but not so good for the sub-processes.

The tolerance is calculated by dividing the difference in readings by the average of the readings and multiplying the result by 100 to turn it into a percentage. So, for example, if we look at "Vet form," the difference between Timekeepers A and B is 4 seconds, the average is 43 seconds, and the resulting tolerance is 9.30% ($4/43 \times 100\%$).

Determining what's good in Gauge R and R terms is somewhat subjective, and no truly right answers exist. We can offer some broad guidelines, but when you decide whether to take action, much depends on the process and the consequences of inaccurate data. Generally, if Gauge R and R exceeds 10 percent, you should look to improve the measurement system, perhaps focusing on a better operational definition, for example, or using more precise measuring equipment.

WARNING

We have described the concept of Gauge R and R here and described a simple approach to evaluate measurement system performance. In many situations in manufacturing, laboratories, and so on, a more formal Gauge R and R study will be needed involving statistical calculations. These are beyond the scope of this book — but the concepts are no different.

As we get further into the Measurement and Analysis aspects of Lean Six Sigma, the type of data being used to measure and understand performance becomes important, as different types of data are used in different ways. Remember that *continuous data* is measured on a continuous scale, such as, for example, processing time or the size of a component. *Attribute data* is used to understand whether or not something is present, or is right or wrong, to categorize items, such as types of compensation claim, complaint, and financial standing. Attribute data is the result of classifying items and then counting the number in each classification.

We use Gauge R and R to assess measurement systems that produce continuous data. To check the accuracy and consistency of discrete (attribute) data, we use *Attribute Agreement Analysis*. So, for example, you ask a number of people in the process team to classify the items in a batch into various categories. You can then compare their assessments both with one another and with an expert's assessments. Doing so ensures consistent classification by the process team and sometimes highlights ineffective standards or definitions as well as training needs.

In Figure 7-6, you can see how assessors Ann and Brian classify claims consistently between each other, but aren't in line with the expert's assessment. The claims need to be coded by category as either AA, AB, AC or BB. This finding indicates a need to improve the operational definitions that specify how to classify the claims correctly and training given to the assessors so that their classification is in line with the expert's view.

Claim Number	Expert's Classification	Ann	Brian
1	A A	A A	A A
2	A B	A A	A A
3	A A	A B	A B
4	A C	A C	A C
5	B B	B B	B B

FIGURE 7-6: Attribute data in action.

© Martin Brenig-Jones and Jo Dowdall

Step 4: Developing the Sampling Plan

One of the important decisions to make in the collection and analysis of data is deciding what data we need to collect and how much data is needed. This is where sampling comes in. Sampling means deciding what subset of all the possible data in the population of interest we need to use in order to fairly draw conclusions (make inferences) about the population.

Figure 7-7 illustrates this simply. A sample is taken from the population, that sample is analyzed, and the results of the analysis are used to make inferences about the population. That sample needs to be chosen carefully; otherwise the inferences won't be right.

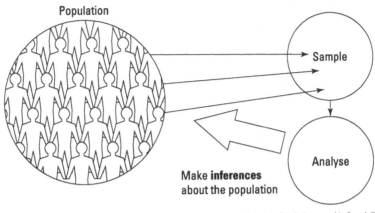

FIGURE 7-7:
Making
inferences.

Sampling is used when collecting and analyzing all the available data is not appropriate, perhaps because it is too time consuming or expensive. Sometimes, collecting the data destroys what's being measured, as with drop-testing mobile phones. Importantly, valid conclusions can be drawn from a comparatively small amount of data if sampling is done well. For conclusions to be valid, the samples must be representative (so that the data you collect represents the population of interest).

Population sampling

As the name suggests, population sampling looks at populations — the entire group. This could mean a customer base, or a population of something that has been processed (for example, loan applications or orders), voting intentions or buying patterns. Using data from the whole population is usually only possible when it is small and the data is easy to get hold of.

For population sampling, it is important to use a random, or segmented random approach. In other words, no systematic differences should exist between the data you collect and the data you don't collect, so every item stands an equal chance of being included. If this is not the case, your sample will be biased (see Figure 7-8).

If you don't understand the segmentation factors of the population, you could take an inappropriate sample.

FIGURE 7-8:
Understanding the segmentation factors is vital.

The segmentation factors (sometimes called "stratification factors") might include demographic factors (age, gender, ethnicity, and so on), geographic factors, factors based on the behaviors and habits of people, or any other aspect of the population of data you're interested in such as size or product type.

Process sampling

The purpose of process sampling is to understand not just a "snapshot" of performance, as was the case with population sampling, but what is happening over time. It is important to use a systematic rather than a random approach when process sampling as you need to collect your data in time sequence in order to be able to display it in time sequence, which we need to do in order to understand process behavior.

As shown in Figure 7-9, you could take a regular, systematic sample (for example, every third or tenth item) or take a sample at regular time intervals (for example, every hour). This can be relatively easy to do, but be aware of the risk of introducing bias, such as, for example if every third item is processed by the same person, or if the one hour interval coincides with staff break times. The data obtained could be displayed in a type of control chart known as the X moving R chart (XMR), described in Chapter 8.

Process sampling involves subgroup sampling (see Figure 7-10), which requires you to take a regular and representative sample of items. This type of sampling is used for high-volume processes (for example, where thousands of calls are coming in to the help desk, or thousands of components are being manufactured). Here, sampling every third or tenth item isn't enough, so an appropriate subgroup size and frequency is determined, such as, for example, five items per hour. The data obtained from the samples in the subgroup can also be displayed in a control chart. So the average and range of the five data points measured in the subgroup could be plotted on an X bar R control chart (which we cover in Chapter 8).

Taking a regular sample, for example every third or tenth item or so on. This can be relatively easy to do, but may introduce bias.

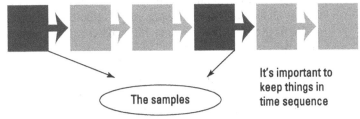

The samples

It's important to keep things in time sequence

FIGURE 7-9: Using a systematic approach.

© Martin Brenig-Jones and Jo Dowdall

Subgroup sampling from a process

Take a regular and random sample of five items, every hour or two, or every day, for example.

Items processed in time sequence on Monday

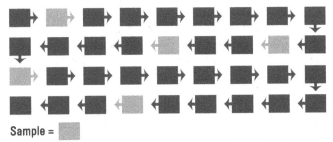

Sample =

FIGURE 7-10: Subgroup sampling from a process.

© Martin Brenig-Jones and Jo Dowdall

Subgroup sampling is also used when we have discrete data. We might count the number of errors per day and plot these on a C chart, or we can measure the proportion of items that fail inspection every hour on a P chart.

Determining the sample size

It is beneficial to only collect a subset of all the data, but there is a consequence that needs to be managed. Whenever sample statistics are calculated (the sample average, for example), although the figure obtained will be the exact average of the *sample*, it will only be an estimate for the mean of the *population*. The uncertainty associated with the estimate can be quantified using a *confidence interval*. We have influence over how wide the confidence interval is by the size of the sample that we specify: The confidence interval is narrower when the sample size is larger, and vice versa.

Let's say we measured time for 50 orders and the sample average was 30 days. Depending on the sample size and standard deviation, you might end up with a confidence interval with endpoints at 27 and 33. You would say, "I am 95-percent confident that the population mean time is between 27 and 33 days." This is being honest about the extent of what you truly know. If this interval is too wide, you would need to collect more data. If it is narrower than you need, you have collected more than what was needed.

So before we collect the data, what we need to do is determine the width of confidence interval we would like and then collect the corresponding amount of data, which is very much a case of beginning with the end in mind.

When we do the calculation to determine sample size, what we actually input is the *precision* (also known as the *margin of error*). Precision is simply half the width of the confidence interval.

For example, you might want to understand the process cycle time to within 2 hours (precision = 2 hours), or understand the proportion of defective products being produced to within 3 percent (precision = 3%). The precision needed will vary according to your requirements. Why do you want the data? What decisions will you be making as a result? You may be using the knowledge you have gained from measuring the sample to determine staffing requirements, establish plans or set budgets. The tighter the precision you will need, the bigger the sample size will be.

The *confidence interval* is determined by the precision value you have set. For example if you have set the precision value at 2 hours, the confidence interval will be 4 hours wide. Say the data you have measured shows the average cycle time of the process is 50 hours, then your confidence interval will be from 48 to 52 hours (in other words, within +/− 2 hours of the mean).

The *confidence level* is another important element when sampling. This is a percentage figure that shows how confident you can be if you repeatedly drew random samples of the same size. In general, a 95-percent confidence level is used in most business sampling situations. Returning to the example above, with a 95-percent confidence level, you'd be able to say that you were 95-percent confident that the mean of the population which the sample was taken from lies somewhere between 48 and 52 hours. There is a 5-percent chance of being wrong. Want to be 99-percent confident? This would result in a bigger sample size.

Now that we've got to grips with the basic elements of sample size calculations, let's work through an example. This example uses continuous data and uses the sample size formula shown in Figure 7-11.

FIGURE 7-11:
Formula for
Continuous Data.

Estimate average cycle time $n = \left(\dfrac{2s}{d}\right)^2$

© Martin Brenig-Jones and Jo Dowdall

Imagine your team wants to understand the mean query response time, and 15,000 queries have been processed. How many should we sample? Start by establishing the precision you require. Do you want to understand mean response time to within 10 minutes, 5 minutes, or 5 seconds? 10 minutes doesn't give you the precision you require, and 5 seconds is too much. Let's say you want to understand mean process time to within 1 minute. The precision value is represented by d in the formula. Sometimes it is represented by delta or Δ.

Next you need to understand how much variation exists within process cycle times. You need to know the sample standard deviation (which we cover in Chapter 1 if you need a refresher). This is significant in sampling because the more variation there is, the bigger the sample size will be.

TIP

This may seem quite strange! You haven't measured anything yet, so how can you know the standard deviation? If you have some "historical" data, you could have a look at that, or you could take a small number of data points and calculate the standard deviation from those. You could also use the standard deviation from a similar process, or obtain an estimation from the process operators by asking them for the highest and lowest values they typically see (the range) and dividing that by 6.

In this example, let's assume you know the standard deviation and it's 3 minutes.

Figure 7-12 uses these values and tells us that the sample size needed is 36. If we then measure 36 queries and calculate the average, we will be 95-percent confident that the true average of the entire population will be within +/− 1 minute of this value.

Now look at what happens if we want to increase the precision. Changing the precision value (d) to half a minute (0.5) results in a sample size of 144. If we want to be even more precise than that (to the nearest 7.5 seconds, which is 0.125 of a minute), we'd need a sample size of 2304.

Incidentally, the 2 in the formula is what makes it a 95-percent confidence interval, as 95 percent of the items in a normal distribution lie within 2 standard deviations of the mean. Strictly speaking, this gives you 95.40 percent, and the correct figure should be 1.96 rather than 2. However, we feel that if you're just getting into this subject, it's easier to use 2, and the answers will be close enough!

$$n = \left(\frac{2 \times 3}{1}\right)^2 = 6^2 = 36$$

$$n = \left(\frac{2 \times 3}{0.5}\right)^2 = 12^2 = 144$$

FIGURE 7-12:
The formula in
practice.

$$n = \left(\frac{2 \times 3}{0.125}\right)^2 = 48^2 = 2304$$

© Martin Brenig-Jones and Jo Dowdall

Now let's look at the sample size formula for "discrete" data, which is in Figure 7-13.

FIGURE 7-13:
Formula for
discrete data.

Estimate Proportion
(e.g. % defective) $n = \left(\dfrac{2}{d}\right)^2 (p)(1-p)$ n = Required Sample Size
d = Precision
p = Proportion

This formula assumes that we are using a 95% confidence level.

© Martin Brenig-Jones and Jo Dowdall

As with continuous data, the "usual" convention is to use a 95-percent confidence level.

With this type of data, we are working with proportions, such as, for example, the proportion of defective items that are generated by the process. The tricky bit in this formula is determining the value of this if you haven't measured anything yet. As with the example above (where we were using continuous data and wanting to know the standard deviation), you will need to look at historical data or collect a small sample up front and use that to get a value for p.

The value of p will have an impact on the size of sample you need to collect. The largest sample size occurs when p = 0.5, or 50 percent. If you have no idea what p is, use 50 percent, but you may end up with a sample size that is larger than necessary.

Incidentally, the proportion defective is a phrase that we use for this type of sample size calculation, but it doesn't just describe defective items. It may relate to the proportion of customers who are likely to purchase a new product or service, for example.

Figure 7-14 provides an example of the formula in action. In this example, we start with an expectation that the proportion defective is 0.10, or 10 percent, and we want the estimate to be within 3 percent. To be 95-percent confident that the percentage defective in our sample lies within plus or minus 3 percent of the percentage of the whole of the population of data, we'd need to measure 400 items. Now look what happens to the sample size when the precision is "tightened" to 1 percent.

The answer with a 3% precision

$$n = \left(\frac{2}{d}\right)^2 (p)(1-p)$$

$$n = \left(\frac{2}{0.03}\right)^2 (0.10)(1-0.10)$$

$$n = 4444.4 \times 0.10 \times 0.90 = 400$$

The answer gets a lot bigger with precision at 1%

$$n = \left(\frac{2}{d}\right)^2 (p)(1-p)$$

$$n = \left(\frac{2}{0.01}\right)^2 (0.10)(1-0.10)$$

$$n = 40000 \times 0.10 \times 0.90 = 3600$$

FIGURE 7-14: Precision is a key factor in sample size.

© Martin Brenig-Jones and Jo Dowdall

Sampling from a finite population

The sample size formulas we've looked at assume that the sample size (n) is small relative to the population (N). If you are sampling more than 5 percent of the population, n/N is greater than 0.05. This may be more than you need, and you can adjust the sample size with the formula shown in Figure 7-15.

Sampling from a limited (finite) population

$$n\text{finite} = \frac{n}{1+\frac{n}{N}}$$

FIGURE 7-15: Adjusting the sample size.

© Martin Brenig-Jones and Jo Dowdall

See how this reduces the sample size of 2,304 that we calculated earlier in this section. Remember the population size in this example was 15,000. As you can see, we can reduce the sample size to just under 2000, as shown in Figure 7-16.

FIGURE 7-16:
Bringing the sample size down.

$$n\text{ finite} = \frac{2304}{1 + \frac{2304}{15,000}} = \frac{2304}{1.1536} = 1997$$

© Martin Brenig-Jones and Jo Dowdall

You may have worked out the sample size needed for the precision you'd like, but how big a sample can you afford to look at? If it's less than the sample size should be, what will the affordable sample size provide in terms of precision? And will that be precise enough? By moving our formula around, as shown in Figure 7-17, you can calculate the precision provided by the sample size and make a business decision as to whether it will be sufficient.

Calculating precision from the affordable sample size

FIGURE 7-17:
Precisely what can we afford?

◆ For an average within ± d units

$$d = \frac{2s}{\sqrt{n}}$$

◆ A proportion within ± d%

$$d = 2\sqrt{\frac{(p)(1-p)}{n}}$$

© Martin Brenig-Jones and Jo Dowdall

Note that the calculations above were developed for population sampling but can also be used for process sampling provided the process is stable.

Step 5: Collecting the data

Step five of the data collection process covers how you actually collect the data. This may include collecting some of it manually. Data collection sheets make the process straightforward and ensure consistency. A data collection sheet can be as simple as a check sheet that you use to record the number of times something occurs.

The check sheet is best completed in time sequence, as shown in Figure 7-18. This real example shows data from the new business team of an insurance company processing personal pension applications from individual clients. It captures the main reasons why applications can't be processed immediately; daily recording the number of times these different issues occur. On a daily basis, you can see the number of "errors" and the number of application forms, and in Figure 7-18 we've calculated the rate of errors per forms. By adding stratification (that is, breaking it down by day of the week) in this way, we may be able to gain some additional insights about the potential causes of the issues. Also, each day forms a subgroup (see process sampling earlier in this chapter), so we will be able to assess any time-related patterns over the two-week period, such as an upward trend.

Ref	Characteristic	M	T	W	T	F	M	T	W	T	F	Total	%
A	form not signed	2	1	0	1	0	1	1	0	0	1	7	8.3
B	no part number	1	0	2	1	1	2	0	0	0	0	7	8.3
C	address missing	5	2	3	2	3	4	3	5	3	3	33	39.4
D	no cheque	1	0	1	1	1	0	1	1	1	1	8	9.5
E	wrong amount	3	4	1	3	1	2	3	3	4	5	29	34.5
Total errors		12	7	7	8	6	9	8	9	8	10	84	100
Total forms		24	20	21	18	18	24	16	20	14	22	197	
Defects per form		.5	.35	.33	.44	.33	.37	.5	.45	.57	.45	.43	

FIGURE 7-18: Checking out the check sheet.

© Martin Brenig-Jones and Jo Dowdall

Looking across the check sheet from left to right, you can see that we've recorded the total errors by type and have determined their percentage in relation to the whole. This check sheet links neatly to a Pareto analysis, which we show in Chapter 8.

TIP

Even if you use a computer system to automatically measure and generate your data, it may help to design a data collection form on paper first. Doing so helps you think through all the details you may need, such as whether and to what extent to take account of stratification factors (see Chapter 3), which could include different customer or product types, for example.

A defect *concentration diagram* provides another simple form of data collection. This technique is good for identifying damage to goods in transit, for example, by recording where on the product or packaging marks and holes occur. Car rental companies often ask customers to complete defect concentration diagrams. On a picture of the car, customers have to highlight existing damage, such as dents and scratches. Upon return of the vehicle, the leasing company then checks to see whether any further damage has occurred, as shown in Figure 7-19.

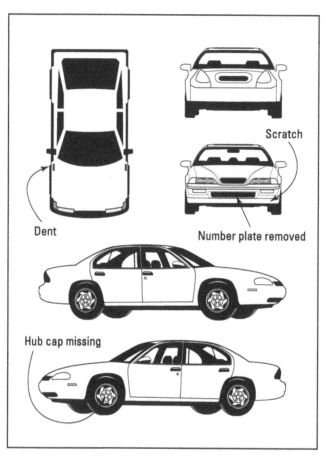

Scratch

Dent

Number plate removed

Hub cap missing

FIGURE 7-19: Coming up to scratch with the concentration diagram.

© Martin Brenig-Jones and Jo Dowdall

EXAMPLE

An American colleague recently rented a car and, when filling out the form identifying existing damage, inquired about a small indentation. The agent replied "Buck and a quarter." When asked what that meant, the agent explained that if the indentation was larger than a quarter, it was a dent; otherwise it didn't matter. It wasn't considered a scratch unless it was longer than a one-dollar bill. So here we see operational definitions in practice, with readily available references for both the customer and the agent.

Identifying ways to improve your approach

The fifth step in the data collection process reminds you that data collection is a process and needs to be managed and improved just like any other.

Figure 7-20 provides a data collection summary. Use it to ensure you've covered all aspects of your data collection plan; doing so should lead you to collecting data that is accurate, consistent and valid.

Data Collection summary						
Type of measure	What? What are we measuring?	Why? Why are we measuring this?	How? How do we collect and record the data?	When? When do we collect the data?	Where? Where in the process?	Who? Who will collect it?
Output						
In-process						
Input						

© Martin Brenig-Jones and Jo Dowdall

FIGURE 7-20: Pulling the data collection plan together.

TIP

Enhance your data collection summary by using icons to show how you present your data. For example, you can use images of Pareto diagrams or control charts that show the variation in your performance. We describe these in detail in the next chapter.

Chapter **8**

Presenting Your Data

This chapter outlines the importance of understanding and identifying variation. If you can identify what type of variation you're seeing in your process results, you can determine whether action is needed or not, and avoid taking inappropriate action and wasting effort.

We introduce control charts in this chapter. They can be used to identify types of variation in your process and provide an effective way to display the data in order to tune into the "Voice of your Process." We focus on the most commonly used type, the X moving R, or "individuals and moving range" control chart.

We also include some other data display tools: histograms and Pareto charts.

Delving into Different Types of Variation

Things are seldom exactly the same, even if at first glance they appear to be so. Variation is everywhere! For example, it exists in people's heights, in the many shades of the color green, in the number of words in each sentence of this book, and in the time different people take to read it.

Variation comes in two types: common cause and special cause.

>> **Common cause or natural variation** is just that — natural. You should expect it, you shouldn't be surprised by it and you shouldn't react to individual examples of it.

>> **Special cause variation** isn't what you'd typically expect to see, so in the context of your processes, something unusual has happened that's influencing the results. Special cause variation can also result from a process change you've made to improve performance. In this instance, it will be the evidence you're looking for to confirm that the improvement has had an impact on performance.

You can use statistical process control (SPC) and control charts to identify and define variation in your business processes, and we explain just what these are and how to use them in the section "Recognizing the Importance of Control Charts."

WARNING

Identifying the type of variation is important as it ensures you take action only when you need to. Confusing one type of variation with the other creates problems.

Understanding natural variation

Natural variation is what you expect to see as a result of how you design and manage your processes. When a process exhibits only natural variation, it's in *statistical control* and *stable*. Being in statistical control doesn't necessarily mean that the results from the process meet your customer CTQs, the Critical To Quality elements of your offering, which we cover in Chapter 4, but it does mean that the results are stable and predictable. If the results don't meet your CTQs, you can improve the process using DMAIC (Define, Measure, Analyze, Improve and Control), which we cover in Chapter 2.

TIP

To determine whether the variation is natural or special, try the following simple experiment with some colleagues.

First, ask the team to write down the letter *A* five times. This in itself forms the basis for an interesting discussion on giving clear instructions so that everyone understands the requirement. You may find that some people write their *A*'s across the page, and others down the page. Some use capital letters, and others lower-case. One or two may even write "the letter *A* five times"!

Now look at the letters and ask whether they're all the same. Each *A* is probably slightly different, but generally they're likely to be pretty similar and can clearly be identified as a letter *A*.

The difference between each colleague's letters is natural variation, and their process for producing the letters is stable and predictable. If you repeat the exercise, you're likely to see the same sort of variation. To reduce the variation, you need to improve the process, perhaps by automating your writing or introducing a template. We continue this exercise in the "Avoiding tampering" section later in this chapter.

Spotlighting special cause variation

Special cause variation is the variation you don't expect. Something unusual is happening and significant enough to affect the results. Special cause variation is sometimes called *assignable cause variation*. It is an unexpected occurrence.

When a special cause exists, the process is no longer stable and its performance becomes unpredictable. You need to take action to identify the root cause of the special cause, and then either prevent the cause from occurring again if it degrades performance, or build the cause into the process if it improves it.

TIP

Not all special causes are bad. Sometimes they improve performance or provide evidence that an improvement has worked. We describe how you can identify special causes later in this chapter, but first we need to stress why doing so is so important.

Distinguishing between variation types

You need to be able to tell the difference between the two types of variation. If you think something is natural variation when it's really special cause, you may miss or delay taking an opportunity to improve the process. If you think something is special cause variation when in fact it's natural, the changes you make in response may inadvertently increase the amount of variation. This is known as tampering.

Avoiding tampering

In the "Understanding natural variation" section earlier in this chapter, we asked you to experiment with colleagues by writing down the letter A five times as an example of natural variation. In this section we show what happens if you tamper with the process by reacting to an individual example of common cause variation.

Imagine that your manager doesn't understand the importance of distinguishing between natural and special cause variation. They wander through the work area to see the output being produced and feel that your letter A's show too much variation. As you begin to demonstrate the process, your manager asks you to stop writing and points out that using your other hand is much better — after all, this is the hand they use!

If you try writing with your other hand, your results probably show increased variation, and chances are you take longer to produce the output.

Unfortunately, tampering happens all the time in many organizations. Managers often feel their role is to respond to performance changes when actually the variation being seen is natural cause.

Tampering and pointless discussion often go hand in hand. You may often see reports comprising pages of numbers that somebody expects you to understand and perhaps base decisions on. In Figure 8-1, we show a typical set of information that is practically meaningless.

	Sales Performance - **May**									
	Location A					Location B				
PRODUCT	Previous month	Target	Current month	Target	% change from last year	Previous month	Target	Current month	Target	% change from last year
1	34	30	37	30	-5.4	59	50	56	55	-7.6
2	260	250	230	250	3.3	226	250	267	250	12.8
3	75	75	65	70	0.4	125	130	133	135	5.9
4	3	2	4	2	2.7	16	15	18	15	-6.7
5	4678	4750	4978	5000	10.6	1657	1600	1753	1700	5.9
6	930	950	1006	975	2.9	975	1000	952	1000	-1.5
7	950	975	1100	1050	-3.9		975	950	975	-6.2
8	43	45	48	45	-2.8	75	75	78	85	8.4

FIGURE 8-1:
A typical data set that doesn't reveal very much.

© Martin Brenig-Jones and Jo Dowdall

Figures relating to sales activity often provide good examples of pointless data. You may hear statements such as "This week's figures were better than last week's, but not as good as those of the week before that." Almost certainly the differences in the weekly figures are a measure of the natural variation in the process and not due to special causes.

Using control charts can help you make sense of the figures by enabling you to distinguish between natural and special variation.

Displaying data differently

The data in Figure 8-1 don't tell you much. But if you present the data in a more visual form, you may begin to understand what's happening. Figure 8-1 shows a typical set of row-by-column data, highlighting the sales performance for two different locations in the month of May. The figure refers to eight different products. You can see the number of actual sales, along with some targets.

Instead of giving the figures for only one month, a more useful method is to plot a graph, called a *run chart*, using figures for a series of months. A run chart plots the data in time order, which makes it easier to spot any patterns or trends, such as seasonal changes and when to expect "peaks." A run chart is a simple and helpful method for data display but it doesn't tell you whether the variation is natural or special, so to know that, you use a control chart.

In Figure 8-2 we use the figures for Location A and Product 3 to create a run chart that presents data through to the following March.

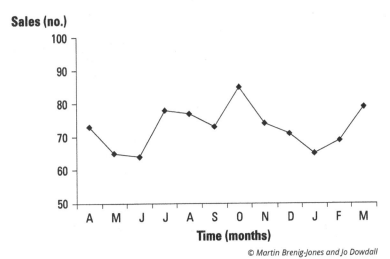

Sales (no.)

Time (months)

© Martin Brenig-Jones and Jo Dowdall

FIGURE 8-2: Presenting data as a run chart.

Recognizing the Importance of Control Charts

Control charts provide the only definitive way of identifying the type of variation in a process, which is essential for really understanding what is going on.

Walter Shewhart developed control charts in the 1920s. He felt that businesses wasted too much time confusing the types of variation and taking inappropriate action. Shewhart envisaged the control chart as a way to simplify identification of variation. He wanted to display the data in the modified form of a run chart, showing the grand average and also the upper and lower control limits (UCL and LCL). These upper and lower control limits show the natural range of the process results, but he was uncertain where to place these control limits.

Shewhart conducted thousands of experiments to determine the most appropriate position for the control limits. He discovered that the best positions were at plus and minus three standard deviations from the process average. We explain standard deviations in Chapter 1, but essentially, one standard deviation tells you the average difference between any one process result and the overall average of all the process results. (Chapter 1 describes how to calculate these, square roots and all.) It's a measure of variation, and at plus one and minus one standard deviation from the grand average, you're likely to incorporate almost two-thirds of your total results. At plus and minus two standard deviations, you cover approximately 95 percent of the results and setting the control limits at plus and minus three standard deviations includes 99.73 percent of the data.

This is only part of the story. Shewhart chose to place the control limits at these points because he discovered that here they work most effectively and economically to distinguish between natural and special cause variation. Over time, many process experts have reviewed Shewhart's experiments and concluded that Shewhart got his limits exactly right.

It's important to note that the percentages described above (where 95 percent of your data will fit between plus and minus 2 standard deviations and so forth) only apply if your data is "normally distributed." Check out Figure 1-3 in Chapter 1 for an illustration.

Creating a control chart

Control limits are calculated using the actual results from your processes. The control limits are not what your manager would like them to be, or what the customer is looking for. They represent the voice of the process and enable you to see what's happening for real.

Using the results from a process, you can calculate the average of the first 20 points, represented by a central line on the control chart, together with the control limits, denoted by UCL and LCL. These control limits represent the natural variation of the readings. We show the details for calculating the control limits in Figure 8-7 later in this chapter.

Building on our example from Figures 8-1 and 8-2, we've included some more data for Location A and Product 3 to develop the control chart for the sales performance in Figure 8-3. The chart shows that the sales process exhibits variation, but that the variation sits within the upper control limit and lower control limit shown on the chart. We use the rules of statistical process control (SPC) to distinguish the types of variation. We cover SPC rules later in this chapter, but for now, work on the fact that because all the data fall within the control limits, the readings reflect natural variation. This won't always be the case, and you'll need to look out for unusual patterns in the data. These patterns are part of the rules we describe in the "Spotting special causes" section.

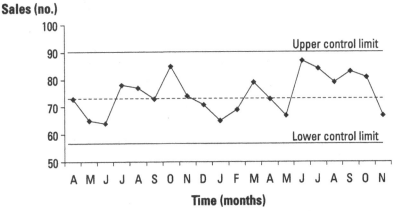

Sales (no.)

Time (months)

© Martin Brenig-Jones and Jo Dowdall

If a process exhibits only natural variation, then it is in statistical control and is *stable*. Being stable means that the process results are predictable and you'll continue to get results that display variation within the control limits. Not reacting to individual data items is the key.

WARNING

Just because all your readings reflect a process that's under control, stable and predictable, doesn't mean your results are necessarily good. For example, you may find a large gap between the voice of the process and the voice of the customer. (See Chapter 4 for more on these voices.) You might not realize it, but your processes are trying to talk to you and you need to listen! Control charts provide an effective way to understand the voice of the process.

Because the process is stable, you can at least review the whole process to find improvement opportunities.

When you take action to improve the process, you must update your control chart to show the changes. Charts should provide a "live" record of what happens. You can add notes and comments to the chart to reflect it. Some say that a "clean" control chart probably isn't being used properly!

Spotting special causes

You can identify special causes of variation in a number of ways. Noticing when a data point appears outside the control limits is an obvious one, as we show in Figure 8-4.

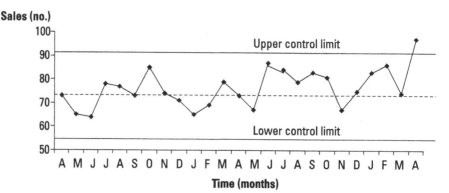

FIGURE 8-4: Occurrence of a special cause outside a control limit.

You also have some special causes to contend with if you spot seven consecutive points that are all:

>> Going up

>> Going down

>> Above the mean

>> Below the mean

Also watch for two other anomalies:

>> The middle third rule, which is based on the assumption that approximately two-thirds of the data will appear in the middle third of your control chart. This brings us back to standard deviations. The middle third of the control chart covers plus and minus one standard deviation, approximately two-thirds of your population data. If the spread of the data is out of line with this pattern, a special cause may be responsible.

Most special causes result in a point outside the control limits or a run of seven points above or below the mean.

>> Unusual patterns or trends, where, for example, something cyclical is occurring or data is drifting upwards or downwards over time, but isn't by itself offending any of the other rules.

When you identify special cause variation, you need to find the root cause and then either prevent the special cause from occurring again (if the result is bad) or build the special cause into the process (if the result is good). If you can do this systematically, over time, your process will become more stable.

TIP

Statistical process control is a broad subject, and in this chapter we provide only the key points. We could tell you for example that some process experts use a rule of eight data points above the mean and eight details below the mean to signify special causes, rather than seven! For more detail, grab one of our companion editions: *Six Sigma For Dummies* or *Six Sigma Workbook For Dummies* (both published by John Wiley & Sons, Inc.).

In Figure 8-4, you can see a point outside the control limits. This probably indicates a special cause and you need to investigate it, but be aware that very occasionally you'll find a point outside the control limits that is a natural part of the process and lies in the small proportion of data outside the 99.73 percent covered by the control limits. This is known as a false alarm, though you won't know that, of course, until you've investigated.

Maybe you know why the April sales figure is unusually high. Perhaps you ran a special promotion, resulting in a sales figure out of line with the previously expected values and therefore outside the control limit.

Sometimes you find a reason for an out-of-control signal that you can integrate into your improvement program. As with this example, if you have a very high sales figure, and you know why, you can integrate this reason into the system and use it as part of an improvement strategy. (Of course, if it's the result of a special promotion, it shouldn't be done.)

A special cause that most people are pleased to see is the proof that a change in the process has been successful. Figure 8-5 shows a situation where a process review has been carried out and an improvement action taken. In this chart, the numbers on the vertical axis refer to the number of errors produced in sequential documents — perhaps the sales order forms.

FIGURE 8-5:
New control limits set after a process review and improvement action.

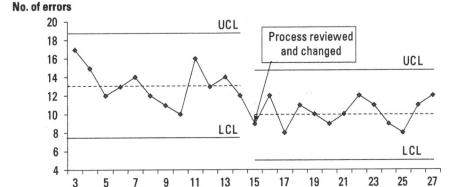

© Martin Brenig-Jones and Jo Dowdall

The results that follow the change to the process are all below the original average (the dotted line), reflecting an improvement in the process. The control chart gives us evidence of a change for the better — in this case, seven consecutive points below the original mean. You can now recalculate the control limits. Reducing variation is one of the key principles of Lean Six Sigma — and that's exactly what you're seeing in Figure 8-5.

Choosing the right control chart

You can use a number of different SPC charts depending on the type of data and volume of data you have, but broadly, they all follow the same concepts and rules. *Variable charts* display data that's been measured on a continuous scale, such as time, volumes or amounts of money, while *attribute charts* track data that's counted, or whether a particular characteristic is present, or right or wrong. Each type of chart has its own standard formula for calculating control limits, but generally the same rules for interpreting the results, and the presence of a center line, the grand average, apply to all.

Of the available control charts, the *X moving R*, or *individuals*, chart that we're focusing on in this chapter is the most versatile. In the X moving R chart, the "X" represents each of the data points recorded — perhaps a series of sales volumes or the time taken to process each order. "Moving R" describes the *moving range*, which is the absolute difference between each consecutive pair of Xs, as shown in Figure 8-6.

FIGURE 8-6:
Determining the
moving range.

X	47	38	7	57	45	59
Moving R		9	31	50	12	14

© Martin Brenig-Jones and Jo Dowdall

This chart is ideal for measuring a variety of things, such as cycle time performance and volumes, and to present attribute data such as proportions or percentages by treating them as individual readings.

Figure 8-7 shows the formulas for the X moving R chart control limits. The UCL and LCL represent the upper and lower control limits for the X data. The X with the little bar above it is the grand average of all the Xs in the data you're using to construct your chart. mR bar (the mR with a little bar above it) is the average of the moving range values you calculate, which you can see in Figure 8-7.

The formula for the control chart:

$$UCL = \bar{X} + (2.66\,\overline{mR})$$
$$LCL = \bar{X} - (2.66\,\overline{mR})$$

$\bar{X} = X\ bar = $ Average of the X values
$\overline{mR} = mR\ bar = $ Average of the moving range values

The formula for the Moving Range part of the chart:

$$UCL = 3.267\,\overline{mR}$$
$$LCL = 0$$

For the moving range part of the chart the Lower Control Limit will always be 0

© Martin Brenig-Jones and Jo Dowdall

In addition to the control chart for the X values, you can also create a chart for the moving range values. Control chart formulae make use of "standard constant" values, in this case 2.66 for the X moving R control chart and 3.267 for the Moving Range chart. These have been calculated using statistics to provide shortcuts in the calculations.

REMEMBER

Control charts are a key technique in the analysis, control and improvement of processes.

Examining the state of your processes

You can use control charts to review performance and help make more effective decisions.

A process can be in one of four states. Understanding the state of your process can provide the basis for more effective discussion and action, as shown in Figure 8-8. Here, we overlay the customer requirements onto the control chart to understand not only whether the processes are in statistical control but whether they are meeting the CTQs. The CTQs are represented as upper specification limits and lower specification limits. You may not always have both an upper and lower limit — maybe just an upper limit.

>> In an **ideal state**, the process is in statistical control and meets the customer's requirements. If you use a traffic-light or RAG (Red, Amber, Green) system, you can think of this state as "green," which means you need no discussion about why this week's numbers differ from last week's. By continuing to use the control chart, you can monitor the process and make sure it remains in

the ideal state. You may also want to improve on ideal — perhaps by delighting the customer, reducing variation, or reducing the costs associated with the process — but to do that you need to implement an improvement project that looks at the whole process.

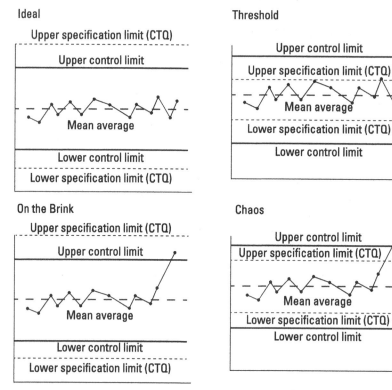

Ideal

Threshold

On the Brink

Chaos

FIGURE 8-8:
The four states of a process.

© Martin Brenig-Jones and Jo Dowdall

» A **threshold state** — or "amber" — describes a process that's in statistical control but doesn't meet the customer specifications. Your discussion can focus on the action that you need to take to bring the process into an ideal state. Again, you don't need to discuss the variation between this week's and last week's numbers, because the process is predictable. Assuming a DMAIC improvement project is initiated (see Chapter 2), your ongoing discussions will concern the progress you make. By continuing to use the control chart, you can monitor the effectiveness of your improvement efforts and, in due course, provide evidence that they're working, perhaps with the identification of a special cause, similar to that in Figure 8-5.

>> When a process is in the **on the brink state**, it meets the customer's requirements but is not in statistical control. The process has special causes and is unpredictable. Here, the traffic light would be red, which means that at any moment, the process may slip into chaos.

>> Chaos — the serious **red state** — describes a process that's not in statistical control and doesn't meet the customer's specifications. By continuing to use the control chart, you can monitor the removal of special causes and the eventual improvement and stability of the process. Removing these special causes from the process before you begin to change is important; if you don't, it's highly likely they'll impede your efforts to improve.

TIP

In a culture of continuous improvement, moving to an ideal state via a threshold performance is fine. Improvement efforts should always focus on bringing the process into a state of statistical control first as special causes can confuse your improvement efforts if you don't understand the interactions they are causing.

Take a bite-sized approach to improvement, monitoring as you go. As your use and understanding of control charts increases, you may wish to incorporate additional information concerning the capability of your processes. Capability indices help you understand more about how well your processes are doing in terms of meeting the CTQs.

Considering the capability of your processes

As we've seen, a process in statistical control does not necessarily meet customer CTQ. Two *capability indices* can be used to help assess your performance.

The capability indices compare the process performance and variation to the CTQs (or specification limits) and provide both a theoretical and actual measure to demonstrate the relationship. They tell you precisely how capable the process is of meeting the CTQs.

These indices are relevant only when your process is in control and the process is predictable. The first capability index — the C_p *index* — looks at the variation in the process compared with the specification limits of the CTQs.

Using the C_p index is like gauging whether or not you can get your car through a gap. Imagine that the width of the control limits in your control chart is represented by the width of the car in Figure 8-9, and the arch represents the width of your customer's specification limits, the CTQ. Consider whether you can drive through the arch.

Is the process 'inherently capable'?

The width of car represents the control limits for 'the process'.

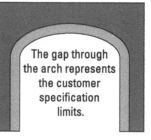

The gap through the arch represents the customer specification limits.

FIGURE 8-9: Taking your driving theory test.

The process is 'Inherently Capable' but only if it's 'centred'.

© Martin Brenig-Jones and Jo Dowdall

In Figure 8-9, you can see that driving through the arch is possible — but only just. You need to drive very carefully and "center" the car. In other words, you need to line up the mean of the control chart with the mid-point of the customer's specification. The C_p index tells us how many times the car can, in theory, fit inside the arch. In our example, the car fits inside the arch just once, with no room to spare, so the C_p value is 1.0.

C_{pk} is the second capability index and it includes information on the process location versus the specification limits. Cpk tells you how well you're "driving" — that is, how well you manage your process. The location describes the position of your process performance as presented by your control limits when compared to the CTQ specification.

In Figure 8-10, the driving needs some improvement. The car could fit into the arch in theory, but in practice, it is off center. Here, the C_{pk} value is less than the C_p value. If C_{pk} is less than 1.0, it doesn't meet the CTQ. In process terms, you need to shift the mean by improving this threshold process. Reducing the variation also makes the "fit" of the car in the arch that little bit easier.

How well is it being driven?
If the process is off centre,
it isn't capable.

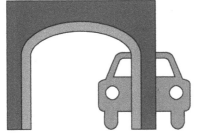

FIGURE 8-10:
The driving needs
improvement.

To fully assess a process you need both the C_p and the C_{pk} values. The process needs to be in control for these indices to be meaningful. The C_{pk} value is never greater than the C_p value. When the process mean is running on the "nominal" — the mid-point of the customer specification — C_{pk} and C_p are the same value. This involves good management of the process, or, continuing our car analogy, some careful driving.

Figure 8-11 shows the formula for calculating the C_p and C_{pk} values for the X moving R chart (which is covered in the "Choosing the right control chart" section earlier in this chapter). The difference between the control limits, the UCL and the LCL, on your control chart covers six standard deviations (three above the mean and three below the mean). The difference between the upper and lower customer specification (USL–LSL) is usually referred to as the *tolerance*. The USL and LSL represent the range of the customer's CTQ. For example, they may want a product delivered within five days, but describe the requirement as an upper specification of five days and a lower specification of one day. Three days would be the nominal value of this specification, the mid-point, and the tolerance, the difference between the specification limits, would be four days.

Dividing the tolerance by the distance between your control limits (six standard deviations), you have the C_p value — the theoretical number of times you can fit the car within the arch. Your C_p value must be at least 1.0 if you are to meet the CTQ, though this really is the minimum. Some organizations specify that their suppliers maintain a minimum target of 1.33 or higher for the goods or parts they provide to them.

Figure 8-11 describes how the formula for working out your C_{pk} depends on the position of the mean on your control chart.

TIP

To put the capability indices into context, think location, location, location! You need to manage your processes in a way that tightly controls variation and *locates* the mean of your control chart on the nominal of the customer specification. Figure 8-12 shows the effects of doing so.

The Cp Index

$$Cp = \frac{USL - LSL}{UCL - LCL} = \frac{\text{Tolerance}}{\text{6 standard deviations}}$$

- For the process to be inherently capable, the Cp index needs to be at least 1.0.

- It may be inherently capable, but how well is it located? You need to use the other capability index, Cpk to find out precisely.

You need to use one or the other of the following formulae: Which one depends on the position of the mean on the control chart.

- If the mean is closer to the customer's upper specification limit, you use

$$Cpk = \frac{USL - \bar{X}}{\text{3 standard deviations}}$$

- If the mean is closer to the lower specification limit, you use

$$Cpk = \frac{\bar{X} - LSL}{\text{3 standard deviations}}$$

- 3 standard deviations is the distance from the mean of the control chart to the upper control limit; 6 standard deviations is the distance between the upper and lower control limits.

FIGURE 8-11:
The capability
formula.

© Martin Brenig-Jones and Jo Dowdall

In Figure 8-12, the process has a C_p value of 2.0. In theory, it can fit inside the arch twice. If the C_{pk} is also 2.0, the process is very capable of meeting the customer specification and does fit inside the arch twice. On the other hand, if your driving isn't so good — that is, you don't manage your process well enough — you can see the effect as the C_{pk} value reduces, moving from left to right in the figure. When C_{pk} is below 1.0, you're unable to consistently meet the customer's specification.

The capability indices help give you a complete picture of performance. They can help you prioritize improvement action, too. By comparing the C_p and C_{pk} values of different processes, you can decide where to focus your improvement efforts, perhaps concentrating on those processes for which the values are less than 1.0.

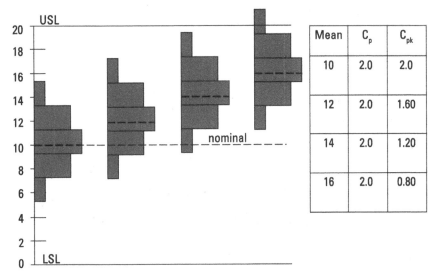

Mean	C_p	C_{pk}
10	2.0	2.0
12	2.0	1.60
14	2.0	1.20
16	2.0	0.80

FIGURE 8-12:
Location,
location, location.

EXAMPLE

We encounter this in practice when we receive parcel deliveries. The delivery of items from distribution centers to our homes is planned and managed with C_p (in theory we can deliver the parcel within this time period) and C_{pk} (when the parcel was actually delivered).

Handling a histogram

As we explain in this chapter, process data may be presented in control charts, enabling you to determine the state of the process and its capability of meeting CTQs. This information provides you with a clear picture of the action needed, if any.

Alongside the control chart, you can use other charts to examine the data. The histogram, shown in Figure 8-13, is a chart frequently used to display continuous data to understand the "shape" and "spread" to look at large (>50) samples.

Histograms can be helpful in providing a picture of the average and range of performance, and indeed the distribution of the data; they don't help you determine the *type* of variation that you're seeing, however, which is why we use a control chart. In Figure 8-13, the data appear to be distributed symmetrically, (information on distributions is provided in Chapter 1), but this isn't always the case.

Sometimes you might see examples of skewed data, where, perhaps, a lot of items are processed quickly but a long tail of data reflects items that are delayed for some reason (see the chart in Figure 8-14). These delayed items may be creating customer complaints or increasing your processing costs in some way — or both! With a skewed distribution, the mean is pulled to the right or left of the average.

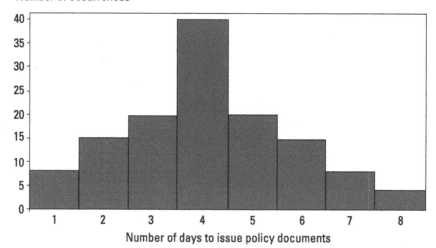

Number of occurrences

FIGURE 8-13:
An example
histogram.

Number of days to issue policy documents

© Martin Brenig-Jones and Jo Dowdall

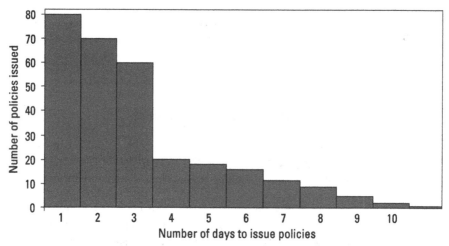

Number of policies issued

FIGURE 8-14:
Looking at a
long tail.

Number of days to issue policies

© Martin Brenig-Jones and Jo Dowdall

You need to understand the reasons for the delay, perhaps using a check sheet and Pareto diagram to present your results. The histogram can also help you identify the need to segment your data, as shown in Figure 8-15.

Looking like a camel with two humps, this *bimodal distribution* (two peaks) contains two "populations," and to fully understand what the results are showing you need to separate them. The two populations could well be two different product lines, where one takes longer to process because of its increased complexity, for example, or the results might be from different locations dealing with different processes.

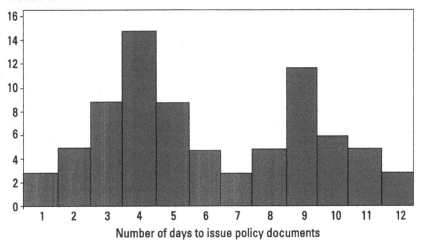

Number of occurrences

FIGURE 8-15:
Twin peaks.

Using Pareto charts

A Pareto chart can help you to identify the "vital few" significant situations in your data. You may have come across the 80:20 rule, also known as the *Pareto Principle*. It claims that 80 percent of all outcomes (or outputs) come from 20 percent of all causes. This is what we're looking at here: It's typical that 80 percent of the errors are caused by 20 percent of the error types. A Pareto chart has been developed from the data we looked at in Figure 7-18 in the previous chapter. In this example, the main causes of the problem, C and E, account for almost 75 percent of the errors made. The Pareto chart in Figure 8-16 highlights this.

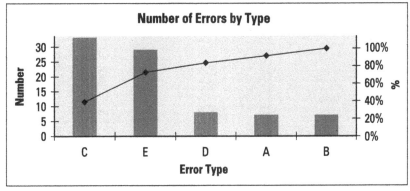

FIGURE 8-16:
Looking at the
vital few with
Pareto.

The Pareto chart is a bar chart with the bars displayed in descending order (longest bars on the left hand side and shortest bars on the right). It includes a cumulative percentage (the vertical axis on the right hand side of the graph) to help you to identify the percentage of the total that each category contributes. The cumulative percentage line on the Pareto chart is plotted from left to right, finishing at 100 percent of course. Your analysis won't always result in a precise 80:20 split. Here, if you tackle type C errors, you'll address 39.4 percent of the problem, but if you also tackle type E errors, you'll cover 73.9 percent. You could tackle types A, B, and D later on. Note that recasting the Pareto chart by cost per error type rather than by error type may give you a different picture!

Displaying your data as a graph or a chart makes it easier to understand. A picture paints a thousand words, so always visualize your data.

TIP

Chapter 9

Identifying Root Causes

Whether you manage a day-to-day operation, are involved in a DMAIC (Define, Measure, Analyze, Improve, and Control) improvement project, or are seeking to solve a problem effectively, you need to understand what factors are affecting performance, especially if you encounter problems in meeting your customers' requirements. In this chapter, we introduce a selection of tools and techniques to help you identify the "guilty parties."

Unearthing the Suspects

People often jump to conclusions about the causes of problems. In organizations where a "firefighting" culture prevails, there is such a feeling of urgency that people don't think they have time to get to the real causes of problems. All they can do is tackle the effects. And sometimes getting to the bottom of something means that people have to admit they don't yet know the solution, which can be difficult for some. However, getting to the root cause of a problem means it can be addressed effectively, and you won't have to "put out the fire" again. Usually, a whole range of suspects influence performance and affect your ability to meet customers' CTQs (Critical To Quality requirements), but the chances are only a vital few are actually "guilty." Taking the time to unearth and investigate root causes is invaluable.

EXAMPLE

A Lean Six Sigma Green Belt (see Chapter 2 for an explanation of Lean Six Sigma belts) was investigating down-time on a production line. The team identified that some of this time was due to the recurring need to replace a sensor. Because the sensor was low cost, no one had questioned why it needed replacing so frequently, as that was just the way it was. An improvement team member who didn't have much knowledge of the process came up with a brilliant question that no one else had thought to ask: "Why is the sensor located on a moving part of the machine?" The team investigated and found that the sensor needed replacing so often because of fatigue caused by movement. By relocating the sensor to a fixed position, the frequency of replacement was reduced and down-time decreased. A fresh pair of eyes and a questioning mindset are great assets when it comes to root cause analysis.

Generating Your List of Suspects

To find the guilty party (or parties, as sometimes there is more than one), you generate a list of possible causes, explore each possible cause, and gradually narrow down the list. In this section, we look at the methods available to help you root out the suspects.

Creating a cause and effect diagram

The fishbone, or cause and effect, diagram (see Figure 9-1) was developed by Dr. Ishikawa and provides a useful way of grouping and presenting ideas arising from a brainstorming session.

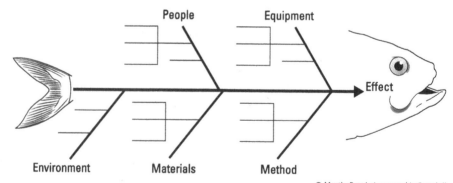

FIGURE 9-1:
The fishbone diagram.

© Martin Brenig-Jones and Jo Dowdall

The head of the fish contains a question that describes the effect you are investigating. (Make sure you choose a narrowly focused question or you'll end up with a whalebone!) For example, you might ask, "What are the possible causes of delays in delivering customer orders?" or "Why are there so many errors in our invoices?" You can group the possible brainstormed causes under whatever headings you choose. In Figure 9-1, we use People, Equipment, Method, Materials, and Environment as the headings on the fish bones. You may find these headings useful in prompting ideas during the brainstorming session, or you may want to use other headings that you feel are more relevant to the problem you're investigating.

After you've constructed your fishbone and added the headings, the team comes up with their ideas on the possible causes. Writing the ideas on sticky notes is a good idea so that you can move them around easily during the subsequent sorting process.

For each possible cause, ask the question "Why do we think this is a possible cause?" and list the responses as smaller bones coming off the main cause. You may have to ask "Why?" several times to identify the probable reason, though you might still need to validate this with data.

Applying affinity mapping

Affinity mapping (or creating an "affinity diagram") is a helpful technique if you don't want to use the PEMME headings (People, Equipment, Methods, Materials, Environment) in your fishbone and don't know where to start.

Begin with a silent brainstorm of all the possible answers to the question written in the head of your fish. These guidelines are useful for affinity mapping and brainstorming in general:

>> Write one idea per sticky note.

>> Write statements rather than questions.

>> Write clearly.

>> Don't write in upper case. (Reading lowercase words is easier.)

>> Avoid one-word statements. (Your colleagues won't know what you mean.)

>> Include a noun and a verb in each statement.

>> Don't write an essay.

Once everyone has finished writing their sticky notes, maintain the silence and place them on the wall (or virtual whiteboard/collaboration space), as shown in the first part of Figure 9-2. Next, move the notes into appropriate themes or clusters. Finally, give each theme or cluster a title to describe its content. This title can now form the heading on your fishbone diagram. You can move your sticky notes under the headings and continue to consider more possible causes until your fishbone is complete.

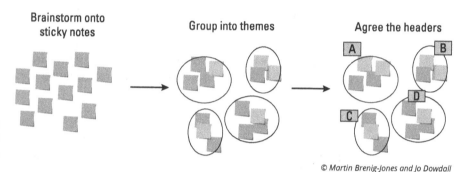

Brainstorm onto sticky notes → Group into themes → Agree the headers

FIGURE 9-2: Creating an affinity diagram.

© Martin Brenig-Jones and Jo Dowdall

TIP

There can be lots of situations in a Lean Six Sigma project where affinity mapping is beneficial. For example, you could use it to gather information from customers about their CTQs. Or you could use it at the very beginning of your Lean Six Sigma journey where you might brainstorm "what issues are involved in introducing Lean Six Sigma in our organization?"

Digging deeper with the Five Whys

Asking the question "Why" is extremely effective when it comes to understanding more about what's causing the effect you're seeing. Remember to leave your assumptions at the door and be prepared to get right back to basics. Five Whys are usually enough to help you get past the symptoms of a problem down to the underlying cause, though you might need more or less.

Here's an example of the Five Whys in action, where a customer has had to wait a long time for some information to be provided. You might have assumed that the supplier was at fault, but with the benefit of the Five Whys, we can see that this is not the case.

Why did it take three weeks to provide the information that had been requested? We had a lot of information to read and redact before the file could be provided to the customer.

Why was this so time consuming? There were 43 pages of information.

Why were there so many pages when the customer has been quite specific about what they need? When we requested the information from the supplier, they sent the whole file rather than just the specific items we needed.

Why did the supplier send the whole file? They left it to us to sort out what was needed.

Why did they leave it to you to sort out? When we asked for the information, we were in a rush and didn't actually specify the items needed.

Understanding the key drivers

An interrelationship diagram can help to analyze and prioritize the items on your fishbone diagram by enabling you to understand the relationships between them.

In Figure 9-3, the key suspects from the fishbone have been arranged in a circle. Now work your way around, looking at the relationship between pairs of items. As you do so, you need to consider whether a relationship exists or not, and, where it does, determine which has a greater effect on the other, such as, for example, "does A drive B to happen?"

If a relationship does exist, connect them with a line. Either there is a relationship or there isn't, so don't use dotted lines and don't use a double-ended arrow.

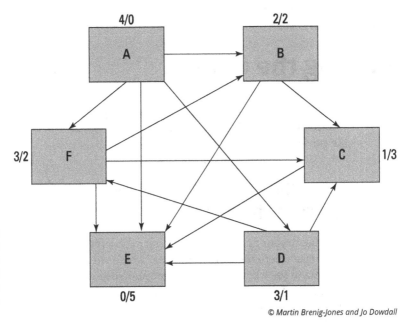

FIGURE 9-3:
The fishbone diagram meets the interrelationship diagram.

© Martin Brenig-Jones and Jo Dowdall

After you've determined the "causal" item, draw an arrow into the "effect" item. In Figure 9-3, you can see that "A" drives "B," but that "B" is the driver of "C." The numbers above each suspect represent the number of arrows out over the number of arrows in. Suspect A has 4 arrows out and no arrows coming in.

The finished diagram can be presented as shown in Figure 9-4, and you can clearly see the key driver is "A," whereas "E" is probably just an outcome of the problem. You need to particularly focus on "A" to address the issues or effects you're facing. This is the root cause.

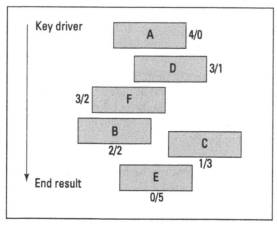

FIGURE 9-4:
Identifying the key drivers.

© Martin Brenig-Jones and Jo Dowdall

Confirming the Causes

Managing by fact is vital, so validating the possible causes highlighted by your interrelationship diagram (see previous section) is the next step. All those possible causes are innocent until proven guilty.

Investigating the suspects and getting the facts

To validate your causes, you may need to observe the process and go to the Gemba (the place where the work gets done, which we cover in Chapter 2), or check out the data to see whether they confirm your suspicions. You'll probably need to collect some additional data to do this. Chapter 4 covers the development of measurable CTQs, which provide the basis for the measurement set of your process, and Chapter 7 introduces the importance of a data collection process.

In Chapter 7, we looked at how Y=f(x) can help you to get to grips with the variables (Xs) that influence the results (Ys) in your process. This is cause and effect. Individually and collectively, the various Xs influence your performance in meeting the customer CTQs, the Y variables. Sometimes, Xs are referred to as "independent variables" and Ys as "dependent variables." Clearly, the Y results depend on you managing the Xs very carefully.

TIP

A SIPOC diagram (see Chapter 3 for the details) provides an ideal framework to help you think about all your process measures. Now you need to pull together a set of X measures, if you don't already have them. A range of X variables will be coming into your process — the input variables. These input variables affect the performance of the Ys, and may include, for example, the number and type of new orders. The input variables may well be related to the performance of your suppliers, perhaps in terms of the level of accuracy, completeness and timeliness of the various items being sent to you.

A range of X variables will exist in the process itself: the process variables. Here, your deployment flowchart or Value Stream Map (see Chapter 5 for details) can help you highlight the potential Xs, including activity and cycle times, levels of rework, the availability of people or machine downtime, for example. Again, these Xs will affect your performance. As you identify the X measures you need, you're building a balance of measures to help you manage your process. You're likely to find that the SIPOC and deployment flowchart are especially helpful here.

Succeeding with scatter plots

Using a *scatter plot* (sometimes referred to as a scatter diagram) can help you strengthen your case. A scatter plot helps you identify whether a potential relationship or correlation exists between two variables and enables you to give a value to and quantify that relationship. The variables are the potential cause and effect — X and Y. You can use this method to explore potential root causes of a problem or, for example, to validate the relationship between an input or in-process measures against your output measures. If your suspected cause (X) is important, then any changes in X produce a change in the effect (Y). Do be careful, however, as correlation does not always imply causation, and you need to use common sense when drawing your conclusions.

In a scatter plot the dependent Y variable is always plotted on the vertical axis and the independent X variable is plotted on the horizontal axis. The data is plotted in pairs, so when X = "this value" then Y = "that value." We show three such pairs in the first example in Figure 9-5. In this example, a relationship seems to exist between speed and error rate: The faster we do it, the more errors we get. This correlation is positive because the values of Y increase as the values of X increase.

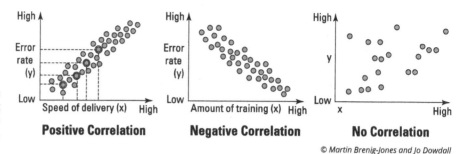

FIGURE 9-5:
Demonstrating
correlation with a
scatter plot.

Positive Correlation   **Negative Correlation**   **No Correlation**

The second example in Figure 9-5 shows a negative correlation: The values of Y decrease as the values of X increase and, in doing so, appear to confirm our theory that investment in training leads to reduced error rates.

In the third example in Figure 9-5, no correlation exists, so the theory being explored here doesn't necessarily hold. Whatever the value of X is, it doesn't influence the Y results. Do make sure, though, that the data has been segmented, or "stratified"; otherwise a pattern might be hidden from view. Chapter 4 covers segmentation.

Measuring the relationship between X and Y

Simply seeing the diagram or plot you've developed may be enough to demonstrate that you have or haven't found the root cause of your problem, but to strengthen your case, you can put a value on the relationship between the variables by calculating the *correlation coefficient,* or *r* value. This value quantifies the relationship between the X and the Y, meaning that it tells you the strength of the relationship, be it positive or negative, in terms of the amount of variation the X is causing in the Y results.

In a perfectly positive correlation, $r = +1$. In a perfectly negative correlation, $r = -1$. Usually the correlation coefficient is less than one, as the possibility of only one X affecting the performance of the Y is unlikely; generally, several will be evident and it's likely you will have determined the correlation coefficient value for each of these.

The correlation coefficient becomes clearer with a little bit more arithmetic. (Don't worry, software such as Excel, JMP or Minitab can do it for you.) The value R^2 (the coefficient of determination) shows the percentage of variation in Y explained by X. For example, if $r = 0.7$, the variable is causing 49 percent of the variation in Y; if $r = 0.8$, the value increases to 64 percent. In either of these circumstances, you seem to have found the important potential root cause of the problem as these values are particularly high, especially considering that a number of other Xs are also influencing the Y values. With a lower value, for example where $r = 0.2$ or 0.3, the impact is relatively small, accounting for 4 percent and 9 percent, respectively.

Figure 9-6 shows the line of best fit, which can help you see the likely values for data that you don't currently have. Drawing a line through highly correlated data such as that in the first two examples in Figure 9-5 is easy. You can do it with a ruler and pencil. You can calculate the line more precisely using the regression equation, $Y = b_0 + b_1 x_1$, where b_0 = the intercept (where the line crosses the vertical axis, $X = 0$) and b_1 = the slope (the change in Y per unit change in X).

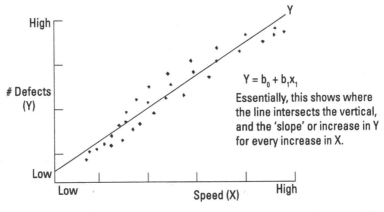

$Y = b_0 + b_1 x_1$

Essentially, this shows where the line intersects the vertical, and the 'slope' or increase in Y for every increase in X.

© Martin Brenig-Jones and Jo Dowdall

FIGURE 9-6: Working out the line of best fit.

Here you can use the data to help you predict things, but remember the potential for a threshold point that changes the picture.

You'll see this equation presented in a number of ways, but whichever letters you use, the slope will look the same! Figure 9-6 identifies the need to be aware of a threshold point because the straight line of best fit might not always continue into the future as circumstances change.

While you can be somewhat confident in predicting Y values between the smallest and largest X values, it is not good practice to extrapolate — that is, to go beyond the available data values and assume what the next will be. As figure 9-7 shows, relationships between X and Y may be linear over a short range, but over a larger range may become curved in either direction or simply break down all together.

When just one X is involved, this calculation is known as *simple linear regression*. *Multiple linear regression* extends the technique to cover several Xs, as does *Design of Experiments*, but these more involved statistical techniques are outside the scope of this book. (Take a look at *Six Sigma For Dummies* and *Six Sigma Workbook For Dummies*, both published by Wiley.

Linear regression enables you to make predictions for the value of Y with different values of X, though remember that the straight line might not continue forever. As indicated earlier, a threshold may exist where things change dramatically, as we show in Figure 9-7.

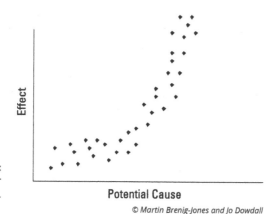

FIGURE 9-7:
Looking out for thresholds.

TIP

Scatter diagrams are easy to produce using programs such as JMP, Excel, or Minitab. However, be aware of some of the common errors and pitfalls associated with them, such as mixing up the X and Y variables and axes or making the assumption that correlation implies causation. *Correlation does not always imply causation,* and you need to use common sense to draw your conclusions.

The example in Figure 9-8 shows data from the German village of Oldenberg, for the years 1930 to 1936. As you can see, the figure shows that the old legend is true; storks really do bring babies! A relationship does exist in these data, but the X and Y axes are the wrong way round. The village expanded in this period, people built new houses, and the increase in the number of tall chimneys proved to be an attraction for nesting storks. More usefully, we could plot the number of houses on the X axis and the number of storks on the Y axis.

Handling hypothesis tests

From time to time, and particularly where you've been segmenting your process data, you need to know whether a statistically significant difference exists between data sets. The data might show, for example, the results from different teams or perhaps from varying locations. This can help you identify whether the team operating the process is a significant X in the Y=f(x) of your process. Or you may have been experimenting with improvement ideas and want to know whether the apparent improvement in your results is real.

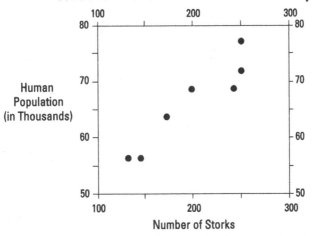

Correlation between Number of Storks and People

FIGURE 9-8:
Bringing home
the baby.

Source: Box, Hunter, Hunter. *Statistics*
For experimenters. New York, NY: John Wiley & Sons. 1978.

You may be able to see a difference by viewing the shape of the data in a histogram, for example, or by comparing the average or standard deviation, or indeed, the amount of variation on a control chart. Even if you appear to see a difference, you may want to determine whether the difference is "real" or just the result of natural variation. You can use a hypothesis test to help you find out.

Hypothesis testing helps you find out whether a statistically significant difference exists or not. This chapter provides only a brief overview of the tests, which are well-supported by software programs such as Minitab or JMP, for example. Check out the Minitab or JMP websites for more details about hypothesis testing.

Creating two hypotheses for your tests, the null hypothesis and the alternate hypothesis, is the first step. The *null hypothesis*, usually expressed as H_0, proposes that no difference exists between the groups. The *alternate hypothesis*, H_A, states that there is a difference. The alternative hypothesis is sometimes presented as H_1.

Hypothesis tests don't look at ongoing data (like control charts do), but rather take a sample at a point in time. Usually, a 95-percent confidence level is used; that is, you can be 95-percent confident that the results identify a statistical difference or they don't.

There are different types of hypothesis tests to use, depending on what you're comparing. The *t-test* looks at two groups of continuous data (as shown in Figure 9-9), and the *ANOVA* (Analysis of Variation) considers three or more groups of continuous data. A Chi-Square test is used for discrete data.

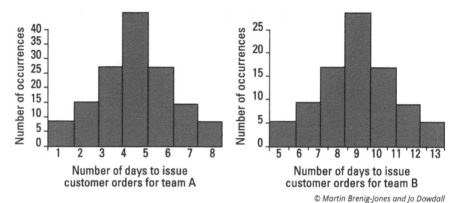

© Martin Brenig-Jones and Jo Dowdall

FIGURE 9-9:
Sometimes the
difference is
clear.

An example of using a t-test is determining whether an input variable (for example, a new battery) makes a difference to the performance of equipment. You could also use it to test whether a process change has really improved performance, so you'd look at the before and after results. An example of using ANOVA is comparing the results from several teams in order to identify whether any team is performing differently than the others, which perhaps provides an example of best practice to follow.

In hypothesis tests a *p-value* determines whether a statistically significant difference exists. The p-value represents the probability of getting the results we've got if the null hypothesis is true. If the p-value is less than 5 percent (p-value < 0.05), you can be 95 percent confident that a difference exists, so a 5 percent chance of spuriously seeing a difference when one isn't there still exists, but the odds are overwhelmingly (19 to 1) against this being the case. If the p-value is equal to or greater than 5 percent (p-value > or = 0.05), you can conclude that insufficient evidence exists to reject the null hypothesis: There is no evidence of a significant difference.

TIP

To remember these rules you could use this aide memoire: "If the p-value is low, the null must go."

WARNING

Where a statistically significant difference is evident, say, in the performance of teams at different branches, for example, don't jump to conclusions about why. The difference could be related to the way the data is collected, the size of the branch, the number of staff, their experience, the market segmentation, and so on. Through discussion and analysis of the process, you need to find the reasons so that you can build in best practice or find ways to eliminate the root causes of problems. There is some debate in scientific circles about the use of p-values and statistical significance. We encourage you to seek support from an experienced Black Belt or Master Black Belt if you intend to use these tools. It's a big subject which goes beyond the scope of this *Dummies* book. It's also worth remembering that you can make a important improvements to your process without using advanced statistical analysis.

Moving on

It's helpful to bring your findings together so that you can come to some conclusions about the cause of any significant difference. Figure 9-10 presents a simple matrix to show how the various pieces of analysis highlight which of the suspects is guilty.

Evidence	Suspect A	Suspect B	Suspect C
Branch performance data	√	×	√
Complaint analysis	√	×	×
Pareto analysis	√	×	×
Correlation co-efficient	√	×	×

© Martin Brenig-Jones and Jo Dowdall

FIGURE 9-10: Being logical.

This matrix is sometimes referred to as *logical cause testing*, where you summarize the possible causes of the problem, and show whether the various evidence you've gathered from your process and data analysis logically matches the suspects. This process is similar to the way in which a legal trial proves or disproves the guilt of the accused: all the evidence is assembled and tested against the (suspected) final causes.

It's almost always possible to carry out further analysis, but these two questions can help you decide whether doing so is sensible:

» Do you feel that you understand enough about the process, problem and cause(s) to be able to develop effective solutions?

» Is the value of additional data worth the extra cost in time, resources and momentum?

If you can answer "yes" to the first question and "no" to the second question, you understand enough about the causes and you can move on. You could also consider undertaking some process-based analysis, so you may want to check out Part 4 for some process analysis tools.

Chapter **10**

Identifying Non-Value-Adding Steps and Waste

W hen Taiichi Ohno described the Toyota Production System, he talked about reducing the timeline of processes by "removing the non-value-adding wastes." Removing waste is clearly beneficial in lots of ways, but how do we know what's meant by "value-adding," and how do we spot a waste?

This chapter focuses on waste. We describe how to tell whether a process step adds value and introduce the "eight wastes" popularized by Toyota's Taiichi Ohno. (These are now often referred to as the TIM WOODS wastes, and we'll explain that acronym later in the chapter.) Addressing waste will not only help to reduce the timeline of processes, but it will reduce costs, remove frustrations, and improve service to the customer. Let's not waste this opportunity!

Defining Value-Adding

Lean Six Sigma focuses on providing value for the customer, so knowing what value actually means in your organization is crucial. Chapter 4 covers the CTQs, those critical to quality customer requirements that your organization needs to meet. In examining how your processes try to meet those CTQs, you need to assess whether all the steps involved are really necessary, and whether they occur in the best sequence. For determining whether each step adds value to your process, a standard definition that everyone in your organization can use and understand is a prerequisite.

Providing a common definition

For a step to be value-adding, it must meet each of the following three criteria:

>> The customer has to care about the step.

>> The step must either physically change the product or service in some way or be an essential prerequisite for another step.

>> The step must be actioned "right first time."

The first criterion in this list is rather subjective. Put yourself in the shoes of the customer: if they knew you were doing this particular step, would they be prepared to pay for it? In providing value for your customer you need to give them the right thing, at the right time and at the right price (see Chapters 2 and 4 on meeting CTQs).

TIP

You need to look at your process from your customer's perspective. You may be processing orders in batches, for example, and waiting until you've completed the entire batch before dispatching the products. The step of putting an individual customer's order to one side while you finish processing others hardly adds value from their perspective.

Consider another example. You have to refer your customer's mortgage application to a senior underwriter to approve the loan. The customer won't be happy to pay for this step, especially if it involves sending their papers to another location and having to wait longer as a result.

The second criterion — the step must change the product or service — means that activities such as filing, copying, checking, revising, expediting, and chasing are clearly non-value-adding. Challenging your process steps with this criterion helps to prevent unnecessary checking and the movement of items back and forth between different steps in the process. As the saying goes, "don't confuse movement with progress."

Chapter 5 describes a Process-Stapling exercise for highlighting non-value-adding steps. Some steps in your process may be completely unnecessary, so remove them. Ensure the removal won't cause an unexpected effect elsewhere in the process, though. If you carry out the process stapling thoroughly, you can see all the vital elements in your process and how they interrelate and can make a simple improvement with no unforeseen adverse effects.

TIP

Often, people (with the very best intentions) have "bolted on" unnecessary steps as a knee-jerk reaction to something going wrong in a process, such as, for example, building in a checking step or an escalation. It was almost certainly the wrong thing to do, but before too long, it became recognized as an important step in the process. Our experience is that checking work to avoid errors can be a pretty hit-and-miss affair, so we always recommend trying to build quality in through prevention and error proofing rather than "inspecting" faults out.

Making sure a step is done right first time is the third criterion in checking value-adding. Rework costs time, effort, and money and is definitely a non-value-adding activity. Chapter 13 looks at addressing errors using prevention and error proofing.

Carrying out a value-add/ non-value-add analysis

With this common definition for value-adding, you can review your processes and see if any non-value-adding steps can be removed. This section describes how to go about a value-add/non-value-add analysis (or VA/NVA analysis) but bear in mind that you're likely to need to keep some of the non-value-adding steps you discover. For example, some regulatory requirements may be in place that the customer may not be interested in, but which you must adhere to. These are usually described as "essential NVAs." Some organizations feel it appropriate to add an additional category to their VA/NVA analysis to capture this. In Table 10-1, it could be included in the column "Essential Value-Add."

You need to analyze your process, so looking at process mapping (which is covered in Chapter 5) may be helpful. A value-add analysis really is as straightforward as it sounds though. Just look at each step in your process, with the three criteria outlined above (see "Providing a common definition" earlier in this chapter) to determine whether it adds value. Use the matrix in Table 10-1 to capture your data. Completing and analyzing the detail might create some surprises; typically, very few steps add value.

As part of your analysis, assessing the unit or activity time (also known as processing time) for each of the process steps is sensible. Unit time is the time it takes to complete a process step (we cover unit time in more detail in Chapter 5). The unit or activity time is the sum of the value-added and non-value-added time, including the "Essential Value-Add" if you chose to show it as a separate column.

TABLE 10-1   A Value-Add Analysis

Process Step	Unit or Activity Time	Value-Adding Time	Non-Value-Adding Time	Essential Value-Add
Vet application				
Enter on system				
Run credit check				
Issue offer				
Diary follow-up				
Client confirms				
Issue funds				
Total Time				
Percentage Time	100%			

If you know how long a step takes to complete and the salary costs and other costs associated with the people working in the process, you can work out the approximate cost of that non-value-adding activity, which may well encourage you to improve the step or eliminate it.

Understanding the unit time is relevant for all of the non-value-adding steps, but perhaps especially so in terms of rework activity. Chapter 5 looks at mapping your processes. Very often process maps are produced assuming the work is carried out right first time. Unfortunately, this isn't always the case, as you can see in Figure 10-1 (where the dotted lines represent rework).

Mapping the rework loops in your process (perhaps in a different color so they stand out) and recording how often they're used can be very revealing. In possession of your cost information, you can then start to prioritize your efforts to prevent these expensive errors. (See Chapter 13 for more on preventing errors occurring in the first place.)

Once identified, many non-value-adding tasks can probably be eliminated. However, some will remain necessary for regulatory, health and safety, or environmental reasons. Termed "essential non-value-adds," these activities need to be carried out as quickly and efficiently as possible. Ensure your process allows this to happen.

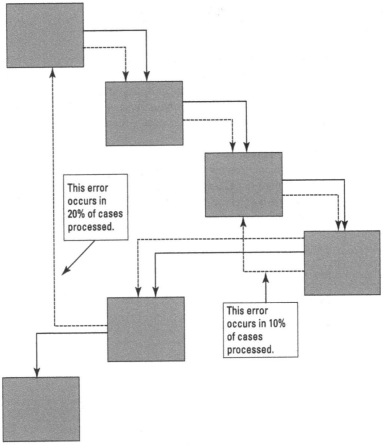

This error
occurs in
20% of cases
processed.

This error
occurs in 10%
of cases
processed.

FIGURE 10-1:
Mapping the
rework loops.

Assessing opportunity

Typically, only 10 to 15 per cent of the cycle time of a process is spent on value-adding activities. These numbers may sound surprising, but the scope for improvement is huge, especially in reducing the time it takes to deliver the products or services customers want. As Taiichi Ohno said (and we repeat from Chapter 1),

> *All we are doing is looking at a timeline from the moment the customer gives us an order to the point when we collect the cash. And we are reducing that timeline by removing the non-value-adding wastes.*

If reducing the timeline between a customer's order and receiving payment is your mission, the value-add analysis described in this chapter is a good starting point.

Looking at the Eight Wastes

Muda is Japanese for waste. In any process, you're likely to find some steps that add value and some that don't. Some of these non-value-adding steps have to stay, however, perhaps because of limitations in available technology or resources. Others can be eliminated immediately, perhaps through a DMAIC (Define, Measure, Analyze, Improve, and Control) project (which we cover in Chapter 2).

Toyota's Taiichi Ohno developed a list of seven wastes to identify all of the forms of muda that could occur in a manufacturing plant. These have since been developed into a list of eight wastes that applies to any type of process in any type of organization. We use the mnemonic TIM WOODS to sum them up and make them easy to remember:

>> **T**ransportation

>> **I**nventory

>> **M**otion

>> **W**aiting

>> **O**verproduction

>> **O**verprocessing

>> **D**efects

>> **S**kills Waste

In the following sections, we look at each of these categories of wastes.

Troubling over transportation

Transportation waste involves the movement of things (people, materials, information, and so on) from one place to another. Transport can contribute to waiting times (for example, waiting to receive a part), it consumes resources, and it can increase the risk of items being transported getting lost or damaged. Examples of transport waste include moving products from one area to another, moving information between systems, and travelling between sites and locations to attend meetings.

Overproduction (covered later in this chapter) might result in transportation waste. You might develop a need to move things around in order to find space for other things, for example. (Chapter 11 covers pull production systems, whereby items are only requisitioned when they're actually needed).

Investigating inventory

Inventory could take the form of stocks and provisions, such as, for example, materials that have been requisitioned in advance to ensure a future order can be fulfilled, or items that have been ordered in bulk to achieve a discounted price. Even though it has been amassed for good reason, inventory might be problematic. For example, was it necessary to order the materials in advance because the supplier is unreliable? Will the items ordered in bulk actually be needed? Inventory in this form ties up the organization's cash. It also takes up space. The items being stored could get damaged or could become obsolete if stored for too long. You might not be able to see your inventory. Storing data and information in the cloud also takes up space, costs money, and has an environmental impact.

Inventory can also take the form of "work in progress." Where batch work is being undertaken, there will be more inventory. Chapter 5 looks at the use of triangles to represent inventory (work in progress or WIP) between process steps when developing a Value Stream Map. The amount of work in the queue can have a big impact on how long the customer has to wait to receive the output of the process.

Moving in on motion

Time for some ergonomics. Motion waste covers unnecessary movement, perhaps because of the siting of equipment, resulting in too much bending, twisting, reaching, or walking, or the need to click on too many links to access necessary information.

Motion waste includes movement caused by a poorly designed workspace, such as positioning of computer screens or the height of a desk or work bench, for example. It is a particular focus in assembly plants, where saving even a few seconds in the various stages of assembling a high-volume product can be vital in enabling reduced costs and increased production.

EXAMPLE

Some years ago, researchers compared the relative positions of the controls on a lathe with the size of an average male worker. They found that the lathe operator had to stoop and move from side to side to operate the controls. The "ideal" person to fit the lathe would measure 4 feet 6 inches tall, 2 feet across the shoulders and have an arm span of 8 feet!

People come in all shapes and sizes, and ergonomics takes this variability into account in the design process. Ergonomics is about ensuring a good fit between people, the things they do, the objects they use and the environments in which they work, travel, and play. A range of best practice guidelines is available on the Internet, covering areas such as lifting and the ideal design of workstations.

One goal of ergonomics is to design jobs to fit people. Job design in ergonomics recognizes that everyone is different. Variability in height, weight, length of arms, size of hands, and so on needs to be taken into account, and study of the human body (*anthropometrics*) provides data on how these vary across the population.

TIP

Applying ergonomic principles involves following a logical process:

1. **Analyze the job.**

   What is required to do the job properly and safely?

2. **Identify any stressful elements of the job, focusing on issues related to physical movement.**

   Is machine access too tight for the largest worker? Do shorter workers have to crane their necks to read displays? Do workers have to reach above their shoulders or below their knees?

3. **Determine the relevant body dimensions linked to the problems identified.**

   Height, weight, arm length or hand size can be issues, for example.

4. **Decide how much variability needs to be accommodated in the design.**

   You can use data from various anthropometric studies (studies of the human body) to help you determine the appropriate specifications in your design. Many of these are available on the Internet or from relevant government departments. You may be able to create the design based on the actual measurements of your existing staff, for example, using the extremes of their height and/or weight information.

5. **Involving the operators and users, redesign the workstation as appropriate.**

   Build in adjustment capability to accommodate size or arm-length differences between members of staff. Factor in if they're sitting or standing, and allow the necessary space for maintenance operations around equipment.

Benefits of applying this five-step process are improved efficiency, quality. and job satisfaction. Costs of failure include error rates and physical fatigue, or staff absence as a result of injury.

Playing the waiting game

Waiting essentially means that people are unable to get on and process their work. This delay may be caused by equipment failure, for example, or because people are waiting for the items they need in their part of the process.

Waiting can result from late delivery by external or internal suppliers, or perhaps the incomplete delivery of an order. Overprocessing can also result in waiting. For example, if a sign-off or authorization step has been built into the process, it's likely that the item requiring sign-off will sit in an inbox until the authorizer has the time to address it. This could add hours or days to the process timeline and could seriously upset the customer.

Owning up to overproduction

Overproduction is producing too many items, or producing items earlier than the next process or customer needs. This type of waste contributes to the other wastes.

EXAMPLE

Working with a service organization, we discovered a classic example of *process suboptimization*: improvement or inappropriate targets in one part of the process causing problems elsewhere in the process. The manager of Department A set an ambitious production target and achieved extremely high levels of productivity that earned praise from senior management. Unfortunately, this increase in output created problems in the immediate downstream process step, leading eventually to the work being stored as a two-week backlog because Department B simply did not have the capacity to keep up. Even more unfortunately, the manager of Department B received the blame and was pressured by senior management and those working on the process steps even farther downstream. Overproduction had struck again!

A classic example of overproduction involves printed material. When you see how the unit price for leaflets or brochures, for example, dramatically reduces as the volume increases, over-ordering is really tempting. Ordering the higher volume and paying so much less per unit makes sense. Or does it? Do you have a large amount of printed material that's unlikely to be used, taking up valuable storage space and eventually becoming out-of-date? How much ends up in the recycling bin?

Picking on overprocessing

Overprocessing waste covers performing unnecessary processing steps, involving, for example, irrelevant information or too many fields on a form. Building in steps for checking and authorization are also examples of overprocessing.

Consider situations in which customers filling in order forms, and people processing them, have to provide or input more information than is really needed. Eventually, the processing team identify the "key fields" and, provided they complete those, the application can be processed. So what was the other information for?

Workarounds are an example of overprocessing. Think of the effort involved to create separate spreadsheets to compensate for an IT system that's not fit for its purpose. Tampering is also an example, as we discuss in Chapter 8, where people may be responding unnecessarily to natural cause variation.

Dealing with defects

Defects is the seventh waste, and it deals with rework caused by not meeting CTQs (which are the Critical to Quality customer requirements we looked at in Chapter 4), providing incomplete replies, or simply making errors.

Figure 10-1, in the "Carrying out a value-add analysis" section earlier in this chapter, is a process map showing levels of rework. You can use unit time information to put a cost on rework. American quality guru Phil Crosby referred to PONC, or the *price of non-conformance*. This simple measure puts a price on how much it costs to do things wrong or to not meet customer requirements. When you include the cost of rework and correction, scrap, recall costs, credit notes issued, and so forth, you can see how significant the price of non-conformance can be — not to mention the effect of lost productivity elsewhere and the impact on your reputation. Chapter 13 focuses on how to prevent errors.

Realizing the potential in people

Skills waste is about failing to use the potential of people in the process. The "waste" of human potential can be viewed from two perspectives: misused or untapped.

>> **Misused potential** can result from not properly structuring the way work is distributed and described. So, for example, how often do you see misalignment of individual and departmental goals, causing people to work at cross purposes? And how often do you either hear or say the words, "That's not quite what I meant"? Spending a little more time on properly describing and agreeing to the requirements of the task is time well spent — assuming the task is a value-adding one!

>> **Untapped potential** is often the result of managers assuming their staff leave their brains behind when they come into work. Think about all the things people do in their spare time, like running clubs or societies, acting as the treasurer, organizing social events, raising funds for charity, being members of teams or choirs, being parents, and so on. These activities require skills and talents. And these skills and talents aren't always recognized in the workplace. It's such a waste!

In looking for opportunities to reduce or eliminate waste, you can find a clue in words that begin with "re." Although plenty of "re" words are fine — recycle is one of them — many indicate doing things more than once. Look out for rework, reschedule, redesign, recheck and reject!

Going greener with Lean Six Sigma

Lean Six Sigma can be used to address all sorts of process problems and opportunities, including those based on reducing negative environmental impacts or promoting more sustainable ways of working. Some projects we have coached include reducing packaging and the use of plastic, and exploring energy-efficient systems for cooling a warehouse. Using Lean Six Sigma tools to measure the difference between "before" and "after" makes for some impressive success stories that can be shared inside and outside of your organization.

When you shop with outdoor clothing brand Patagonia, as well as viewing the spec and features of core products, you can also view all of the environmental impacts associated with their production. Patagonia also leads a range of environmental campaigns to repair and recycle items to avoid landfill and donates 1 percent of its sales to environmental organizations.

Other examples of waste are over-heated buildings, machines left turned on or in standby mode, overnight lighting of empty premises, and travel. The shift to working from home that many people have made during the COVID pandemic has resulted in significant environmental savings. Global Workforce Analytics estimates that working from home for half the week can reduce greenhouse gas emissions by 54 million tons every year.

When you are quantifying the benefits of your Lean Six Sigma project, include environmental benefits.

Considering customer perspectives

The various wastes described in this chapter are all seen from an internal perspective. But, given that one of the key principles of Lean thinking is providing customer value, how are customers impacted by waste in your process?

Certainly, customers will experience delays in waiting; consider queues, late deliveries or slow responses. Waiting and delays will also result when they order products that are currently out of stock or when the wrong product is delivered and a reorder is needed. Also think about the effects of poor communication or inadequate instructions, errors and defective products. They all create waste.

Customers are also likely to feel frustrated with the amount of duplication they experience. Having to re-enter or repeat information and details, whether on forms or in telephone conversations, especially in situations where they're transferred from one person to another, is time-wasting for the customer — and the organization.

Acquiring new business is an expensive process, yet organizations then seem quite prepared to let dissatisfied customers walk out of the back door. What a waste.

All forms of waste, whether internal or external, are expensive!

Going for a Waste Walk

Going to Gemba (where the work gets done) and Process Stapling are covered in Chapter 5. Going for a "Waste Walk" through the process, equipped with a checklist of wastes to look out for, is a variation on this theme. Using data to quantify the waste makes the exercise even more compelling. Some of the wastes identified could be tackled with some quick, simple changes. Others might require a DMAIC project.

Use Table 10-2 for recording observed wastes. After reflecting on the process and discussing it with experts, you can add improvement suggestions.

TABLE 10-2   ## A Waste Walk

Waste	Observations	Improvement Suggestions
Transport		
Inventory		
Motion		
Waiting		
Overproduction		
Overprocessing		
Defects		
Skills Waste		

Consider arranging a schedule for such walks so that everyone working in the organization gets involved. This approach means you benefit from lots of fresh eyes and also secure people's sense of engagement and willingness to undertake subsequent improvement. (Chapter 6 covers the people element of Lean Six Sigma).

Chapter **11**

Getting the Process to Flow

We have seen that *flow* — keeping the work moving smoothly through the process — is a key principle. In this chapter, we focus on those points in the process flow where demand exceeds capacity. They say a chain is only as strong as its weakest link. A process is only as fast as its slowest steps. These steps are referred to as bottlenecks or constraints, and they dictate the pace of your process and determine the rate of your output. Put simply, either you manage them, or they manage you.

Applying the Theory of Constraints

This section looks at how to identify the *pinchpoints* in your process, prioritize them for action, and reduce or eliminate their effect using Eli Goldratt's five-step approach known as the "theory of constraints." There is a subtle difference between a bottleneck and a constraint, though the terms are often used interchangeably. A bottleneck is a step that doesn't have the capacity to meet the demand being placed on it. A constraint is a step in the same situation, but which limits the performance of the system so that it can't meet its goal. Goldratt entitled his famous book about the theory of constraints *The Goal*. It's a classic!

Identifying the weakest link

Think of your organization as a chain like the one in Figure 11-1. It's a series of processes that are dependent on each other, even if the people within the organization don't recognize and accept that fact. For example, you don't ship parts until they're packaged, and you don't package parts until they're manufactured, and so on. Answering the question "How strong is the chain?" is easier than you may think: The chain is as strong as its weakest link. Find your constraint and you find the weakest link in your chain.

FIGURE 11-1:
Working on the
chain gang.

© Martin Brenig-Jones and Jo Dowdall

Conventional wisdom supports the idea that improving any link in the chain improves the chain overall, and "global" improvement is the sum of the local improvements. But time for some different thinking: this local improvement approach actually leads to *process suboptimization*, where apparent improvements in one part of the process actually make things worse in another part. Here, if improvements were to be made in Sales, resulting in lots of new business, you might be celebrating. But if nothing is done to lift the capacity in Service, the organization will be unable to deliver. You need to make your improvements with an understanding of the end-to-end process, or the chain. And you need to take only those local actions that strengthen the chain, by focusing potentially scarce resources on the constraint.

Improving the process flow

Eli Goldratt suggested a *theory of constraints* involving a five-step approach to help improve flow:

1. Identify the constraint.
2. Exploit the constraint.
3. Subordinate the other steps to the constraint.
4. Elevate the constraint.
5. Go back to Step 1 and repeat the process.

A *constraint* is a pinchpoint that occurs wherever and whenever capacity cannot meet demand and the overall throughput of the process is limited. You can *identify* constraints where you have a build-up of people (a queue), material (inventory), units to be processed or work in progress (a backlog).

When you find the bottleneck or constraint, you can then find ways to improve the processing capability at that point in the process flow. You need to *exploit* the constraint, that is, maximize its potential, ideally without major expenditure.

For example, if your constraint is a machine, try to keep the machine running during the working day. Don't close it down for servicing or routine maintenance tasks; you can do that after hours. If the constraint is a person, then make sure their work is covered during breaks for lunch, for example. Any time lost at the constraint has a big effect on the whole process, which takes you to Step 3 of the theory.

To *subordinate* the other steps to the constraint, you use the constraint to dictate the pace at which the upstream activities send their output to the constraint, which tells the downstream activities how much they can expect to receive from the constraint.

As an example, consider the deployment flowchart in Figure 11-2, featuring Ann, Brian, and Clare.

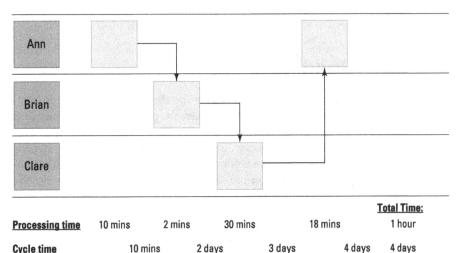

FIGURE 11-2: Brian the Bottleneck.

					Total Time:
Processing time	10 mins	2 mins	30 mins	18 mins	1 hour
Cycle time		10 mins	2 days	3 days	4 days	4 days

Brian's step is the main process pinchpoint. Ann producing more than Brian can deal with is pointless, as doing so will simply create an increasing pile of work in progress. You can see how productivity measures and targets could drive the wrong behavior here. You get what you measure, and if people are measured on productivity, then you'll get it! But where does the output go? And at what cost?

This situation encourages "push" whereby people are focused on hitting their targets, never mind about the backlog downstream in the process. In the Ann, Brian and Clare example, the queue of work building up for Brian will get worse if Ann keeps pushing work through, but if she's trying to meet productivity targets, that's almost certainly what she'll be encouraged to do. Now imagine what it would be like if Brian was *pulling* the work at his pace, rather than letting Ann *push* it through. This would mean that Ann can steady her rate of production and take on some alternative tasks, possibly even helping Brian out, to ease the flow of work through the process.

Let's get back to the *theory of constraints*. To elevate the constraint means to improve it, and, in doing so, increase its capacity. You can introduce improvements that remove this particular pinchpoint, possibly through a DMAIC (Define, Measure, Analyse, Improve, and Control) project (covered in Chapter 2). Of course, once you initiate changes, a new constraint will appear somewhere else in the flow, so you start this improvement cycle again.

Step 5 takes you back to the beginning of the five-step process so that you *repeat* it — a route to driving continuous improvement. In the Ann, Brian and Clare example, if we now assume that the constraint has been removed at Brian's step, you'd then need to address the "new" bottleneck in the process, which appears to be with Clare.

Building a buffer

The constraint sets the pace for the process. Subject to the external customer requirements, it tells the upstream process steps the rate of production needed, and the downstream process steps how much work to expect, as well as their production rate. However, imagine if one of the upstream steps wasn't able to produce things on time. For example, a machine could break down or a system could go offline. The downstream step would be starved of work. Placing a small buffer (an amount of inventory) in front of the constraint to ensure sufficient work is always available is a good idea, just in case an upstream process step experiences problems. This upstream step can work faster than the constraint if necessary, so things should soon catch up, but in the meantime the process flow is uninterrupted. This concept is called *drum, buffer, rope*.

The imaginary "drum" is the beat of production set by the constraint, rather like the drum beating the pace for the oarsmen on a Roman galley. The "buffer" provides the contingency that keeps the constraint working even if one of the upstream steps slows or fails temporarily. The "rope" cordons off, or controls, the flow of work by preventing too much coming through to the constraint. This image also helps you imagine the work being pulled through at the right pace. In Figure 11-3, the drum equates to the production of 40 items each day; even though the process steps both upstream and downstream of the constraint could produce more, their output will each be reduced to 40 items.

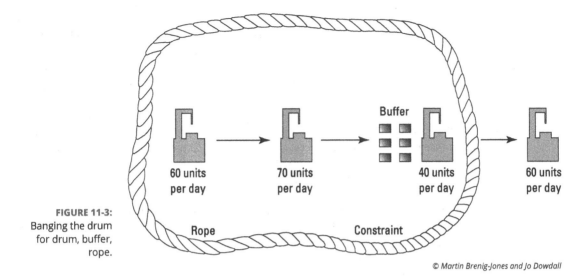

60 units per day

70 units per day

Buffer

40 units per day

60 units per day

© Martin Brenig-Jones and Jo Dowdall

FIGURE 11-3:
Banging the drum for drum, buffer, rope.

Rope

Constraint

Managing the Production Cycle

Whether you work in a manufacturing organization or in the service sector, you need to understand and manage the production process.

Using pull rather than push production

Pull production is a system in which each process takes what it needs from the preceding process exactly when it needs it, and in the exact amount necessary. The customer thus controls the supply and avoids being swamped by items that aren't needed at a particular time. In our example in Figure 11-2 in the preceding section, Brian began to pull the work through at his pace when he wanted it, not when Ann could send it. Pull production reduces the need for potentially costly storage space. For example, in an environment where pull production isn't in use, overproduction in one process, perhaps to meet local efficiency targets, may result in problems downstream, increasing work in progress and creating bottlenecks. Symptoms of overproduction include the following:

>> **Too many:** Making more items than needed.

>> **Too soon:** Making them earlier than needed.

>> **Too fast:** Making them faster than needed.

Pull production links naturally to the concept of *Just in Time*, which provides the customer with what they need, when they need it and in the quantity demanded. This concept applies to both internal and external customers, but it requires a very closely managed relationship with suppliers.

In a pull system, signals are needed. The downstream activities signal their needs to the upstream activities through some form of request, for example a *kanban* (Japanese for a card) or an electronic *andon* board (Japanese for paper lantern). An andon could take the form of a light that flashes when more stock is required, for example, or you could use a kanban to signal that a goods-in tray needs materials.

Whatever signal is agreed, nothing is produced upstream until the request is made and a signal is flagged. If the activity is being processed within a "cell" (see the "Using cell manufacturing a.k.a. autonomous working" section later in this chapter), seeing and managing the pull operation is more straightforward as everyone is working closely together.

A simple example of the kanban signal in practice is the stationery supply cabinet. A reorder card is placed in an appropriate position within the stock and when the card is revealed as someone takes a new memo pad from the remaining pile, for example, a reorder is made to ensure the stock of memo pads doesn't run out. Kanban is used effectively by the Agile movement to manage the flow of work through the project team. You can read more about this concept in Chapter 16.

Moving to single piece flow

Single piece flow (or one piece flow) refers to processing one piece of work at a time between the steps in a process or work cell. The alternative would be working in batches, processing "like" pieces of work together and moving them to the next process step as a group. You might for example set aside time once a week to deal with invoice queries, manufacture a specified amount of product in one run, or print statements overnight. Single piece flow is considered to be a Lean ideal. Let's have a look at why.

Recognizing the problem with batches

Single piece flow moves you away from processing in batches, but it may be difficult to achieve and organizational logistics may mean you need to continue with batches. If that's the case, you need to be aware of the pitfalls associated with it.

When working in batches, groups of individual cases or items are processed and are passed along to the next step of the process only after an entire batch has been completed. This has an impact on inventory, as the number of items of work in progress will reflect the number of items in the batches.

Lead time is increased as a result of batch work. At any given time, most of the cases in a batch are sitting idle, waiting to be processed. Transport time and costs, as well as storage costs, may also be significant.

In batch processing, errors can be neither picked up nor addressed quickly. If errors occur, they tend to occur in large volume, which further delays identifying the root cause. In single piece flow, the error is picked up immediately. With the trail still warm, you can get to the root cause analysis faster and prevent a common error recurring throughout the process.

As mentioned earlier, it may not be possible to adopt single piece flow, and there may be logical reasons for batch working, such as set-up costs or changeover time. Use the Lean Six Sigma principle of "manage by fact" to examine the data and determine the optimal batch size for your process.

Looking at Your Layout

In many organizations, the various people involved in a process often aren't located together. They may even be located on different floors, in different buildings, or in different countries. This type of layout could result in delays as people and work travel around the organization. This section takes a look at the fundamentals of layout.

Identifying wasted movement

People and materials lose significant amounts of time travelling between different locations (Chapter 10 covers waste and how to eliminate it). Use the spaghetti diagram in Chapter 5 (Figure 5-1) to help you reduce wasted travel time.

Using cell manufacturing (a.k.a. autonomous working)

Cellular manufacturing organizes the entire process for similar products into a group of team members, with all the necessary resources. This group and its resources is a *cell*. A cell shouldn't feel like a prison; rather, it should feel liberating for the team members who have real control over what they produce. An alternative name for cell manufacturing is *autonomous working*.

In a manufacturing environment, cells are arranged to easily facilitate all operations, often adopting a horseshoe shape, as shown in Figure 11-4. Outputs or parts are easily passed from operation to operation, often by hand, eliminating set-ups and unnecessary costs, and reducing delays between operations.

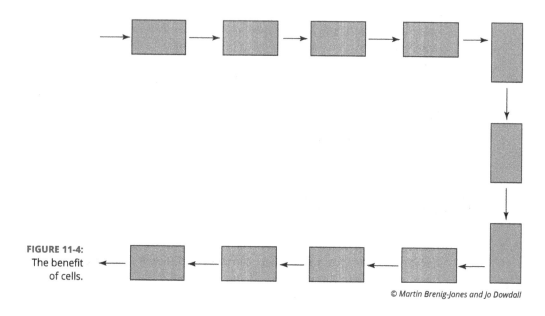

FIGURE 11-4:
The benefit
of cells.

© Martin Brenig-Jones and Jo Dowdall

Working in cells offers the following benefits:

>> The facilitation of single piece flow and a reduction in the use of batches.

>> Faster cycle times and less work in progress (where single piece flow is used), which in turn results in a reduction in floor space.

>> Reduction of waste and minimization of material-handling costs resulting from less movement of people and materials.

>> More efficient and effective use of space.

>> A heightened sense of employee participation.

>> More efficient and effective use of people in the team, empowering them to take responsibility and control. Daily team meetings are easier to arrange, helping to create a culture of continuous improvement, which results in a positive team attitude and an enrichment of job satisfaction.

>> The ability to identify bottlenecks.

>> The facilitation of visual management (see Chapter 13). With everyone in the process working closely together in the same area, the team's performance results can be displayed easily for all to see.

Applying cell manufacturing in the office

Don't be put off by the term "cell manufacturing" as this concept also applies to non-manufacturing processes. Team members managed as cells may not be situated in the same location, but their work is focused on a particular product or service, or the delivery of a number of services to a particular customer or "family" of customers. This type of specialization facilitates communication between various parts of the process and can reduce waiting time between process steps. Without this approach, where work crosses between teams or functions — with different priorities and objectives — it could easily "fall between the cracks." It is possible to apply this approach even when team members are located in different places or working remotely. For example, kanbans can be applied digitally or through workflow management systems to provide visibility and support the process flow.

Identifying product families

Within cellular arrangements, identifying and processing common *product families* makes sense. So products or services involving identical or similar processing steps (that previously might have been seen as different activities, each processed by different teams), can be brought together. To identify the appropriate product families, you need to create a matrix detailing the process/value stream steps across the page and the different products or services down the page, as shown in Figure 11-5.

	Vet application	Enter on system	Run credit check	Issue offer	Diary follow up	Client confirms	Issue cheque
Bronze plus	X	X	X	X	X	X	X
Silver edge	X	X	X	X	X	X	X
Gold	X	X	X				X
Platinum	X	X					X
Platinum plus		X					X

FIGURE 11-5: Keeping it in the family.

This matrix highlights where the process steps are identical or essentially the same for the different products. These steps can then be processed by the same team, increasing your flexibility and processing capability. When we look at the product families and processes, we should be aware of the need to address the three Rs — in this case, the runners, repeaters, and rarities.

Runners are regular and predictable work activities; the repeaters are also regular work activities, but are fewer in number and frequency than the runners. As their name suggests, rarities are exactly that, occurring every now and then. They need to be addressed as one-off work activities. Some organizations refer to these as *strangers*.

Naturally, the process and Value Stream Maps (see Chapter 5) should take account of these differing activities.

Taking takt time into account

Takt is German for rate — the rate at which a product or service must be completed in order to exactly meet customer needs. The takt time formula is the available production time divided by customer demand, as shown in Figure 11-6.

Calculating Takt Time

$$\frac{\text{The available work time per shift}}{\text{The number of customer orders per shift}}$$

- You have 100 customer requests each working day, where you have an 8 hour shift for 10 people
- 8 (hours) x 60 (minutes) = 480 available minutes
- 480 divided by 100 (customer requests) = 4.80 takt time

© Martin Brenig-Jones and Jo Dowdall

FIGURE 11-6:
Calculating
takt time.

The available time is independent of how many resources are available. It represents the number of working hours in the day or shift. For example, if an organization works for 480 minutes per day and customers demand 100 outputs per day, takt time is 4.80 minutes, as shown in Figure 11-6. If demand is for 240 outputs, the takt time would be 2 minutes. Similarly, if customers want two new products per month, takt time is 2 weeks.

Recognizing the effect of rework is important. Imagine that a 10-percent error rate exists in the first-pass output of the work, but is being identified and corrected. In effect, this increases the number of customer requests from 100 to 110. The available minutes are unchanged at 480, but the impact on takt time is to reduce it to 4.36 minutes. Rework takes up valuable time!

An important relationship exists between takt time, cycle time, and activity time. If cycle time is greater than takt time, you have a problem, which could be tackled using DMAIC. Removing waste may be part of the solution; preventing it in the first place might be another.

When takt time equals cycle time, *perfect flow* exists. But be aware that if the flow is not balanced, bottlenecks or constraints could disrupt your ability to meet customer demand. Figure 11-7 shows a process experiencing bottlenecks. In order to meet the takt time the level of non-value-adding activities will need to be addressed and a better balance will be required too, as shown in Figure 11-8.

TIP

Standardization is an important pre-requisite when using takt time.

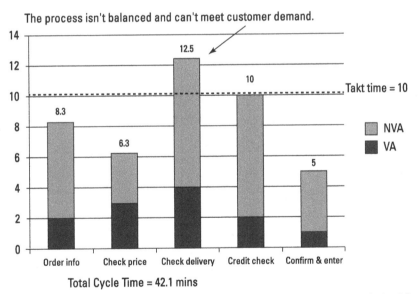

FIGURE 11-7: Visualizing cycle time versus takt time.

© Martin Brenig-Jones and Jo Dowdall

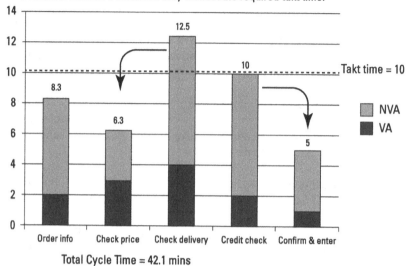

Distribute tasks in a balanced way to meet the required takt time.

Takt time = 10

NVA
VA

FIGURE 11-8:
Balancing the
flow.

Total Cycle Time = 42.1 mins

Combine tasks, reduce NVA and simplify things where possible.

© Martin Brenig-Jones and Jo Dowdall

4

Improving and Innovating

Use tools and techniques to inspire creativity, encourage "different thinking," and generate solutions.

Explore tools for risk analysis and error proofing.

Take a look into Business Process Robotics.

Understand Design for Six Sigma and how DMADV is used to design new processes.

Discover Design Thinking, see how it compares with Design for Six Sigma, and explore how it can be used to boost aspects of your Lean Six Sigma project.

Chapter **12**

Thinking Differently and Generating Solutions

When the root causes of problems have been identified, we can consider how to address them. In this chapter, we focus on "different thinking" and explore a range of tools and techniques for creativity and ideation. As the adage goes, "If we do what we've always done, we'll get what we've always got." So by thinking differently, we can drive innovation and boost the performance of our processes beyond their current levels. Let's start with a shower. . . .

Getting Immersed in Ideas

It has been reported that the majority of people have their best ideas in the shower, and we know that Archimedes was in the bath when he had his Eureka moment. But instead of taking a chance and hoping for inspiration to strike, it's beneficial to build time for solution generation into your process-improvement plan. You might have identified some "obvious" improvements during process mapping or going to Gemba (see Chapter 5). But you can still benefit from thinking differently and applying creativity to drive improvement.

Showering and storming

One of the most widely-used tools for generating ideas and solutions is the brain-storm or thought shower. While it is generally the most well known, it is not always used to its full potential. When brainstorming, and when using the other techniques included in this chapter, try the following:

» **Establishing a relaxed atmosphere.** It helps to put people at ease so they're feeling comfortable about being creative. The authors of *The Design Thinking Playbook* suggest that before beginning brainstorming, people must laugh at least once. Give it a go!

» **Making people feel equal.** Everyone should be able to contribute, whatever their grade or position in the hierarchy. Avoid introductions that reference job titles.

» **Establishing a clear and unambiguous outline of the "subject" to ensure that everyone is focused.** Make this visible to everyone.

» **Encouraging everyone to participate.** Use some of the facilitation tech-niques outlined in Chapter 17.

» **Resisting the urge to critique the ideas as they come.** Encourage the flow of ideas first, and work on them later.

» **Capturing comments verbatim.** If you are the scribe, don't try to translate the input into your own words. Use the exact words of the contributor.

» **Making everything visible.** Use a flipchart, a whiteboard, or online collabora-tion tool.

» **Following up.** What happens next is important! Group similar ideas together, build on them, and prioritize them. Share the outputs with the group and let them know what the next steps will be.

Negative brainstorming

Often in a brainstorm, starting with a blank page can be daunting, and solutions might take a while to trickle through. Turning the process on its head and starting with a list of what *not* to do can be tremendously helpful here. Instead of asking "How can we fix this?", try asking "How could we make this even worse?" For example, how could we slow the process down even further? How could we ruin the customer experience? This can feel quite audacious, and you can expect some unusual and interesting contributions. Next, seek to turn the negatives into posi-tives, and continue to build on the ideas raised.

Using words and pictures

Random words or pictures can provide effective triggers for ideas, as they encourage you to address issues from different angles.

1. Find a picture in a magazine or online, or pick a random word. If using a word, pick a verb or noun rather than a conjoining word (and, the, and so on). It helps to choose pictures or words with positive associations rather than those which might trigger a negative response.

2. Ask the team to make a list of associations they have with that word or that picture. For example, if the word is "holiday," people might think of sunshine, ice cream, or relaxation. If you're using a picture, do the same thing. What do you think of when you look at the picture? Whether it's a word or a picture, encourage the team to use all their senses. What would it sound like? What does it feel like? And so on. Make a list of the associations where everyone can see it.

3. Now think about the problem you are trying to solve. Do any of the words on the list trigger ideas and inspirations? You might be surprised with what comes up! Record these, keep the ideas coming, and never dismiss an idea that's raised.

4. After the generation of ideas, discuss and develop them. Even the most unusual suggestions can be built upon.

Brainwriting

Brainwriting requires written rather than verbal contributions. Like the other tools explored in this chapter, it can be done "virtually" as well as in face to face by using a shared online collaboration space. Brainwriting encourages the group to build on the ideas generated by their team members and works best with a group of six people. There is some flexibility here of course, but avoid too large of a group. Here's a step-by-step guide:

1. Ask everyone in the group to write a problem clearly at the top of their form (shown in Figure 12-1) so that everyone involved can understand it. (Some guidance on developing problem statements is included in Chapter 2.)

2. Now let everyone contribute three suggestions or ideas for solving the problem in the first row of the form, allowing five minutes in total.

3. After five minutes have passed, each participant passes their idea to the next member of the team. You could pass them physically, or if working virtually, exchange them in alphabetical order of names. The team members will now populate the second row, seeking to build on the ideas generated in the first row, or add any new ideas that arise.

4. Repeat the process row by row until everyone in the team has contributed to each form.

5. If six participants have generated three suggestions each in each five-minutes provided, you will have 108 ideas! Follow up the session using the best practice guidelines outlined above.

Problem Statement:		
Write the problem statement here. Remember, a good problem statement should be specific and easy to understand.		
1 The first team member writes their solution suggestion here.	The first team member writes a second solution suggestion here.	The first team member writes a third solution suggestion here.
2 The second team member can build on the suggestion above, or write a new one here.	The second team member can build on the suggestion above, or write a second new one here.	The second team member can build on the suggestion above, or write a third new one here.
3 The third team member can build on either of the suggestions above, or write a new one here.	Etc.	Etc.
4 Etc.		
5		
6		

© Martin Brenig-Jones and Jo Dowdall

FIGURE 12-1: A template for brainwriting.

Identifying the attributes

Attribute listing encourages you to break the thing that you wish to improve down into smaller parts so that alternatives for those parts can be identified. It works really well with physical objects. For example, if the object is a laptop bag, you might break its attributes into material, color, shape, texture, size, pockets, straps, and so forth. List as many attributes as you can. You could then identify the positives and negatives of the attributes and start to consider alternatives. Instead of being made from neoprene, could the laptop bag be made from rubber, sea grass, or recycled flip flops?

The technique also works when the thing you want to improve is not physical. For example, if you want to improve the effectiveness of team meetings, the attributes might include the frequency, the method, the location, the attendees, the materials used, the inputs, and more. Work on these and consider how they could be modified.

TIP

Whether you're working on a physical or non-physical item, study the suggestions to see how they could result in a better or worse situation and whether the attributes can be recombined in a different formation altogether. You'll find that there are many possibilities.

Additional tools for idea generation

There are plenty of tools and techniques available for generating ideas. You may want to practice a few and see if your team has any preferences. You may even go on to develop your own! Here are some further suggestions for tools you could apply:

» **Using analogies:** Drawing parallels between things can help with creativity. For example, you could compare managing your team with driving a bus. In each case, you'd want to make sure all the right people were on board, and they'd need to know where they were going.

» **Using archetypes such as, for example, the hero, the thinker, the magician, the caregiver:** How would each of these archetypes tackle the problem in hand?

» **Wishing:** Ask the team to capture their list of wishes about the process you are working to improve. Encourage them to be imaginative and let go of perceived restrictions. Next, work on ways to make it possible. You could use other methods listed in this section to help.

» **Imagining aliens:** Ask the team to imagine themselves as aliens who have just landed from a far-off planet. What aspects of the problem process or situation might they find strange? This technique helps you to identify and challenge assumptions and adds some "psychological distance," as it's easier to solve problems when you look at them from other perspectives.

» **Creating a mood board:** Ask the team to collect and arrange images or words that represent different solutions. This is particularly helpful when it's difficult to find the words to express ideas. Look at the themes that have emerged from the boards and consider how they can be brought to life in the process or the situation you're looking to improve. Mood boards can be created digitally as well as physically.

» **Looking outside:** Learning about how other organizations do things can be illuminating. You could look at "world class" organizations and see how they approach the processes or problems that you want to address. The organizations don't need to be the same size or in the same sector as your own.

TEN TOP TIPS FOR BOOSTING CREATIVITY

There are many more tools and techniques available to support thinking differently and generating solutions. You can also try giving your creativity a general boost in the following ways:

1. Move away from your normal work environment, or rearrange the space.

2. Go for a walk. It's scientifically proven to boost creative inspiration.

3. Don't just "accept" facts or information. Challenge everything.

4. Be prepared to take risks and embrace failure. Not every idea might be a winner, but every idea can spark another.

5. Collaborate with others.

6. Ask a child and observe their creative "process."

7. Write down new ideas, or parts of ideas, as they emerge,

8. Listen to classical music. Einstein found that listening to Mozart was particularly effective.

9. Silence your inner critic. There really is no such thing as a bad idea.

10. Make the time to practice. The more you use the creativity muscle, the stronger it gets.

Prioritizing the Ideas

If the ideas generation stage of your process-improvement or problem-solving work has gone well, you will have lots of potential solutions to consider. You can now evaluate and prioritize them to identify which are most effective.

TIP

Addressing this task as a team will bring transparency to the decision-making process, which will help you build acceptance for the changes your improvement ideas will bring about. Remember the importance of acceptance, covered in Chapter 6.

If you have lots of ideas, you could use a simple voting technique to reduce your long list to a more manageable number before using a more detailed criteria-based approach. A simple voting approach is effective for a first-round reduction.

Feeling dotty with n/3

The n/3 or *mutivoting* technique can help trim a long list of ideas down to manageable size. N is the number of ideas that have been generated. Divide this number by 3 to arrive at the number of votes each team member gets to assign across the list, with one vote (or dot) per idea. The team can then use a marker pen or a virtual marker pen to apply their dots to their preferred options (see Figure 12-2). Once all the dots have been distributed, there is a reduced number of ideas/solutions to work with, making further analysis easier to undertake. Of course, you can discuss the outcomes to ensure they are appropriate.

Another approach is to use *paired comparisons*. This tool is covered in Chapter 4, which is a good reminder that lots of the tools included in this book are multipurpose. You can use the prioritization tools described here when deciding which improvement projects to take forward, when prioritizing customer requirements, or when evaluating solutions. You can also use them to make procurement or recruitment decisions, or to decide where to go on your next holiday.

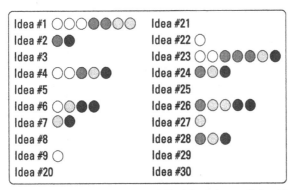

FIGURE 12-2:
Multivoting
in action.

© Martin Brenig-Jones and Jo Dowdall

Using a criteria selection matrix

Establishing criteria for evaluating the improvement ideas is important as it promotes openness and transparency and reduces the potential for "personal favorite" solutions to make the cut, or those that won't fully hit the mark when it comes to improving the process.

A weighted criteria selection matrix (shown in Figure 12-3) can then be used to consider how well each of the improvement ideas on your shortlist addresses the criteria. First, agree on the selection criteria with the team. Input from your sponsor can also be helpful here. Try to keep the number down to no more than six criteria. You can then agree any weightings to be applied. For example, if speed of implementation is a critical consideration, giving it a weighting of 2 will have the effect of doubling the score awarded.

Now evaluate the ideas against the weighted criteria as described below, making sure the more preferable options are awarded the higher scores.

1. **List the ideas.**

2. **Identify the important criteria in the decision.**

3. **Weight these on a scale (if you choose to apply weightings).**

4. **Look at how each option impacts the factors and score out of ten.**

5. **Multiply the score by the weighting.**

6. **Add up the weighted scores and group into high, medium, or low.**

7. **Reject the low-scoring options.**

8. **Evaluate the rest and decide.**

Criteria	Weights	A	B	C	Score (weighted)	Rank	%
Options		1	3	5			
Idea one		6 / 6	5 / 15	7 / 35	56	3	62
Idea two		3 / 3	7 / 21	6 / 30	54	4	60
Idea three		1 / 1	8 / 24	8 / 40	65	1	72
Idea four		8 / 8	6 / 18	5 / 25	51	5	57
Idea five		7 / 7	7 / 21	6 / 30	58	2	64

FIGURE 12-3: A criteria selection matrix.

© Martin Brenig-Jones and Jo Dowdall

Even where you've identified a clear winner, making sure that it's an effective option and not simply the best of a bad bunch is still worthwhile. The percentage column on the right side of the diagram helps you keep a check and balance on things, and perhaps encourages you to look for ways of improving the preferred choice.

TIP

Make sure the solutions identified address the root causes! Some people use the term "countermeasure" to describe the solutions because countermeasures are designed to reduce negative effects.

Testing the Ideas to See What Will Fly

It may be appropriate to undertake a test or "pilot" to make sure the solutions are suitable and effective. This process will highlight the consequences of solutions and provide a valuable opportunity for learning. Make sure you don't create an "unreal" test. Before the test you will need to consider the following:

>> Where to do the test

>> What barriers might be in the way

>> How you will measure the effects of the pilot

>> What you expect the results to be

Afterwards you can look at the results to ascertain the answers to these questions:

>> How well the results matched up to your expectations

>> What knock-on effects occurred

>> How the solution might need to be amended

>> How the approach to implementing the solution might need to be amended

>> Whether a further test or pilot is needed

Use what you learned from your test or pilot to develop a detailed plan for the implementation of the solutions. Be sure to consider issues associated with "scaling up" if your pilot was confined to a small area.

TIP

Plenty of tools and techniques for planning are included in *Project Management For Dummies* by Stanley E. Portny (Wiley).

Chapter **13**

Discovering the Opportunity for Prevention

The concept of prevention has been in existence for a long time. Even before our grandmothers told us that prevention is better than cure, and probably even before Lao Tzu highlighted its importance back in 600 BC:

Before it moves, hold it,

Before it goes wrong, mold it,

Drain off water in winter before it freezes,

Before weeds grow, sow them to the breezes.

You can deal with what has not happened,

Can foresee

Harmful events and not allow them to be.

Closely related is the concept of "no fault forward," meaning that mistakes should be identified as soon as they happen rather than be allowed to travel downstream through the process. This chapter examines how prevention and detection can be applied in our processes.

Looking at Prevention Tools and Techniques

You can prevent or at least reduce the impact of problems by using a whole range of tools and techniques.

Introducing Jidoka

Jidoka is a Japanese word associated with building quality into the process, and preventing defects. Jidoka is often referred to as *autonomation,* which is a means of preventing defective items from passing to the next process. We highlight the "no" in autonomation to remind you that *no* defects are allowed to pass to a follow-on process.

Without Jidoka, automation has the potential to allow a large number of defects to be created very quickly, especially if processing in batches.

Jidoka works on the principle that once a defect or error occurs, the process is stopped to ensure no further defects or errors are produced until the cause of the problem is remedied. In 1902, Sakichi Toyoda, the founder of the Toyota group, invented an automated loom that stopped each time a thread broke. This immediate halt prevented the thread coming out of the loom and so saved time that previously was wasted in sorting out the mess. A printer stopping when its ink runs out is a modern example of Jidoka.

Autonomation allows machines to operate autonomously by shutting down if something goes wrong. *Automation with human intelligence* is another term for this concept.

Jidoka embraces the concept of "Stop at every abnormality," which means a manual process stops whenever an abnormal condition occurs. In some manufacturing organizations, every employee is empowered to "stop the line," perhaps following the identification of a special cause on a control chart (see Chapter 8 for more), but the concept applies to any type of process in any type of organization.

REMEMBER

Forcing everything to stop to immediately focus on a problem is an effective way to quickly get at the root cause of issues. In batch processing, discovering problems immediately is crucial.

Recognizing risk with Failure Mode and Effects Analysis

Failure Mode and Effects Analysis (*FMEA*) is a prevention tool that helps you identify and prioritize potential opportunities for taking preventive action. Identifying the things that might go wrong — the *failure modes* — is the first step.

By looking at what might go wrong (the failure modes), you can assess the impact of what happens (the effects) when it does go wrong, how often it is likely to occur, and how likely you are to detect the failure before its effect is realized. For each of these potential events you assign a value, usually on a scale of 1 to 10, to reflect the risk. FMEAs can be applied to processes, systems and designs. They are used to manage quality, ensure safety and reduce the cost of poor quality (see Chapter 10).

Table 13-1 provides a typical rating scale for a service organization.

TABLE 13-1   Weighing up the risk

Rating	Severity of Effect	Likelihood of Occurrence	Current Detectability
1	None	Remote	Immediately detected
2	Very minor effect	Very low	Found easily
3	Minor	Low	Usually found
4	Low to moderate	Low to moderate	Probably found
5	Moderate	Moderate	May be found
6	Moderate to high	Moderate to high	Less than 50% chance of detection
7	High	High	Unlikely to be detected
8	Very high	Very high	Very unlikely to be detected
9	Hazardous	Extremely high	Extremely unlikely to be detected
10	Disastrous	Almost certain	Almost impossible to detect

These ratings are used to calculate a *risk priority number* (*RPN*), which helps you to prioritize your actions. This value is the result of multiplying your ratings for the severity of the risk (from Table 13-1), the frequency of occurrence, and the likelihood of detection. When all the RPN values have been calculated, you can identify which to work on, and find ways to reduce the RPN. Figure 13-1 provides an example of an FMEA template. It includes columns that enable you to consider the failure modes and their effects, determine the RPNs, allocate the responsibility for improvement, and recalculate the RPN once the improvement actions have been taken.

Failure Modes and Effects Analysis template

Process: _____ Team: _____ FMEA Date (original): _____ (revised): _____

	What?			Why? When? Where?				How?	Who?	Action Results				
Item/process step	Potential failure mode	Potential effect(s) of failure	Severity	Potential cause(s) of failure	Occurrence	Current controls and measures	Detection	RPN	Recommended actions	Responsibility and completion target date	Action taken	Severity	Occurrence	Detection	RPN

FIGURE 13-1:
Weighing up the risk with FMEA.

TIP

In determining ratings for the various failure modes in your processes, working with members of the relevant process team and looking at each step in the process is sensible. There may be multiple failure modes for each step. To ensure you identify each step, we recommend you use a deployment flowchart rather than a Value Stream Map, as the latter might not have sufficient detail for a process FMEA.

Your ratings against the descriptions in Table 13-1 are based on your experience rather than absolute fact, so when you complete the exercise, step back and make sure the numbers seem sensible. It's important to rate each failure mode consistently.

EXAMPLE

A scheduling team for a utility company regularly operated workarounds because the IT system used to schedule technicians' jobs wasn't considered fit for purpose. Members of the scheduling team would alter aspects of the data in the system to overcome the algorithm it used to plan the day's jobs. For example, they might change the address details of a job to allow the technician to undertake work in a postcode that would otherwise have been "out of their area." One of the failure modes identified in the FMEA was forgetting to change the postcode back again, which resulted in an incorrect customer address being held in the system. Ratings for severity and likelihood were fairly low, but the rating score applied to Detection was high, since only the scheduler knew the data had been changed.

Examine your own processes to see if FMEA creates any opportunities for improvement. Consider each step in your process and identify its failure modes. In coming up with your RPN, remember that these numbers are subjective; use common sense in determining the action needed.

Error proofing your processes

Error proofing — sometimes referred to as *poka-yoke*, (Japanese slang for "avoiding inadvertent errors") — could be used to address risks highlighted in the FMEA or to help process users get it right every time.

Poka-yoke approaches either prevent mistakes from being made or make the mistakes detectable. The best poka-yoke approaches are:

>> Inexpensive

>> Very effective

>> Based on simplicity and ingenuity

Poka-yoke doesn't rely on operators catching mistakes, but it does help to ensure quick feedback 100 per cent of the time, leading to process improvements and reductions in waste.

Consider the 1-10-100 rule, which states that as a product or service moves through the production system, the cost to your organization of correcting an error multiplies by 10. Looking at the processing of a customer order, for example:

>> Order entered correctly: $1

>> Error detected in billing: $10

>> Error detected by customer: $100

The 1-10-100 rule fails to pick up the additional costs associated with dissatisfied customers sharing their experience with others, something that can escalate rapidly on social media, for example. Error proofing is definitely worth doing!

Examples of prevention and error proofing are observable in everyday life. These include the warning sound you hear if you don't use the seat belt, or elevator buttons you can press with your feet to reduce the transference of bacteria and viruses.

Three types of error proofing approaches exist: contact, fixed value, and motion step.

>> **Contact error proofing** involves products having a physical shape that inhibits mistakes, as shown in Figure 13-2.

The physical design makes installing parts in any but the correct position impossible. Electronic equipment design, and that of its various attachments and extensions, for example, ensures the right cables can only go into the right sockets. This situation is achieved through a combination of part sizes and shapes, as well as color-codes. Although the latter is an example of visual management and might not prevent you from trying to plug something into the wrong socket or location, the concept is trying to prevent you from doing so! Another example is a fixed diameter hole through which all products must fall. Any oversized product is unable to pass through, and the potential defect associated with it is thus prevented.

>> **Fixed value error proofing** identifies when a part is missing or not used and essentially ensures appropriate quantities. A simple example is the French fry scoop used in fast food outlets, which is designed to ensure a consistent number of fries fit the package served to the customer. A further example is "egg trays" used for the supply of parts: Spotting that something's missing is as easy as seeing that one compartment is empty.

>> **Motion step error proofing** automatically ensures that the process operator has taken the correct path or number of steps, possibly by breaking a photocell light sensor, stepping on a pressure sensitive pad during the assembly cycle, or through remotely tracked pedometer style technology. A different example is spell-checkers providing automatic warnings when words are incorrectly spelled and the operator needs to click on the highlighted word to change it.

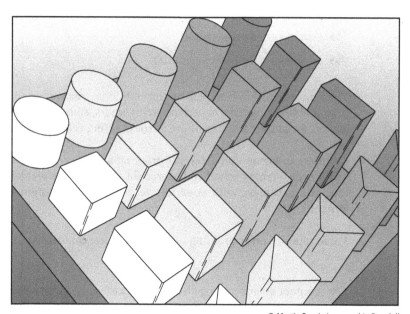

FIGURE 13-2: Square pegs and round holes: Contact error proofing.

Workplace Organization

Organizing the workplace well can reduce waste, improve productivity and prevent errors and accidents. The 5S methodology can be used here to provide structure and ensure sustainable results. In fact, Sustain is one of the 5Ss!

Introducing the Five Ss

The 5S method consists of five steps to be taken, in order, to organize a physical or "virtual" workspace. You could use it anywhere, including the office, storage areas, and the cloud. Implementing 5S leads to a safer and more pleasant working environment that encourages both self-management and team working. Here are the five steps:

>> **Sort** (sometimes referred to as Separate) encourages you to look at the tools, materials, equipment. and information you need to do your job, and separate them into those used "frequently," "occasionally," and "never." You can sort based on your experience, but "tagging" the items in some way can be helpful (see the "Carrying out a red-tag exercise" section later in this chapter). After sorting, remove unnecessary items from the work area.

>> **Set** (or Straighten) means straightening things up and arranging everything you use frequently so that it's easily to hand. This may include toolkits, files or email folders, or moving a printer to a more convenient location. Things that you don't use frequently need to be put somewhere else, recycled, or thrown away. Decide how many items need storing, how they should be stored, and where. Naturally, these stored items should be appropriately labeled to facilitate their easy access in the future.

>> **Shine** (or Scrub) concerns keeping the things you use, and the environment you work in, clean and tidy and appropriately maintained. Make your workplace shine, so get rid of rubbish and dirt, and don't leave scrap lying around. Make sure your tools are current, safe, and clean, and that all the information and documents you use are up-to-date and well-presented. Check that equipment and machinery are routinely serviced and maintained.

>> **Standardize** (or Systemize) means that processes described above become standardized. Design a simple way of working so that your information and tools stay sorted, straightened, and shiny. Essentially, this involves regularly redoing the first three Ss! Doing so helps identify the reasons why the workplace becomes messy and cluttered, and prompts preventive thinking to find ways of stopping the problems recurring.

>> **Sustain** (or Standardize) is about keeping the whole process going. Stick to the system, train everyone in the application of 5S, regularly review the standard, implement improvements, and tell others about your effective method of working so it becomes a way of life.

Carrying out a red-tag exercise

A *red-tag exercise* is a tracking process to identify unneeded items. If you use 5S, which we describe in the previous section, red-tagging can become a useful element of "Sorting." You could, for example, tag the various items on your desk on a particular date, see when you use them next and then update the tag with the time and date. If you haven't used them in, say, one month, then move to "Set" so they can be appropriately relocated. After all the obvious things have been thrown away, recycled, or relocated, you'll be left with only those things that you regularly use and need to hand.

TIP

You can use red-tagging at home as well, such as, for example, to keep your wardrobe from bursting.

You may need to form a team to work on red-tagging your wider working areas, appointing a champion and team members. Identify the areas to tackle, such as, for example, inventory, files stored in the cloud, equipment, stationery, or supplies. And then agree upon and communicate the criteria and timeframe of the exercise.

Visual management helps ensure that items in use can be returned to the right place, and that missing items are easily identified. See the "shadow board" for tools in Figure 13-3.

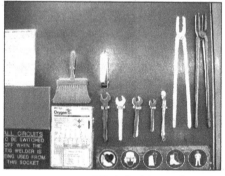

FIGURE 13-3: A shadow board helps you see at a glance if any tools are missing.

© *Martin Brenig-Jones and Jo Dowdall*

Using Visual Management

5S is a basic form of visual management. In a well organized work environment you can recognize if anyone needs help, or if action is required, far more easily than in a chaotic environment.

Visual management takes many forms in the workplace and also outside of it. Traffic signs are an obvious example. A variety of displays, charts, signs, labels, color-codes and markings can be utilized. Using a visual approach helps everyone see what's going on, understand the process, and know that tasks are being carried out or items stored correctly.

Visual management can also support the communication of information and the identification of issues or abnormalities. Visual displays could include data or information for the people working in a particular area, keeping them informed of overall performance or focused on specific quality issues. Visual controls could also cover safety, production throughput, material flow or quality metrics, for example.

Essentially, visual management is a technique that enables improvement; it ensures the workplace is well organized and that things can be easily found. It provides a very effective way of communicating results and involving people, and makes it clear when action is required.

Understanding and acting on these signals is vital. This is where the discipline of regular, frequent meetings comes in. These meetings are one of the secret ingredients to success that organizations and teams use to expose and understand issues, and make timely decisions based on fact.

Some call them daily huddles, stand-ups, lean daily management meetings, or fit-to-fly sessions. It doesn't really matter what you call them. What matters is holding them regularly and making them focused, as shown in Figure 13-4. These meetings should take no longer than 15 minutes and should take place where the work gets done rather than in a meeting room. They can also be done remotely of course.

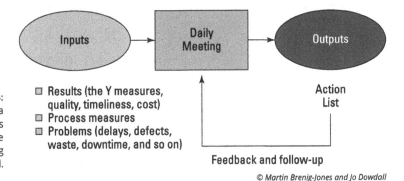

FIGURE 13-4:
Keeping a process performance review meeting tightly focused.

© Martin Brenig-Jones and Jo Dowdall

Apart from reviewing performance and the activity for the day ahead, process performance review meetings also provide a forum to discuss improvement opportunities and ideas. They have been embraced by the Agile movement, which incorporates "daily scrums" into the Scrum framework (which we cover in Chapter 16).

TIP

If you're using physical displays of information, include "use by" dates on the displays to ensure the information remains current and empower everyone to remove an item if they see that it's out-of-date. Place a silhouette behind each item (see the shadow board in Figure 13-3) so that it's immediately obvious that an issue must be updated.

Figure 13-5 provides an example of how to structure an activity board that then forms the agenda and focus for the team meetings. Make sure the meetings are actually held in the same location as the board is displayed!

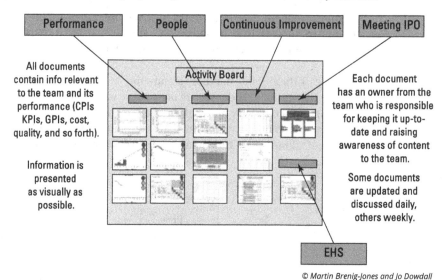

FIGURE 13-5:
An activity board approach to team management.

© Martin Brenig-Jones and Jo Dowdall

In this example, you can see that five key areas are highlighted for discussion. Whatever form your visual display takes, aim to keep the information simple, easy to read and understand, and up-to-date. You shouldn't need to spend time interpreting the message.

Profiting from Preventive Maintenance

Preventive maintenance means being proactive to avoid equipment failure and system problems. Contrast this approach to diagnostic or corrective maintenance, which is performed to correct an already-existing problem. If you own a car, you may understand the concept of preventive maintenance: You don't change your oil in response to a problem situation; you do it before things go wrong, so your engine lasts longer and you avoid car troubles down the road.

Preventive maintenance requires a schedule of planned maintenance actions aimed at the prevention of breakdowns and failures. It is designed to preserve and enhance equipment reliability by replacing worn components before they fail and activities include equipment checks, partial or complete overhauls at specified periods, oil changes, lubrication, and so on. In addition, workers can record equipment deterioration so they know to replace or repair worn parts before they cause system failure. Recent technological advances in tools for inspection and diagnosis have enabled even more accurate and effective equipment maintenance.

An ideal preventive maintenance program prevents all equipment failure before it occurs. For example, in an airport, preventive maintenance may be in place in critical service areas such as escalators, lighting and aircraft bridges.

REMEMBER

Preventive maintenance results in savings by increasing the service life of effective systems. Long-term benefits of preventive maintenance include the following:

>> Improved system reliability

>> Decreased cost of replacement

>> Decreased system downtime

>> Better spares inventory management

You can't always prevent things from going wrong or equipment from failing. But when they do, your ability to recover from problems quickly is key.

Avoiding Peaks and Troughs

This section focuses on dealing with work activity to avoid too many peaks and troughs in the volumes and types of work being processed. Leveling the work isn't easy, but it is the foundation of Toyota's celebrated production system. The Japanese refer to the concept as *Heijunk*a.

Introducing Heijunka

Heijunka is the Japanese word for leveling. It is an underlying concept of the Toyota Production System (TPS), shown in Figure 1-1 in Chapter 1.

Heijunka involves smoothing processing and production by volume and by work type. The following elements are included:

>> **Leveling by volume** involves smoothing the volume of production in order to reduce variation. If demand fluctuates daily, processing the average number of customer orders over the week allows you to achieve a steady flow and meet the average demand by the end of the week. Amongst other things, this seeks to prevent "end-of-period" peaks, where production is initially slow but then quickens in the last days of a sale or accounting period, for example.

>> **Sequencing** involves mixing the kinds of work processed so the average demand for product types can be met. So, for example, when setting up new loans, the type of loan being processed is mixed to better match customer demand and help ensure applications are actioned in date order. In a manufacturing process, a producer may be able to hold a small buffer of finished goods to respond to the ups and downs in weekly orders. Keeping a small stock of finished goods at the very end of the value stream, near shipping, this producer can adjust to small changes in demand for its plant and for its suppliers, making for more efficient utilization of assets along the entire value stream while still meeting customer requirements.

EXAMPLE

Getting to see the doctor provides a good example of Heijunka. The demand for appointments is high and growing. To balance this out, telephone triage is offered, along with email consultations, online services, preventive services, and specific offerings at specific set times during the week where the work is standardized (for example, vaccinations).

Spreading the load

Keeping things balanced and level means your process flows are smoother and your overall processing times faster. But be warned: This situation isn't easy to achieve. A balance of other lean concepts and techniques are required to make it work, such as managing inventory and buffer, quick changeover, takt time, batch sizing, and standardization.

TIP

In the workplace, you need to try to avoid peaks and troughs in activity, if you can. The month-end or quarter-end cycles in many organizations highlight the difficulties of peaks. Actioning financial reconciliations, for example, on a daily or weekly basis may be possible, thus avoiding the monthly or quarterly peak of activity. You need to determine whether an opportunity to change frequencies exists in your organization.

In Chapter 10, we talk about waste, or *muda*. This expression is often used together with two other words, *mura* and *muri*. Mura describes unevenness in an operation; for example a piece of work that flows quickly through some steps in a process, but then slows right down. Muri means overburdening. An example might be placing excessive demand on a particular team or individual within a team, or overburdening a piece of equipment.

Consider mura and muri in the context of maintaining a smooth and level flow at a transport depot. You have several three-ton trucks, but you need to transport six tons of material to your customer. You have four options:

>> All six tons on one truck = muri and a probable broken axle.

>> Four tons on one and two on another truck = muri, mura, and muda.

>> Two tons on three trucks = muda.

>> Three tons on two trucks = muri-, mura-, and muda-free!

So this last option is the optimum way of delivering the material to your customer. It uses an evenly distributed approach, no waste occurs and trucks aren't overburdened. Now relate this back to your own processes. Are they free of muda, muri, and mura too?

Carrying out work in a standard way

Standardized work is another of the elements that forms the basis of the Toyota Production System and provides stability for the rest of the structure. Once the "current best way" of operating the process has been identified, standardizing the process delivers the improvement gains and leads to stability and predictability. Actually, without standardization, there is no real improvement. Throughout this book, through the phases of the DMAIC methodology, there are many tools you can use to understand what is happening in your processes and how to improve them. In Chapter 5, we look at techniques such as process mapping to help you document the "current best way" so that it can be adopted as the standard.

TIP

Standardizing the current best way is key, but in a culture of Continuous Improvement, you may find better ways to do the work that become the new "current best way." If defects occur, your first question needs to be "Has the standard process been followed?" If it has, then there are opportunities for improvement. Keep improving your process and encourage ideas from the people working within it. As you grow increasingly confident in applying the Lean Six Sigma principles and tools, you'll recognize that no end exists to the process of improving processes.

Building in Business Process Robotics

Robotic Process Automation (RPA) is the name given to the development of software robots or "bots" to deliver processes. An RPA system can be used to carry out particular tasks in an application's interface with no errors, in high volume, and at high speed. This releases process operators to undertake more value-adding and interesting work elsewhere. This kind of thinking is not new. Taiichi Ohno of Toyota wanted workers to eliminate the "tedious and boring tasks" so that they could be free to focus on adding value for customers.

Where the process steps are of a routine and repetitive nature, and if they use data that's available digitally, RPA can be beneficial. It can be used to support customer facing processes (such as answering frequently asked questions) or in the "back office" to automate time-consuming tasks such as taking data from a system and filing it.

This area is rapidly evolving as the technology becomes more cost efficient. Automation tools are now available for use at our desktops, rather than being the domain of specialists.

Our advice is to make sure the process is optimized before seeking to automate it. Remember that there are ongoing costs associated with RPA, so any changes to data fields or systems can knock your bot off course, and it will need reprogramming. If the requirement is purely to transfer data from one system to another, it could be better to investigate other types of data interface such as API (application programming interface). These types of data feed are often more stable once in place and are more likely to survive upgrades and patches compared to bots.

We also advise making sure people know how to deal with "exceptions" in processes where RPA is applied, though in the future, self-learning systems will have the ability to pick these up too. Artificial Intelligence can already drive a car, recognize emotion in speech, handle insurance claims, and win at Texas hold'em poker.

Things are changing quickly, so there's likely to be a whole lot more to say about RPA over the next few years!

Chapter **14**

Introducing Design for Six Sigma

W hen a brand new process, product or service is to be created, or when a radical change is required to get a process, product or service in shape to meet requirements, Design for Six Sigma rather than Lean Six Sigma is used. This chapter provides an introduction to Design for Six Sigma (DfSS). It is simply an overview because the topic could easily form a book of its own. In this chapter, we look at DfSS and the DMADV method —Define, Measure, Analyze, Design, and Verify — as well as take you on a tour through the House of Quality (otherwise known as Quality Function Deployment, or QFD). But we stress that it's only a tour and not a full structural survey!

Introducing DfSS

In Chapter 2, we look at how to improve existing processes and make incremental changes using DMAIC: Define, Measure, Analyze, Improve and Control. However, you may be working to develop a completely new process, product, or service. Or you may find that the existing process has so much scope for advancement that instead of improving what is already in place, it is beneficial to start again and build it from the ground up. Here, DMADV is used: Define, Measure, Analyze, Design and Verify. The approach is called Design for Six Sigma (DfSS). There are some similarities and some differences between Lean Six Sigma and Design for Six Sigma.

In the circumstances described above, you have the opportunity to begin with a blank canvas. You can design products and services, and the processes that support them, that will delight your customers from day one. Many organizations set a goal for the expected Process Sigma level for a product or service developed using DfSS of at least 4.5. (See Chapter 1 for more on calculating Process Sigma.) DfSS often concentrates on the "delighter" curve in the Kano model that we describe in Chapter 4. Think about introducing these new products and services quickly, and to a consistently high standard. You can focus on those organizational processes that create the highest value-adding outcomes.

Design is a funny word. Some people think Design means how it looks. But, of course, if you dig deeper, it's really how it works.

—STEVE JOBS

To design something that works, DfSS requires high levels of customer involvement from the outset, so it's vital that customer needs are understood and clearly defined as CTQs (covered in Chapter 4).

However, when designing a new service or product, a customer may not exist yet. In this case, it is important to identify and concentrate on the demands of the (potential) marketplace.

Where the customer is involved, we mean both end-user customers and internal business stakeholders and users. Customer requirements and the resulting CTQs are established early on and the DMADV framework rigorously ensures that these requirements are satisfied in the final product, service or process.

Introducing DMADV

As with DMAIC (see Chapter 2), managing by fact and not speculation ensures that new designs reflect customer CTQs and provide real value to the customers in line with the principles of Lean Six Sigma.

TIP

As DMADV projects are often concerned with introducing something new or radically changing something that already exists, a well thought out Change Management plan is vital to support the change. Our elements of change model described in Chapter 6 provides a helpful framework.

Figure 14-1 shows the DMADV phases involved in a DfSS project.

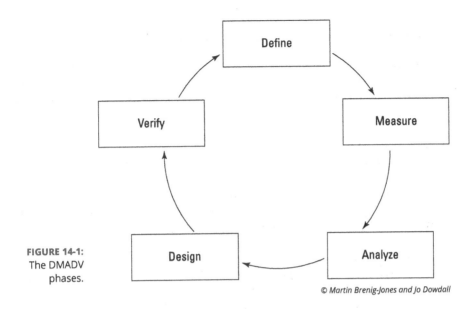

FIGURE 14-1:
The DMADV
phases.

© Martin Brenig-Jones and Jo Dowdall

Defining What Needs Designing

The Define phase is about scoping, organizing and planning your project. Understanding the purpose, rationale and business case is important, as well as knowing who you might need to help you. Understanding the boundaries of the project, including the processes, market(s), customers, and stakeholders involved, is vital.

Customer segmentation (dividing customers or potential customers into smaller, logical categories) is key. The segmentation could be in the form of demographic segmentation (age, gender, and so on), geographic segmentation (location or region), psychographic segmentation (personal beliefs, attitudes, values, and interests) and behavioral (based on spending habits, use of features, frequency of use, loyalty, and so on). Some crucial decisions are required. Which customer segments matter most? Which are most profitable?

You will recognize the tools used in the Define phase of a DMADV project as they include the frame/scope (Chapter 2), the SIPOC (Chapter 3), and the definition of customer requirements (Chapter 4). It is crucial to understand not only what customer requirements are, but also whether it is feasible (and profitable) for the organization to meet them.

Getting the measure of needs

This phase focuses on planning and conducting the research necessary to understand customer needs in detail. You will also translate the needs into measurable characteristics (CTQs) that will become the requirements for the process, product, or service being developed.

As with a DMAIC project, the aim is to fully understand the customer requirements, define the measures, and set targets and specification limits for the CTQs.

DfSS projects typically seek to optimize the design of processes, products, and services across multiple customer requirements, so a detailed understanding of these factors is an essential foundation.

When designing new products or services, you need to make sure the design can be produced with existing processes. If that isn't the case, you'll have to design new processes to accommodate the new design. Considering process capability at this phase, rather than after the design is complete, is a hallmark of DfSS. See Chapter 8 for an introduction to process capability.

Tools and techniques used in this phase include the Kano model and customer research methods (Chapter 4), and data collection and sampling (Chapter 7). The QFD (Quality Function Deployment) is a key DfSS tool, which is covered later in this chapter.

Design scorecards are also used. They help to assess the design against the requirements and predict what performance will look like when the design is implemented. Design scorecards capture the critical performance measures at each level and visibly track the measured performance as the design evolves. A very simple example is provided in Figure 14-2 below.

CTQ	Description	Goal	Predicted Performance	Measured Performance	Goal Met?

FIGURE 14-2: A sample design scorecard.

© Martin Brenig-Jones and Jo Dowdall

Both the QFD and the Design Scorecard are "living" documents that are used throughout the DMADV phases, so keep them updated as you go along.

Analyzing for design

The Analyze phase helps you move from what the customer wants to how you might achieve it. Taking the most promising concepts, you can then start to identify requirements for a more detailed design, creating several high-level blueprints and assessing the capability of each in order to select the best fit.

For a service, this analysis means identifying the key functions. For a more tangible product, it means identifying its key part characteristics. Typically, the subsystem characteristics are developed next, followed by the components (parts) of the subsystem. Thus, top-down design is used.

Functions are what the product, service or process has to do in order to meet the CTQs identified and specified in the design process. In a service environment, functions are best thought of as key high-level processes to be considered. So, for example, the product or service being designed could be an on online ordering service, with a design goal of an order placement within 30 seconds. The functions involved could include "confirm the item is in stock," "add to basket," "check out," and "confirm order." They are typically written as "verb + noun" combinations. You'll need to carry out an analysis of the functions to understand their performance capability and ensure they're fit for purpose.

The development of alternative design concepts is a feature of DfSS projects. The second part of Analyze involves analyzing and selecting the best design concept and beginning to add more details to it. Each element of the design should be considered in turn, and high-level design requirements specified for each. Consideration will also need to be given to how the different components fit and interact with each other.

The design scorecards will help you analyze the design's capability in terms of delivering the CTQs. Assessments might be carried out through simulations, field tests, or pilots, and, where appropriate, involving the customer so that you can capture their feedback.

Based on the outputs of the review, the high-level design requirements can be finalized, and a thorough risk assessment undertaken using Failure Mode Effects Analysis (FMEA, which we cover in Chapter 13). Other tools used in this phase include benchmarking and process mapping, among others.

Developing the detailed design

The Design phase begins by developing the "how" thinking in more detail. The objective is to add increasing detail to the high-level design. The emphasis is on developing designs that will satisfy the CTQ requirements of the process outputs.

The design process is iterative. The high-level design was established in the Analyze phase; now the design is specified at a detailed enough level to develop a pilot to test it. The detailed design activities are similar to those in the high-level design phase but with a lower level of granularity. This step integrates all of the design elements into one overall design.

Finally, the lowest-level specification limits, control points, and measures are determined. These will form the basis of the control plan that needs to be in place following implementation.

Before implementation, however, you need to pilot the design. Enough detail should now be available to test and evaluate the capability of the design by preparing a pilot in the second part of the Design phase. It's important you plan an effective and realistic pilot.

Verifying that the design works

The design is piloted and assessed in the Verify phase, and, subject to any adjustments that follow the pilot, implementation and deployment follow. As with DMAIC, the final step in the cycle is to assess the achievements made and lessons learned.

The results are verified against the original CTQs, specifications and targets. The project is closed only when the solution has been standardized and transitioned to operations and process management.

The tools used in this phase include Process Stapling (Chapter 5), standardization (Chapter 13), control charts, and other methods of data display (Chapter 8).

TIP

You need to ensure that no black holes exist in the handover to the process owner or operational manager. You must work closely with your team to achieve a well-planned and well-documented transition.

Choosing between DMAIC and DMADV

WARNING

It's possible to start a project using the DMAIC method (see Chapter 2 for a description of all the stages) only to find yourself at some point changing to DMADV. Figure 14-3 provides a picture of the likely decision points in transitioning from one method to the other.

DMAIC/DMADV transition points:

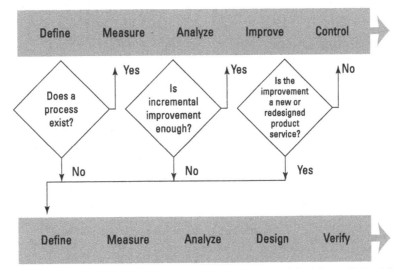

© Martin Brenig-Jones and Jo Dowdall

FIGURE 14-3:
Choosing between DMAIC and DMADV.

DMADV projects call for a range of Lean Six Sigma tools and techniques, including many that you're already familiar with from DMAIC. Perhaps the most important technique, however, is *Quality Function Deployment*, an approach that's often referred to as the House of Quality because of its appearance, which you can see in Figure 14-4.

As with DMADV, QFD merits its own book, so here we provide only an overview of this tool.

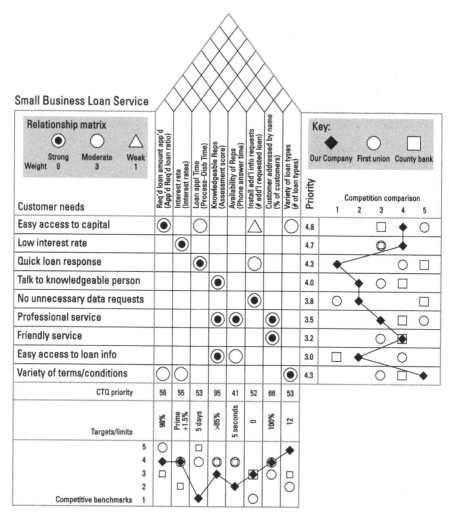

FIGURE 14-4:
The House of Quality.

© Martin Brenig-Jones and Jo Dowdall

Considering Quality Function Deployment (QFD)

QFD is a graphical representation of the logic flow, from identifying customer requirements to the detailed development of actions to ensure those requirements are met. A series of interconnected matrices is developed, moving from the requirements, through to design, and eventual implementation and deployment. They fit together to form a house-shaped diagram. The room numbers in Figure 14-5 represent the order of the logic flow for completing the QFD.

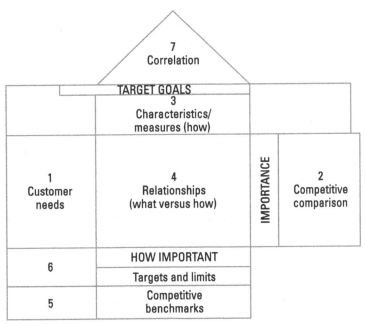

FIGURE 14-5:
Seven rooms
with a view.

© Martin Brenig-Jones and Jo Dowdall

Clarifying the floorplan

Figure 14-5 shows a house with numbered rooms. QFD doesn't stop at just one House of Quality. In the Analyze and Design phases, a second, third, and even fourth House of Quality can be built (which we discuss in the "Undertaking a QFD drill-down" section later in this chapter).

Room 1: Customer needs

Before you get to the QFD stage, you'll have identified and segmented your customers, built a data collection plan, and conducted your customer research, so what you're left with by this stage is a large amount of voice of customer information.

Room 1 focuses on organizing the information that you've collected and then interpreting and translating that information into a set of CTQ statements.

Room 2: Prioritizing needs and looking at the competition

Some requirements will be more important than others. After you've defined the CTQs, their relative importance is established in Room 2. The QFD approach initiates a trade-off analysis. The customer may want the specifications of a Ferrari but is only willing to pay the price of a VW, so which of their requirements are the most important? When you enter the Design phase, you must understand the priorities from the customer's viewpoint.

As part of organizing and prioritizing customer needs, the customers should also be asked to rate you against the competition. Depending on the situation, this may be an internal competitor, the way the needs are met by the customer today, or even an "internal" comparison against the way the organization meets these needs in a different geography or sector. For a redesign effort, the same survey used to determine satisfaction with your current performance can be applied to determine how the competition satisfies needs.

Such a comparison can help you determine the strengths and weaknesses of your current product, service, or process. The resulting information is an input to the target-setting process for CTQs.

Assign a symbol for your own organization and one for each of your competitors, who should be market leaders or the most distinguished organizations you directly compete with. For each need in Room 1, ask your customer to assign a rating between 1 (lowest) and 5 (highest) for both your company and your competitors. The highest rating on the scale is typically reserved for how the perfect service performs. A visual comparison can then very quickly be drawn, as shown in Figure 14-6. Where the customer needs are prioritized you'll notice that our company is not doing particularly well when compared with competitors.

Room 3: Characteristics and measures

In Room 3 (see Figure 14-5), you start moving from the what to the how of the customer requirements. Until now, you've merely understood what the customer requires; now you need to understand the characteristics and measures that are needed to ensure that the end design meets those requirements.

For each customer attribute, ask what characteristics and measures will indicate how well you're meeting their needs. You need to develop measures for which targets and specification limits can be established.

Room 4: Relationships

In Room 4 (see Figure 14-5), some analysis starts taking place. You look at the customer CTQs derived from Room 1 and the characteristics and measures described in Room 3, and then start to draw relationships between them. The purpose of this room is to ensure that the requirements of each characteristic and measure are taken into account. Remembering that Room 1 concerns the whats and Room 3 is all about the hows, the key question you're asking when you build Room 4 is "Can this 'how' achieve that 'what'?"

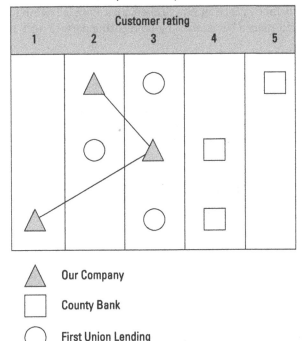

Competition comparison

Customer rating

| 1 | 2 | 3 | 4 | 5 |

△ Our Company

□ County Bank

○ First Union Lending

© Martin Brenig-Jones and Jo Dowdall

FIGURE 14-6:
Competition
comparison.

For each relationship between needs in Room 1 and characteristics and measures in Room 3, perform the following steps and complete the relationship matrix shown in Figure 14-7:

» Figure 14-7 includes symbols representing strong, medium, and weak. Typically, rating the relationships uses a scale of strong (9), medium (3), weak (1), or none (0).

» Calculate the score for each cell by multiplying the priority for the customer need in Room 2 by the (9, 3, 1, 0) value of each related cell.

TIP

Once all of the relationships have been rated, you can add up the individual scores for each measure to determine their importance, carrying out a sanity check and balance at the end to make sure the matrix looks and feels right.

Room 5: Competitive benchmarking

Technical evaluation involves using benchmarking to set appropriate goals and targets for the measures identified in Room 3. However, benchmarking also continues to be valid as you move through the Analyze and Design phases, but the focus then is much more on process benchmarking (searching for best practices) than on performance benchmarking (comparing performance measures).

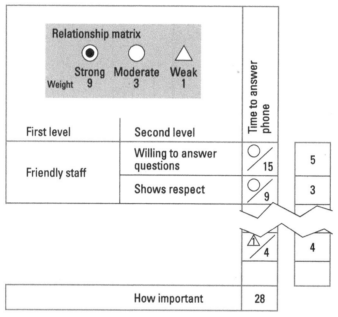

© Martin Brenig-Jones and Jo Dowdall

FIGURE 14-7: The relationship matrix.

The term *benchmarking* applies to the process of looking both inside and outside of your own organization to see both how well others are doing at providing products and services similar to yours (performance benchmarking) and how "best practice" organizations provide their products and services (process benchmarking).

Try to get competitive data for every key measure and analyze it using a 1–5 scale (1 = poor performance, 5 = best-in-class). Use a separate row in Room 5 for each of the 1–5 gradings.

Choose one symbol for your organization and a different symbol for each of your company's competitors. For each measure in Room 3, assign the symbols to the appropriate grading.

Using this exercise, you can gain a very quick visual impression of how your organization is performing against the competition in all of the key measures, as shown in Figure 14-8.

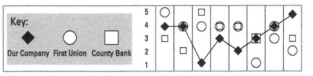

FIGURE 14-8:
Grading
performance.

© Martin Brenig-Jones and Jo Dowdall

At this stage it is important to distinguish between qualitative and quantitative benchmarking. The former was done in Room 2, where customer perceptions of your qualitative performance in relation to the CTQs were established. That situation is different to the requirements of Room 5, where you're looking for a comparison of quantitative performance in relation to the measures established in Room 3. Here, you're looking at actual performance as opposed to perceptions about performance.

Room 6: Targets and limits

Keeping the results of the benchmarking from Room 5 in mind, Room 6 (see Figure 14-5) now looks to set the goals and targets against the measures and characteristics defined in Room 3.

No magic recipe exists for setting targets and specifications. Doing so is a function of business know-how and technical expertise, and the use of tools, including, for example, the analysis of benchmarking data, and a thorough understanding of customer requirements using the Kano model referred to in Chapter 4.

Rooms 3 and 6 in combination formulate the "technical specification" — in other words, the characteristics that your design will deliver and the target performance for each one of the characteristics.

Room 7: Correlation

The final "room" is the attic. It looks at the impact of each of the measures on the CTQs and how the measures affect each other.

To complete Room 7 (see Figure 14-5), you first need to examine each measure and assess the likely impact of increasing, reducing or hitting the target for that measure on customer CTQs.

You then examine the relationship between each pair of measures to understand the impact and effect of any relationships on the final design, assigning one of the following four symbols to represent that relationship:

++ strong positive

+ positive

– negative

– – strong negative

The roof of the house will then look something like Figure 14-9.

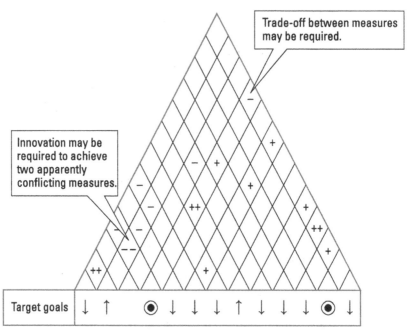

FIGURE 14-9:
Assessing the
impact of
measures on
customer CTQs.

You're now in a position to understand how the various characteristics and measures may impact the end design. The aim is to resolve the conflicting situations before you build the design. Keep in mind the following:

>> Satisfying negatively correlated measures typically requires a lot of time and creativity, though the best solutions and designs will not require trade-offs.

>> Conflict resolution between measures should always focus on meeting the customer needs — not yours!

>> Measures with strong positive correlations can become part of the overall design strategy.

Undertaking a QFD drill-down

A QFD drill-down aims to develop further Houses of Quality, gradually refining the level of detail until the design is specified at an implementable level.

As you move from one house to the next, as shown in Figure 14-10, you carry over the corresponding targets and importance measures. The number of houses used in the drill-down may vary but tends to increase with the level of complexity. For a simple service design, the second house may be enough. Generally speaking, product design is more complex and will require more houses than service design.

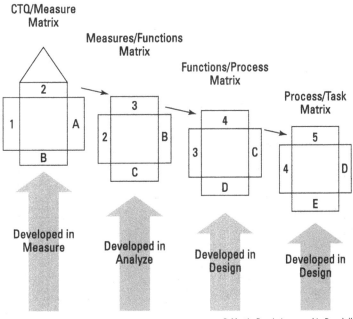

FIGURE 14-10: Developing more Houses of Quality.

The second House of Quality is developed in the Analyze phase, where CTQ measures are mapped onto the functions. The CTQ measures and the targets/importance ratings are taken from the first House of Quality. You find the correlations to enter in the cells in Figure 14-10 by asking the following question: "If I design this particular function correctly, what impact does it have on my ability to meet the CTQ measures/targets?"

The output of the QFD matrix in Figure 14-10 is a prioritization of functions. It helps to identify where the design effort must be concentrated in order to satisfy the CTQs and thereby the customers.

Making Decisions

Throughout the DMADV phases and the evolving constructions of the QFD houses, you make decisions about the various design concepts and ideas. The Pugh Matrix shown in Figure 14-11 is often used to help in this process.

Key Criteria	Concept 1 the datum	Concept 2 E-Loan	Concept 3 Phone Loan	Concept 4	Concept 5	Concept 6	Concept 7	Importance rating
Loan term	S	S	–					3
Interest rate	S	S	–					2
Complexity of information	S	S	S					5
Availability of help desk	S	+	+					1
Time to complete form	S	+	–					4
Staff training time	S	+	–					3
Activity time	S	–	–					5
Unit cost per transaction	S	+	–					3
Opportunity for error	S	S	–					3
Development costs	S	–	+					5
Sum of positives	0	4	2					
Sum of negatives	0	2	7					
Sum of sames	10	4	1					
Weighted sum of positives	0	11	6					
Weighted sum of negatives	0	10	23					

Concept selection legend
Better +
Same S
Worse –

FIGURE 14-11:
The Pugh Matrix.

© Martin Brenig-Jones and Jo Dowdall

Developed in the 1980s by Stuart Pugh, the Pugh Matrix, or *controlled convergence*, provides a simple framework for comparing solutions or concepts against a set of pre-determined criteria. The Pugh Matrix's original intent was to provide a framework to help refine the competing designs by improving the S (same) and – (worse) rankings to + (better) and combining the + attributes into a super alternative. It's often used, however, to aid the selection of the best design.

The tool provides a structured way to evaluate alternative or competing concepts, and benefits from being both non-numeric and iterative. It's most often used during "design projects" and works as described below.

If you face many competing options, try to identify your top five or so favorites. You might find it helpful to represent each concept with a simple sketch and maybe a few words — but ideally not just words alone. The sketches should be produced to the same level of detail and must communicate the key ideas embodied in each option. Finally, give each concept a name.

The list of selection criteria against which the concepts will be evaluated is the crucial part of the matrix. You should already have a detailed understanding of customer needs from your earlier work, and the list of criteria should be straightforward for you to determine. If it isn't, you have some work still to do! Don't forget to include selection criteria that are based upon the needs of the business and internal stakeholders.

The final list of criteria should be unambiguous and must be agreed upon by the full team. Watch out for criteria that are too generic; "cost," for example, may be more effectively assessed if it's broken down into the various cost drivers.

You don't need to have weighted the criteria at this stage, but doing so is a good idea, perhaps using paired comparisons. Weighting the criteria will certainly help you to focus on the key concepts.

Choose one of the concepts as a "datum concept" providing a standard reference point. It doesn't really matter which one, but choosing something that already exists can be helpful. Ideally, use a concept from your earlier benchmarking that represents best-in-class.

In turn, compare each concept with the datum for each of the criteria. If the concept is better or easier, mark it + (plus sign). If it's worse or harder, mark it − (minus sign). Finally, if the concept is similar to or the same as the datum, mark it with the letter S. This process is a bit like trying out different strength lenses when having your eyes tested for new glasses!

For each concept, add up the total number of +, −, and S scores and take the − total away from the + total. Each concept will now have a score, and ranking them in preferential order is possible.

In discussing the merits of each concept, you may well find a basically good concept that suffers from one poor feature. In this case, a minor modification could improve the overall solution. Finding "losing" concepts that outscore the others against certain criteria is also possible. In these circumstances, try to combine the best elements into a "new improved" concept.

As your project unfolds, new concepts may well emerge. If they do, you need to create a new matrix taking one of the stronger concepts as your new datum. If you haven't already done so, weighting the criteria at this stage is sensible.

Naturally, the process is only as good as the team input, the choice of selection criteria, and the quality of the basic concepts. Remembering the importance of the "soft" factors, reflecting on the process is almost certainly worthwhile. Does the team agree on the outcome? Does one solution clearly stand out above the rest? Do the results make sense and do any consistently good or bad features exist? If no outstanding solution emerges, maybe you used ambiguous criteria or perhaps the concepts are too similar.

Although this chapter has provided only an introduction to DMADV, it does highlight the focus and attention needed to introduce new or redesigned products, services, and processes that are defect free.

REMEMBER

More often than not, DMADV projects are significantly more resource hungry than DMAIC projects in terms of people, IT involvement, cost, and time, but despite the potentially higher risks, they do, of course, bring higher rewards.

In a large organization deploying Lean Six Sigma, 20 DMAIC projects will likely be carried out for every one DMADV project.

For most organizations, the initial focus of improvement activity will also probably be on bite-sized DMAIC projects, and it will be some time before DMADV is used, though market factors may demand otherwise.

As the deployment of Lean Six Sigma takes hold, lots of "Lean-based" using DMAIC, a moderate number of more "sigma-based" DMAIC projects, and a few DfSS projects will probably be up and running as the organization gets to grips with reducing rework and waste in general, and improving process flow and reducing cycle times in particular. Where appropriate, rapid improvement projects, again using DMAIC, will also be taking place (which we cover in Chapter 17).

Chapter 15 looks at Design Thinking, which may provide an alternative approach to DfSS and DMADV.

Chapter **15**

Discovering Design Thinking

his chapter delves into Design Thinking, an approach for creative problem solving which shares many of the methods and tools of Lean Six Sigma, Agile and Design for Six Sigma. Although Design Thinking feels like the new kid (or methodology) on the block, work to "scientize design" and understand the methods used by prominent designers began in the 1960s. It is now becoming well embedded in the business world.

As with Lean Six Sigma, there are a number of steps involved: Understand; Observe; Redefine the problem; Ideate; Prototype; and Test. We give you a summary in this chapter.

TIP

Check out *Design Thinking For Dummies* or the *Design Thinking Playbook* (both published by Wiley) for more detail and insight into this fascinating methodology.

The Principles of Design Thinking

A good way to get into Design Thinking is by starting with some simple principles that capture the essence of the approach and apply across every step. You will notice a synergy between these and the principles of Lean Six Sigma outlined in Chapter 2.

>> **Align yourself with people and their needs at an early stage.** This principle is all about understanding customers (or target users) and their requirements. Indeed, Design Thinking is often referred to as *human centric design*. Representatives of the *Lead user* (those users who tend to accept new products first) should be closely involved in the design process.

>> **Develop empathy.** This stage is focused on walking in the target users' shoes to gain an insight into their thoughts, feelings, intentions, and actions.

>> **Illustrate ideas.** Design Thinkers (just like Lean thinkers) seek to make things visual as an aid to understanding. Ideas are tested out and prototypes are developed to make the ideas tangible.

>> **Learn from failure.** Mistakes are considered to be part of the learning process and an important aspect of Design Thinking. This works best within a culture of experimentation.

>> **Ensure diversity in the team.** This principle brings a number of different perspectives, which boosts creativity and innovation. Diversity in terms of age, gender, cultural background, experience, and personality type could be considered.

>> **Offer team-oriented and creative workspaces.** A workspace that supports the three Cs of concentration, communication, and creativity is best.

>> **Make the process flexible.** As you'll see in this chapter, the Design Thinking approach covers a series of steps to be followed. However, you are encouraged to respond flexibly to changes. You can jump forward (for example, if you find solutions early) or jump back (for example, if the customer doesn't like the ideas generated).

Comparing DMADV and Design Thinking

When comparing Design Thinking with DMADV (the Design for Six Sigma approach outlined in Chapter 14), you will note some similarities and some differences. Both approaches are beneficial when you want to develop something new rather than improve something that already exists. Both are based on under-standing people/customer needs and use creative thinking to develop solutions. Both make use of visualization and prototyping, and both encourage collaborative and interdisciplinary teamwork. However there are some differences too. The "Deciding on Design Thinking" section at the end of this chapter can help you to decide which approach — or blend of approaches — is best for you.

Table 15-1 provides a comparison between DMADV and Design Thinking.

TABLE 15-1　　**DMADV and Design Thinking**

DMADV	Design Thinking
Features the phases Define, Measure, Analyze, Design, and Verify.	Features the steps Understand, Observe, Define, Ideate, Prototype, Test, and Realize.
A structured, analytical and linear approach. The team progresses through project toll-gates at each phase.	Less structured, more flexible; there are no preset "stage gates" to be achieved.
Developed to help people solve manufactur-ing and engineering problems.	Developed with people and services in mind.
Strong focus on the detail of the design, implementation and production.	The Design Thinking journey usually ends with the concept; focus on the "minimum viable product" and "minimum marketable product".
Focus on "Functional Analysis" — what work the design must do.	Focus on user stories and the customer journey.

Walking through the Design Thinking Steps

The steps of Design Thinking form two parts: The first is focused on the problem, and the second is focused on the solution (see Figure 15-1). A clever combination of *divergent thinking* (opening up to generate many ideas) and *convergent thinking* (narrowing down to focus on a single aspect) is used to ensure that thinking is wide-ranging and explorative, and that actions are clearly focused.

Understanding the task

Design Thinking begins with learning about the problem that is to be solved. You will recognize the similarities with the Define phase of a DMAIC project and the Design phase of a DMADV project here. And as with Lean Six Sigma, when using

Design Thinking, do not jump into solution mode too soon! In Design Thinking (and with DMADV), a comprehensive understanding of the users' needs and jobs they are trying to get done is required first.

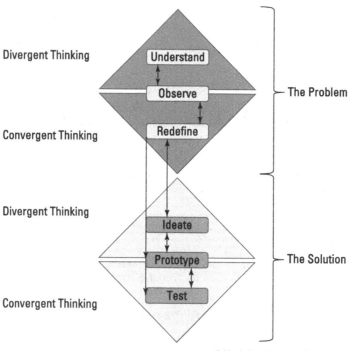

Divergent Thinking

Understand

Observe

Convergent Thinking

Redefine

The Problem

Divergent Thinking

Ideate

Prototype

The Solution

Convergent Thinking

Test

FIGURE 15-1: The double diamonds of Design Thinking.

Design Thinkers start by clarifying what type of problem they are solving, as this helps to determine the next steps. You consider these three categories:

>> **Well-defined problems:** There is a clear problem. There is a single solution. Different paths will be followed to find it.

>> **Ill-defined problems:** The problem is not clear. There may be more than one solution out there. Different paths will be used to seek them out.

>> **Wicked problems:** The information is incomplete or contradictory, and the problem is very broad (like how to end hunger or solve homelessness). Breaking wicked problems down into smaller chunks and looking for connections and relationships between these will bring some clarity. The (smaller) problem statement is then easier to define.

You'll need to identify the "user" or customer and understand their problems or needs in detail. This process could begin with identifying what you don't know and seeking to fill in the gaps through research.

Creating a "persona" provides a clear and detailed understanding of the user or customer. This requires in-depth knowledge and may require data collection, segmentation of customer groups, and creating and testing hypotheses about users/customers. The *persona map* might look something like the one provided in Figure 15-2. You should have a persona map to represent each of your user segment groups. Naturally, there is very likely to be more than one, but you don't want too many. A small handful is generally considered to be enough for most projects.

Name of Persona Name, age and other attributes		
Description of the Persona	**Sketch or Moodboard** Visualise the persona – include images to bring them to life	**Jobs to be Done** Which tasks are supported by the product or service? What social and emotional tasks does the product or service fulfil? What basic needs are satisfied?
Influencer Who they influence and are influenced by? Who pays for the product or service?		**Problems/pains** Difficulties with existing products and services? What might cause a bad feeling?
Trends The wider environment, what trends influence them, future driving forces	**Use cases** Where is the product used by the persona? What happens while using the product? What happens before/after? How do they use it?	**Gains** How do current products and services please them? What makes them happy? What possibilities and advantages might they have?

FIGURE 15-2: The persona map.

© Martin Brenig-Jones and Jo Dowdall

Empathizing and observing

Putting yourself in the customer's shoes is a key focus of this step, and detailed research and observation is undertaken to build on the persona map and build empathy with them. In Chapter 5, we talk about Process Stapling, which is walking through the process from the perspective of the thing going through the process. In Design Thinking, the same applies: You need to do what the customer does in order to feel how the customer would feel. An open mind is essential; otherwise, there is a danger of making assumptions or allowing unconscious beliefs or biases to take over.

An empathy map like the one shown in Figure 15-3 can be developed to capture what has been observed and understood so far. You could capture the outputs of each interview undertaken on this template.

» **Thoughts and Feelings:** What motivates their behavior, what worries them, and what might excite them.

» **Hearing:** The messages they are hearing from friends, colleagues, and other sources. Consider what influences them and who they influence.

» **Seeing:** What is available in the marketplace, what is happening in their immediate environment, what they're watching and looking at on social media, and so on.

» **Doing and Saying:** Attitudes, behaviors, and approaches.

» **Biggest Problems and Challenges and Opportunities and Benefits:** These factors help to sharpen the problem from the user's perspective or capture possible opportunities identified by the users.

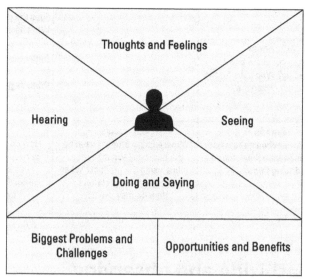

FIGURE 15-3:
An empathy map.

Redefining the problem

Using what has been learned from understanding the problem and observing the user/customer, you can begin convergent thinking to redefine the problem into something more precise. The essentials can be boiled down into these questions: What is the specific need that you want to satisfy, and for who?

In Chapter 16, we look at how user stories are developed to capture requirements from a user perspective as a feature of Agile working. We've also looked at how CTQs (Critical to Quality requirements) are used to define the (measurable) characteristics of a process at the outset of a Lean Six Sigma project. A similar approach is used by Design Thinkers to determine a "point of view." The "how might we?" technique is beneficial here as it paves the way for the next stage by framing the problem clearly. For example, if you are working on the problem of receiving too many calls into the department, the "how might we?" might start with "How might we make sure customers are confident that they have the latest information?"

Figure 15-4 sets out a structure for using the "how might we?" technique. As with writing CTQs (covered in Chapter 4), these questions should be phrased positively and shouldn't include the solution.

How might we_____<what>_____

for _____<who>_____

so that _____<which need>_____is met?

FIGURE 15-4: The "how might we?" template.

Finding ideas (ideation)

As with the Lean Six Sigma DMAIC approach, Design Thinkers don't dive into generating ideas and solutions until they fully understand the problem they are trying to solve. The tools and techniques for ideas generation outlined in Chapter 12 are relevant here (as are plenty of others).

EXAMPLE

Design Thinking puts emphasis on establishing the right environment for creativity. This includes a diverse team and a creative space to work in. The Water Lounge at Google's office in Zurich allowed people to retreat — into a bathtub! — to escape from conscious brainwork and access the unconscious brain.

The SCAMPER method uses a series of questions to support problem solving. SCAMPER stands for Substitute, Combine, Adapt, Modify, Put to other uses, Eliminate, and Rearrange. You don't have to answer all of the questions, but they certainly provide lots of food for thought. This technique can be used in lot of situations and not just in the context of Design Thinking.

Substitute:

What can be substituted?

What can be used in its place?

Who can be involved instead?

Which process could be used instead?

What other material could be used instead?

Combine:

What can be combined?

What can be mixed?

How might certain parts be connected?

Which purposes could be combined?

Adapt:

What other ideas are suggested by it?

Is there anything that is similar and can be applied to the existing problem?

Have there been similar situations in the past?

Modify:

What modification could be introduced?

Can the meaning be changed?

How might the color or shape be changed?

What can be increased?

What can be reduced?

What could be modernized?

Can it be enlarged?

Can it be downsized?

Put to other uses:

For what other purposes could it be used in its present state?

For what purpose could it be used if it were modified?

Eliminate:

What could be eliminated?

What are the things it would still work without?

Rearrange:

What other patterns would also work?

What modifications could be introduced?

What could be replaced?

What could be rearranged?

Designing prototypes

In Design Thinking, prototypes are used to give form to, present, and test out potential solutions. They could take many forms, in 2D or 3D, and support a fuller appreciation of the user and their experience of your design. You can begin by defining what you want to learn from the prototype.

Table 15-2 provides some further insight into prototypes. It also demonstrates another useful tool that could help you in your improvement journey: the Is/Is Not Analysis, which is a simple tool to aid your understanding of something.

TIP

Like a lot of the tools included in this book the Is/Is Not Analysis can be used for lots of purposes. You could use it to scope a DMAIC project (what is and is not in scope?) or draw conclusions from the data you've collected (for example, where is the problem occurring most, and where is it not?).

TABLE 15-2   **What Is a Prototype?**

A Prototype Is	A Prototype Is Not
Something that gives form to an idea	A working model
Useful for identifying strengths and weaknesses	A full test of functionality
Something to "get out there" in front of people (including perhaps, potential customers)	A test to see if customers would buy it
A way to get feedback and to learn	A version we are "wedded to," defensive about, or resistant to changing
A way to help understand the user experience	A demonstration of the product to sales people or the marketing team to get to work on
A route to discovering better ideas	

Testing ideas and assumptions

As with Agile working (outlined in Chapter 16), early feedback from customers about ideas and solutions is essential. This part of Design Thinking is especially experimental as assumptions are formulated and tested, and the feedback is captured to support learning and shape future iterations. It is important to involve "neutral" people in the test because those that had a hand in shaping the prototype might be too involved emotionally to apply a fair test to it. The experiment grid shown in Figure 15-5 provides a helpful format for documenting the results. Remember that there may be a number of experiments involved.

Experiment	Learnings
Step 1: Hypothesis "We believe that …"	**We have learned the following:**
Step 2: Test "To verify this, we will …"	
Step 3: Metrics "and we will measure …"	**Documentation of the test:**
Step 4: Criteria "We are on the right track if …"	

FIGURE 15-5: The experiment grid.

© Martin Brenig-Jones and Jo Dowdall

There are some synergies here with the "Lean Startup" concept (and it links with Agile too, as we discuss in Chapter 16). *The Lean Startup* is a book by Eric Ries that defines the approach to developing, testing, and adapting solutions in a lean way, so as to avoid wasted effort. It is about working quickly and in iterations to validate ideas in order to deliver what customers really want. This concept circumvents a situation where masses of time, effort, and resources are taken to deliver the "perfect" solution to the customer, only to find that needs have changed in the time it's taken to get it there. A spirit of experimentation is adopted and embraced. If you try something and it works fairly successfully, you persevere. If things don't go as planned, you change direction, or pivot.

TIP

The spirit of experimentation is not confined to Design Thinking or Agile. It can be adopted in your Lean Six Sigma projects to add value too. Test out ideas with customers and learn from their feedback to adapt and enhance the process-improvement solutions.

At the end of the Design Thinking process, you will have completed testing and have a clear understanding of how your design solves the problem you began with — unless of course you need to go back to an earlier stage, depending on what your tests have revealed. Note the difference here between Design Thinking and the Design for Six Sigma/DMADV approach outlined in Chapter 14. In a Design for Six Sigma project, the final step is to verify that the approach works, and there is emphasis on planning and preparing the implementation, including the measures of performance post implementation.

WARNING

Don't be put off if solutions don't hit the mark first time. These are great opportunities for learning. In *Design Thinking For Dummies,* some alternative terms for "mistake" are suggested. Using these words can help to drive out the fear of failure. They include deviation, difference, discovery (or learning achievement), discrepancy, improvement potential, or target gap.

Deciding on Design Thinking

We hope this chapter has taught you that there is more to Design Thinking than creativity, and that some brilliant solutions addressing wicked problems can be brought about by using the approach. If you're deciding on pursuing Design Thinking, make sure you understand the approach fully, and get some help at the beginning. Not everyone involved needs to be an expert, but a little training won't be enough. As with Agile (outlined in Chapter 16), the ability to make decisions efficiently is critical, as you don't want to stop the flow of value through the design process. "Old" or existing ways of thinking or working won't cut it. You need curiosity, willingness to change, and freedom from the fear of failure to make Design Thinking work.

You don't have to wait for the opportunity to do a "full project" before you begin to apply the tools and principles of Design Thinking. Many organizations we work with apply aspects of Design Thinking into Lean Six Sigma projects or Design for Six Sigma projects. An example is when they want to develop real empathy with customers. Be a pragmatist rather than a purist and use what works!

IN THIS CHAPTER

» **Understanding the principles of Agile and mastering an Agile mindset**

» **Introducing Agile frameworks**

» **Diving into the scrum**

» **Using kanbans for project management**

» **Considering how Agile practices can support your Lean Six Sigma project**

Chapter **16**

Applying Agile to Lean Six Sigma Projects

I n 2001, a small group of people got together in a Utah ski resort to find common ground in the way software delivery projects were managed. These pioneers developed and signed up to the *Manifesto for Agile Software Development*, and in doing so, they transformed project management. The traditional "waterfall" method of delivering software in a single release (which may take several months) was replaced by a rapid release of value to customers with further releases of software every few weeks. And much more than that, guiding principles for behavior were established. Agile working is about instilling a culture of empirical experimentation (learning what works by trying it out rather than by theory), creating an environment of psychology safety, and working closely with the customer.

Agile principles and practices are clearly applicable beyond the world of software development. These days, Agile ways of working are being applied in many different industries and used to deliver all sorts of projects. This chapter focuses on how Agile can help you accelerate the delivery of a Lean Six Sigma project. You can read more about Agile in *Agile Project Management For Dummies* (Wiley).

Understanding Agile Principles

A good way to get started is to understand the principles that underpin Agile. These apply to Agile working in any type of project in any size or sector of organization. They may help you to understand how aligned your organization really is with the true spirit of Agile.

TIP

Remember that Agile started with software development, so software is referenced within this set of principles. If your project is concerned with delivering something other than software, substitute the word "software" with "value" as you read through this list.

>> Our highest priority is to satisfy the customer through early and continuous delivery of software.

>> Welcome changing requirements, even late in development.

>> Deliver working software frequently, from a couple of weeks to a couple of months, with a preference to the shorter timescale.

>> Business people and developers must work together daily throughout the project.

>> Build projects around motivated individuals. Give them the environment and support they need, and trust them to get the job done.

>> The most efficient and effective method of conveying information to and within a development team is face-to-face conversation.

>> Working software is the primary measure of progress.

>> Agile processes promote sustainable development. The sponsors, developers, and users should be able to maintain a constant pace indefinitely.

>> Continuous attention to technical excellence and good design enhances agility.

>> Simplicity — the art of maximizing the amount of work not done — is essential.

>> The best architectures, requirements, and designs emerge from self-organizing teams.

>> At regular intervals, the team reflects on how to become more effective and then tunes and adjusts its behavior accordingly.

The themes of customer satisfaction, quality, teamwork, and product development (that is, delivering the solution) are clear to see, as is alignment with the principles of Lean Six Sigma, outlined in Chapter 2.

Embracing an Agile Mindset

Agile working goes way beyond the use of tools and frameworks like kanban and Scrum (which we discuss later this chapter). It might call for some changes to the way to the you manage, changes in the way you work with customers, and changes to the way you think!

Not only did the Agile pioneers want to overcome problems with writing software and delivering results, they also wanted to truly "live and breathe" excellence and customer centricity in their work. They worked collaboratively to experiment and share information on what was working and what wasn't, sought to test ideas, learn fast and apply the learning. This is the spirit of Agile.

"Working collaboratively" involves sharing ideas openly, having them questioned (which can feel uncomfortable), and building on those ideas collectively to engender something that exceeds what could have been created by an individual.

This is where *psychological safety* comes in. Psychological safety is the ability (shared in the team) to contribute with a sense of confidence that the team will not embarrass, reject, or penalize an individual for speaking up. Creating a safe environment for people to contribute fully means that it is acceptable for people to ask questions, ask for help, and make a mistake, and it is safe for people to be creative and think differently.

Experimentation is key to an Agile mindset. An experiment is undertaken to discover something, to test a theory, or to prove something. The result of an experiment is not guaranteed, and this brings an air of uncertainty to the experiment process. If this uncertainty is to be accepted, it means that failure should also be accepted, and this may represent a completely different way of thinking. "Fail fast and learn" is a term embraced in the culture of startups, where entrepreneurs seek to test out models or products for viability early on rather than invest years in an ill-fated venture. (See Chapter 15 for the lowdown on the Lean Startup.) This philosophy is embraced in Agile working, where the project, product, or service is developed in increments. It is accepted that not everything is known at the outset, that learning will emerge over time, and that customer feedback can be incorporated and used to determine and shape the next increments.

WARNING

Many people think Agile is an "out of the box" methodology. It is clearly much more than that. If the principles are not applied, and the mindset is not in place, the full benefits of Agile working will not be realized.

Succeeding in the Scrum

As we have seen, Agile is really a set of guiding principles rather than a methodology, series of steps or an "out of the box" solution that can be applied to project delivery. However, certain frameworks and best practices are used to bring Agile principles to life practically and get the work done. The most famous of these is known as the *Scrum*. The Scrum approach preceded the development of the Agile principles and manifesto, but was adopted from the world of manufacturing by Agile thinkers because it promotes flexibility and speed, which are key Agile attitudes.

In scrum working, a sequence of events is followed, over a fixed duration of time, in order to deliver a goal, as you can see in Figure 16-1. The goal could be the development of a piece of software, or other solution, or it could be the delivery of a process improvement.

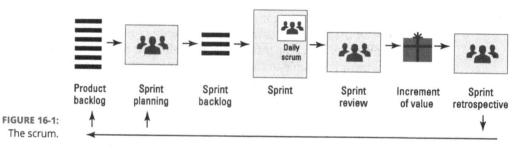

Product backlog   Sprint planning   Sprint backlog   Sprint   Daily scrum   Sprint review   Increment of value   Sprint retrospective

FIGURE 16-1:
The scrum.

© Martin Brenig-Jones and Jo Dowdall

Let's take a look at each event in order to understand the scrum cycle in a bit more detail. This will help you to get into some of the terminology used by Agilists.

» **The product backlog:** In Agile, the stuff we need to deliver to get the project done is thought of as "nuggets of business value." These nuggets are put into a prioritized wish list known as a *backlog.* Before breaking down the nuggets into tasks, first look to see whether they can be broken down into smaller nuggets of value. (Lean thinking again: Small things flow better than large things.) The needs are then prioritized from highest to lowest from the customer's perspective, and the team then pulls through the most valuable work and gets it done. As items are delivered, the team seeks feedback from customers and/or stakeholders and uses the feedback to decide the most important things to work on next.

>> **The sprint plan:** The product backlog can be broken down into segments to support the rapid delivery of value to the customer. These are called *sprints*. The sprint plan is developed to set out the goal, scope and tasks that will be included.

>> **The sprint backlog:** This is the list of requirements and tasks to be addressed in order to achieve the sprint goal. Once the items on the list have been identified, the team will freeze the scope of the sprint in order to provide rigorous focus on the most important items.

>> **The sprint, undertaken by the scrum team:** This is about getting the work done. A sprint has a fixed length of time, at the end of which something useful will be delivered.

>> Team members will meet on a daily basis in the **daily scrum** to review what has been done, agree what will be done next, and address any barriers standing in the way of success. This is a brief meeting, carried out standing up in the workplace or via a call or video call. (In Chapter 18, we look at how daily standup meetings support an effective management system — another example of the synergies between Agile and Lean ways of working.)

>> **The sprint review:** This review takes place at the end of each sprint and is used to demonstrate the work completed (or the increment of value that is delivered to the customer) and to get feedback to help decide what to deliver next.

>> **Sprint retrospective:** This review focuses not on what was done in the sprint, but rather, how it was done. The team will discuss what went well, what could be better, and what actions are required to enhance the next sprint. At the end of the retrospective, the team agrees on one or more things they are going to change about the way they are working together. The team then plans the next sprint, and they go again, as a project includes a series of sprints.

Don't try to change too many things after a retrospective. Better to focus on one improvement and get it done than try too many and achieve nothing.

From what we've observed by using Agile to enable Lean Six Sigma, a "full fat" scrum could be a bit too much for a DMAIC project. But applying certain aspects can really give DMAIC projects a rocket boost!

>> Managing the backlog of work to ensure top priority tasks take precedence

>> Using the kanban to visualize the work and keep it flowing

>> Planning sprints, because of the biggest challenges many organizations face is not applying the DMAIC methodology itself but finding the time to get on with it

>> Holding daily scrum meetings/standups

>> Carrying out retrospectives

We recommend trying sprinting with regular reviews. We have found it can make DMAIC more fun and makes change management easier, since stakeholders feel a heightened sense of openness and transparency as their ideas and insights are actively sought as part of the approach. For the team, the work feels more engaging since the important work is prioritized, and there is a real sense of progress as each sprint is delivered. If you have ever been involved in a rapid improvement workshop (see Chapter 17), you will already have some experience of this.

EXAMPLE

In our organization, we started to notice something interesting happening when teams started using Agile techniques to support their DMAIC projects. They did things differently and got some great results:

>> They worked with a heightened sense of urgency as the scrum approach enabled them to set aside focused time, and the daily meetings encouraged steady progress.

>> They were more pragmatic about the use of the Lean Six Sigma toolbox.

>> They were really good at change management.

>> Much better teamwork (far less of the Yellow or Green Belt acting like a superhero and doing everything on their own).

Understanding Agile roles

Scrum requires specific roles and responsibilities to be established. These are necessary not just to ensure the organized delivery of the work to be done, but also to drive the cultural elements and philosophy of Agile.

Scrum Master

The Scrum Master's role is to teach people about this way of working so that they truly understand it and respect it. Their role is to organize the work and to create an environment of psychological safety within the team. The Scrum Master empowers and enables team members to make their best possible contribution.

Product Owner

The Product Owner is responsible for ensuring customer views are represented. They are ruthless decision makers, who are well connected individuals who manage stakeholders and make sure the work done next is the most valuable, in line with the vision. The Product Owner is responsible for the product backlog.

Team members

Team members play a vital role. They will understand the practicalities of the work and get it done. Team members should be *T-shaped people* who have both a deep and a broad knowledge (see Figure 16-2). Remember that Agile calls for *empowered* teams of people who are self-organizing rather than micromanaged. Without empowerment, there is a real risk of disrupting the flow and delivery of work (that is, value). An example of such a disruption is if everything has to be signed off by the leadership team or if approval is required at every step.

Ability to collaborate across disciplines with experts in other areas and apply knowledge in areas of expertise

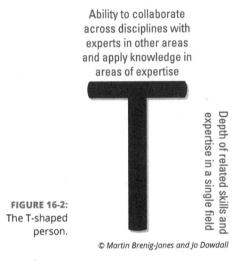

Depth of related skills and expertise in a single field

FIGURE 16-2: The T-shaped person.

© Martin Brenig-Jones and Jo Dowdall

Concentrating on customer requirements

Just like Lean Six Sigma, a compelling feature of Agile is that it enables true customer centricity — and makes actions speak louder than words — through collaboration with the customer from the very beginning in order to understand needs and identify requirements. In Agile projects, customers are also involved in giving feedback throughout the project at sprint reviews (see Figure 16-1).

By releasing product (or value for the customer) at frequent and regular intervals, it gets easier to find out about what is working for customers and what is not, and to address these findings for the next release.

In a DMAIC project, the most important user requirements are called CTQs. In Agile, they are called *user stories.* They're called stories because they encourage conversation, which is the best way to go about understanding what the requirements are. These stories are captured on a card, like the one shown in Figure 16-3. This format could be used to capture the CTQs for your Lean Six Sigma project.

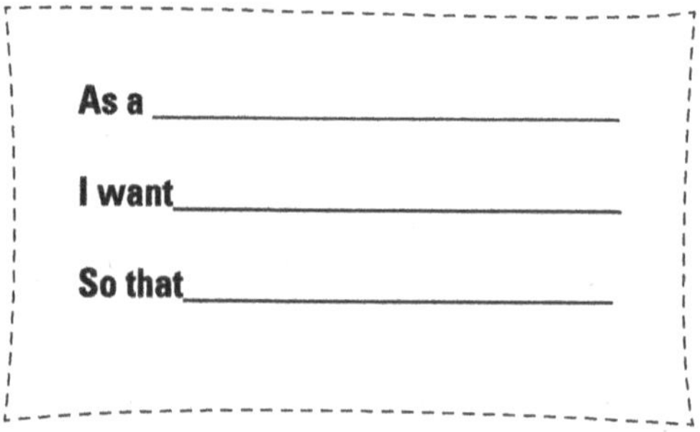

As a
I want
So that

FIGURE 16-3: The user story card.

© Martin Brenig-Jones and Jo Dowdall

Capitalizing on Kanbans

Agile practitioners use *kanban* as a project management method to support scrum working. It is used to display on a board (either physical or virtual) the tasks required (the backlog) and track them through their various stages of completion. This method brings visibility and transparency to project progress, and it incorporates Lean principles like "pull" and "flow" to keep the work (value) moving through to the customer. (See Chapter 11 for more on how this is applied to processes.) A kanban board is shown in Figure 16-4. Each card on the board represents a piece of work.

To Do
Doing
Done

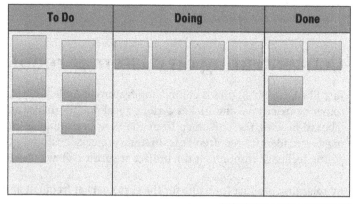

FIGURE 16-4: A simple Agile kanban board.

© Martin Brenig-Jones and Jo Dowdall

In an Agile scrum (and maybe in your Lean Six Sigma project), a team member who has some capacity to do some work pulls a card into the Doing column. This way everyone can see what is being done. When the activity is completed, they move the card into Done — if the conditions of satisfaction have been met. If, for some reason, the flow of work stops or slows down, it is immediately apparent and can be discussed in the daily scrum meetings.

Shifting priorities are managed through this framework as new features and tasks can be added as they become identified as important, unimportant items are removed, and the team pick work in the sequence that is most appropriate in a changing situation.

Kanbans can support DMAIC projects in the following ways:

» Improved transparency on what the team is working on

» Team focus on the most important work items

» Identifying when work is blocked so that the issue can be solved

TIP

Try to limit the amount of work in progress. Can you really do two things at once? Only pull one card through at a time through the kanban.

Kanban cards need to be written clearly so that it is clear what the task is and what the conditions of satisfaction are so that the product owner can determine whether the task has been completed when it is moved into the Done category. Only one item of work should be included on each card.

Include on each card:

» The description of the task

» The due date

» The owner

» The conditions of satisfaction

Make sure each task includes a verb.

The cards should be arranged on the board in order of priority, with those detailing high priority tasks at the top. You could indicate the priority of the task on the card itself. You could even indicate the "size" of the task or estimated effort.

Note that the scrum is only one of the approaches that could be used in agile working. You can read up on "Extreme Programming" in *Agile Project Management For Dummies* (Wiley).

Combining Agile and Lean Six Sigma

. . . and maybe adding some Design Thinking into the mix! Throughout this book, we have presented a broad range of tools and techniques that can be used to solve problems and improve your organization's processes. A number of approaches have also been described: Lean Six Sigma (itself a combination of Lean and Six Sigma); Change Management; Agile; Design Thinking; and Design for Six Sigma. We always recommend being pragmatic, so use what works! You don't have to take an either/or approach. You could think of each approach as a Marvel super-hero. Each has its own superpower, but in combination, they are even more effective. Look what can be achieved when the Avengers assemble! Agile is a huge topic in its own right, but we hope we've inspired you to try some of these techniques on your DMAIC projects.

5

Deploying Lean Six Sigma and Making Change Happen

Learn how Agile can accelerate your Lean Six Sigma project.

Understand the key role that leadership plays in creating the right environment for Lean Six Sigma.

Find out how to manage Rapid Improvement Events and solve problems with Lean Six Sigma

Examine how Lean Six Sigma tools and approaches can be used in day-to-day work.

Walk through DMAIC step by step to understand how it all fits together.

Chapter **17**

Running Rapid Improvement Events and Solving Problems with DMAIC

MAIC provides a systematic and proven approach to improvement that can be applied to projects of all sizes. This chapter focuses on using Lean Six Sigma to address smaller projects and to solve problems on a day-to-day basis. Smaller projects and process problems can benefit from an accelerated approach based on organizing and running a series of workshops, bringing people together to work through the DMAIC stages with a focus on rapid improvement. This requires a high level of facilitation skills and selection of the right tools to use at the different stages. This chapter describes how to make it work.

Raving about Rapid Improvement

Kaizen is a Japanese word meaning change for the better. It's often associated with short, rapid, incremental improvement and forms an important part of an organization's approach to Continuous Improvement. A *Rapid Improvement Event* is the term used to describe a series of facilitated workshops that use the DMAIC approach and the principles and tools of Lean Six Sigma to deliver benefits promptly. You might like to use the term *Kai Sigma* to describe them. The approach makes use of team knowledge rather than detailed analysis. It allows team members to step out from the day-to-day pressure of operating a process and reflect on how the process can be improved.

TIP

The facilitator of rapid improvement events or problem-solving sessions doesn't need to use the "language" of Lean Six Sigma, get too embroiled with technicalities or use any Japanese terminology. The focus is on involving people who have knowledge and experience of the process.

The workshops typically involve the team for anything from one to five days in a series of workshops or in one continuous intensive workshop. A traditional Kaizen event takes place in less than five days. These timescales compare to perhaps three to four months needed for a traditional DMAIC project. Check out Figure 17-1 for an overview.

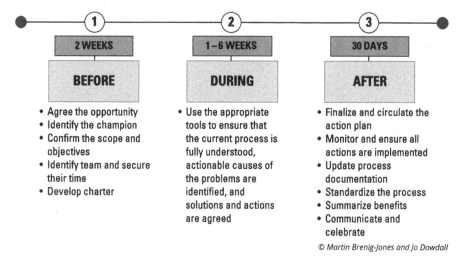

FIGURE 17-1: A typical outline Rapid Improvement Event Plan.

© Martin Brenig-Jones and Jo Dowdall

Good preparation is needed, of course, especially in agreeing on the problem, which should have a narrow focus and be clearly defined. Where appropriate, look to see if relevant data is already available or whether you need to collect some in advance as part of the preparation phase. Rapid improvement workshops are biased towards action and the derived solution to the problem should be put into practice as quickly as possible (within a maximum of 30 days). In fact, some elements of the solution may actually be actioned during the workshops.

As with a traditional DMAIC project, the Control phase is vital to ensure the improvement gain is maintained.

The event involves three phases:

>> Preparation

>> The Workshop(s)

>> Follow-up

In terms of tools and techniques, a set of simple but commonly used tools should handle the problems selected. They include the following:

>> The improvement charter (Chapter 2)

>> Critical to Quality customer requirements (CTQs; Chapter 4)

>> SIPOC, the high-level process map (Chapter 3)

>> Process Stapling (Chapter 5)

>> A process and/or Value Stream Map (Chapter 5)

>> The theory of constraints (Chapter 11)

>> The eight wastes (Chapter 10)

>> 5S (Chapter 13)

>> Visual management (Chapter 13)

>> Measurement and data collection (Chapter 7)

>> Data displays, including check sheets and Pareto charts (Chapter 8)

>> Ideas generation tools (Chapter 12)

>> Fishbone diagram (Chapter 9)

>> Interrelationship diagram (Chapter 9)

>> FMEA and error proofing (Chapter 13)

>> Control plan / process management chart (Chapter 18)

You also need some simple selection and prioritization techniques, including:

>> The 3 × 3 matrix (Chapter 19)

>> Paired comparisons (Chapter 4)

>> The criteria selection matrix (Chapter 12)

DMAIC provides a systematic approach to solving problems and achieving sustainable process improvements in short timeframes. In many ways, the key is clear problem definition followed by the successful completion of the Measure and Analyze phases. Get these phases right and the improvement solution is often very obvious. Sometimes a solution presents itself as a result of the Measure phase, and you can move to a *quick win*. Quick wins bypass the Analyze phase and go straight to Improve, but some care is needed, and you should make sure you truly understand the effects of your change.

Understanding the Facilitator's Role

Good facilitation is critical to the success of the rapid improvement workshop approach. Don't underestimate the skills needed to run effective workshops. The facilitator needs to be experienced and well versed in the Lean Six Sigma toolkit. They also need to be a good trainer as an element of training is inevitable during the workshops.

The role of the facilitator is to:

>> Ensure rapid improvement workshops, meetings and interactions between people are effective and productive.

>> Make the best use of the skills and contributions from everyone involved.

>> Ensure that all aspects of each workshop are orchestrated to ensure success.

Planning and preparation

The facilitator needs to consider the following when planning and preparing for an improvement event:

>> **Purpose and agenda:** Does the event have a clear purpose? Is everyone attending the event clear about the purpose? Does an agenda exist that's

structured to ensure the purpose is achieved? In terms of authority, is everyone clear about what they can and cannot do?

» **Attendees:** Based on the purpose and agenda, are you clear about who needs to attend? If critical inputs need to be made, who is going to make them? Do you need certain people at the event because they have relevant background knowledge that will add to the quality of the discussion? Everyone attending the event should be there for a reason, and they should be clear about expectations for their contribution.

» **Event dynamics:** With knowledge of the purpose, agenda and attendees, it's likely that before the event you can predict potential areas of difficulty. Do some attendees have very strong views for example? Do difficult issues need to be discussed? Either way, you can use stakeholder analysis here to identify key influencers that need some pre-positioning beforehand to make sure they attend the workshop in the right frame of mind. If you can identify these potential difficulties up front, you can structure the agenda and the event to make sure it stays on track.

You first need to identify the stakeholders because they can help make or break your project! Your list will include anyone who controls critical resources or who shapes the thinking of other critical parties. Ask the following questions:

- Who are they?
- Where do they currently stand on the issues associated with this change initiative?
- Are they supportive? If so, how supportive?
- Are they against the change initiative? If so, how much against?
- Or are they broadly neutral?

» **Event structure:** With an outline agenda, a knowledge of how much time you have available and awareness of the likely workshop dynamics, how are you going to allocate that time across the different agenda items? Where does the emphasis need to be placed? How much time needs to be allocated to inputs, to discussion, to decision making? In setting the event structure, you also need to take account of the need for breaks at various points (coffee, lunch, tea), and to be aware of how these breaks will impact the flow of the discussion. For long events, you also need to think about how to keep people engaged throughout the day. For example, consider giving people something interesting to do after lunch.

» **Event roles:** The event will need a champion or sponsor, who is the person who helps establish the purpose and objective of the event. They also clarify the authority given to the team. The role of the facilitator is clearly different.

As part of preparation, the champion and facilitator must agree on their different roles and the overall purpose of and plan for the event. A team member should be appointed as timekeeper during the event to keep an eye on the clock and to ensure that progress is being made. Someone also needs to fulfill the role of note-taker, responsible for capturing information and recording decisions made.

>> **Event venue and atmosphere:** This is a key part of a successful event. What sort of environment do you want to create for the outcome you want to achieve? You need to consider the following issues:

- Whether to host the event on- or off-site, or virtually.

- How to avoid attendees being distracted by operational demands.

- The size and layout of the room, whether it is formal or informal, and the availability of breakout rooms if needed.

- Access to the technology if your event is taking place virtually.

- Equipment needed and its availability.

TIP

Rapid improvement events and problem-solving sessions can also be facilitated online, where teams are working remotely. Make sure everyone has the opportunity get "hands on" with using the tools and techniques via online collaboration apps. Be sure to plan in lots of breaks, and ask attendees to make sure their time and attention are fully committed (for example, by agreeing up front that this will be a "cameras on" session and ensuring they don't get pulled away into other calls).

You need a number of things in the room and outside it. The event toolkit is likely to include some or all of the following:

>> Flipchart and stand

>> Paper and spare flipchart pads

>> Pens

>> Brown paper

>> Sticky notes

>> Camera

>> Laptop and screen

>> Access to online collaboration tools if working virtually

You need to think about refreshments too. Rapid improvement events can be thirsty work!

Running the event

Good preparation means you're clear about the outline process you want to take people through. Of course, you need to be flexible and respond appropriately as the dynamics dictate, but your pre-work gives you a good framework. A successful event requires that the following issues be addressed:

- **Kicking off:** Invite the champion to kick off the session so that everyone understands its importance and relevance.

- **Agenda/timekeeping:** The facilitator needs to ensure the event runs to time. If things are taking longer than planned, they must alter the agenda as appropriate (obviously keeping the overall purpose in mind; after all, the objectives of the event must be achieved).

- **Expectation setting:** At the start of the event the facilitator will find it useful to ask all the attendees for their expectations. These can be logged on a flipchart and referred to throughout the session. Collecting expectations at the start allows the facilitator to make sure that everyone present understands the purpose of the event. This information also highlights different perspectives and allows the facilitator to point out how the event agenda fits with the expectations stated. In some cases it may also result in modifications to the agenda if key influencers express needs that will otherwise not be met (though with good preparation that shouldn't happen very often).

- **Logging issues:** If attendees stray from the issue at hand, threatening to derail the event, their points should be logged visibly and returned to later. The facilitator may be able to work in those points for discussion at suitable slots in the agenda or assign them to clear owners who will take the points away and work on them outside the event.

- **Logging next steps/actions:** It's a good idea for the facilitator to log next steps or actions as the event proceeds. Again, this should be done in a visible way so that every attendee can see what actions have been agreed upon, who's responsible for each, and when they will be undertaken. Doing so prevents confusion, and the facilitator can also return to the list at the end of the event and run through it item by item so that everyone leaves feeling clear about what they have to do next.

>> **Noting pluses and deltas:** At the end of the event, the facilitator can ask all attendees to identify the pluses of the event (what people found useful) and the deltas (what could have been improved). Not only does this activity provide good feedback for the facilitator, but it also allows the attendees to reinforce the positive impact of the event or, alternatively, raise any residual concerns or issues that may not have been picked up during the event itself. The facilitator captures these pluses and deltas. Getting the team to record them on sticky notes is a simple way of doing so. They can then be reviewed, and action taken, before the next event session. Remember that these rapid improvement events are likely to be scheduled as a series of one-day (or half-day) sessions.

Following up and action planning

At the end of the event, or shortly afterwards, the facilitator and the champion will conduct a review. They need to consider what went well, what could've been improved, whether their objectives were met and what follow-up is required. Addressing these issues will help in preparing for the next session. Where appropriate, the facilitator needs to make sure that actions and next steps decided at the event are circulated as quickly as possible. After the improvement solution has been implemented, it will be important to ensure an effective handover has taken place and that a control plan is in place.

WARNING

Do not allow actions to drag on over long time periods. Remember this is all about *rapid* improvement. Set realistic dates for the completion of actions, but the time-frame should not exceed 30 days.

Creating a Checklist for Running Successful Events

The facilitator may find it helpful to have a checklist of questions to refer to. The following list isn't exhaustive and can be added to or modified. The key thing is to think about it!

>> Are the more active participants hogging the discussion?

>> Is anyone who could make a useful contribution being excluded?

>> Is enough being done to encourage quieter members to contribute? Often these people have the greatest insight because they've listened to all the contributions to date.

- » Who are the influential group members? Why is this? Are they influential as a result of their subject knowledge or for other reasons? What are those other reasons?

- » What influencing styles are used within the group? Which are accepted or rejected by other group members?

- » Is someone updating the facts and summarizing the situation to date?

- » Is someone ensuring that all relevant data, whether facts, opinions or alternative solutions, are being collected?

- » Is someone ensuring that the problem-solving technique being used is suitable for the task?

- » Do people keep hopping from one subject to another, thus stopping the group from making progress down its chosen path?

- » Are the physical or virtual "surroundings" having a positive, negative, or neutral effect?

- » Do group members feel able to contribute without fear of being made to look foolish or ignored?

- » What contribution does the leader make to the atmosphere among the group?

- » Are subgroups forming? Are the subgroups helping or hindering the group as a whole?

- » Does an elite exist within the group?

Practicing Problem Solving

When you get familiar with DMAIC, you might find it becomes an in-built, instinctive response to problem solving that you use frequently.

Where DMAIC is used to support everyday problem solving, the A3 method, pioneered at Toyota, provides a helpful format. Taiichi Ono (Toyota leader and founding father of the Toyota Production System) was known for insisting on reports that were no longer than one page. The A3 approach is named after the sheet of paper used to work through the problem-solving process and record each stage. An example A3 is shown in Figure 17-2.

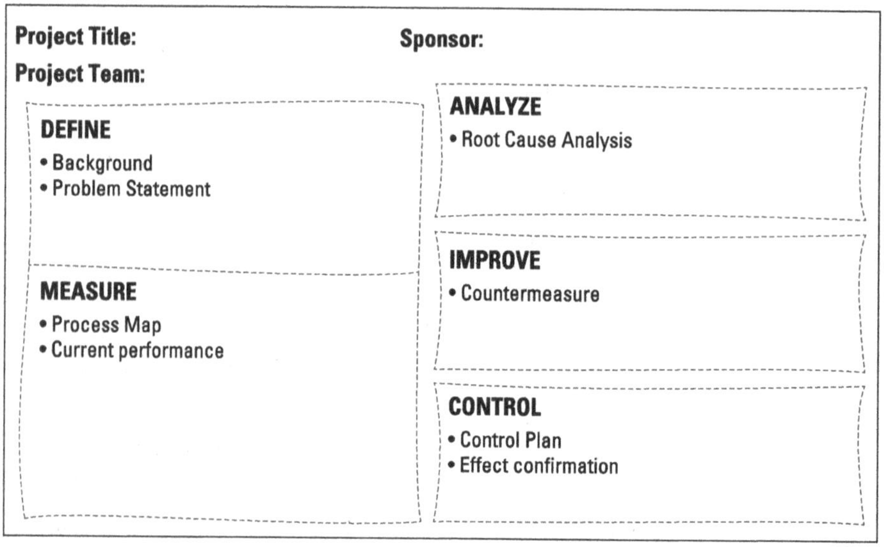

| Project Title: | | Sponsor: |

Project Team:

DEFINE
• Background
• Problem Statement

MEASURE
• Process Map
• Current performance

ANALYZE
• Root Cause Analysis

IMPROVE
• Countermeasure

CONTROL
• Control Plan
• Effect confirmation

FIGURE 17-2:
An example A3.

© Martin Brenig-Jones and Jo Dowdall

Working through the problem-solving steps in a logical way in this format supports a thorough, effective, and consistent approach. The A3 outputs can be shared easily, providing a record of the improvements made, which are something to be proud of.

Chapter **18**

Ensuring Everyday Operational Excellence

The Control phase of a Lean Six Sigma DMAIC project deals with implementing and embedding the solution(s) in order to realize the improvement benefits. This moves the focus from process improvement to process management or "business as usual."

The handover of the improved process to a suitable "owner" in the organization is an important Control phase activity. This individual will now be accountable for its performance. This chapter addresses how processes are managed after the handover to ensure they continue to meet customers' requirements.

It's important to remember that Lean Six Sigma isn't just about DMAIC and DMADV projects. The principles, concepts and tools also provide a framework for operational excellence to become a reality in everyday life. You can also apply what's in this chapter to day-to-day management, aiming for "everyday operational excellence."

Standardizing the Process

In Chapter 13, we looked at how standardization forms the basis of the Toyota Production System and makes it possible to apply the other aspects of Lean that are included.

When the best way of operating the process has been identified it makes sense for other people to follow it. Otherwise, the full potential and benefits of the changes that have been made won't be realized. Quality Management guru Masaaki Imai summarized this nicely:

> *Where there is no standard, there can be no improvement. For these reasons, standards are the basis for both maintenance and improvement.*

In order to standardize the process, you will need to deploy it fully wherever the process is being carried out. The process steps will need to be clearly captured in suitable format so that everyone can understand what to do and how to do it. (See Chapter 5 for more on process mapping.) And everyone with responsibility for operating the process will need to be informed and trained. Going back to the Gemba (also in Chapter 5) will provide insight into how the standard is being applied, and data obtained by measuring key aspects of the process will highlight how well it is performing.

Perfecting the process handover

Establishing *who* the improved process will be handed over to is clearly an important consideration! Your organization may not use the term "Process Owner," but here we're talking about handing the improved process to the individual who will be accountable for the performance of the process going forward. (George Eckes refers to them as "individuals who experience the greatest pain or gain in the process.") This person may have been the sponsor of your Lean Six Sigma project.

Items to hand over will include the documented process and information on which aspects of the new process will be measured, along with when and how the measurements will be taken. The Process Management Chart provides an effective format for this information.

TIP

Throughout the DMAIC project you are likely to have come across additional opportunities for improvement in and around the process you've been working on. Document these and hand them over to the process owner so they don't get lost. These could become future process improvement projects.

Populating the Process Management Chart

The Process Management Chart, shown in Figure 18-1, brings together the key information required to manage the process, which includes the following:

>> The process map

>> The monitors and measures that will be used track how well the process is working

>> The corrective actions that will be taken if the aspects of performance being monitored differ from the aim

The Process Management Chart could also show the following:

>> Who carries out the process steps.

>> Where more detailed work instructions can be found.

>> What the measures are and how they will be taken.

>> Who will take the measurement.

>> Who will take actions based on the data.

TIP

You don't have to wait for a process improvement project to start making use of a Process Management Chart. Why not create one for the processes you are managing so that all key process collateral can be brought together in one place?

Process	Performance	Action
Deployment Flowchart	Checks and Measures	Corrective Actions
	Plot time on each step; should be two hours or less; check for special causes	If time exceeds two hours, alert team leader and organize investigation
	Count errors	If more than one per order, stop process, contact team leader and investigate

FIGURE 18-1:
The Process
Management
Chart includes
essential process
information.

© Martin Brenig-Jones and Jo Dowdall

Making Everyday Operational Excellence a Reality

Using Lean Six Sigma to improve business processes is clearly beneficial. You can ensure that customers' requirements of the process are fully understood and that your process is designed to meet them. But what about the other processes in your organization? When it comes to deploying Lean Six Sigma in your organization one of the most important things to do is to establish a process management system.

All organizations are made up of a system of processes that fit together. By defining this system, the interrelationships between processes, and the way customers experience the processes becomes easier to understand. An example of a high-level picture of an organization's processes is included in Chapter 3. Does your organization have a picture like this? We love creating these pictures with our customers and could write an entire book about process management systems!

Here's our definition of a well-managed process:

>> It's owned.

>> There's a clear customer-focused objective with prioritized customer requirements.

>> The process has been documented.

>> There's a balance of input, process and output measures.

>> It's in statistical control, or there is an improvement plan in place to do so.

>> It meets the CTQs, or there is an improvement plan in place to do so.

>> It has been error-proofed.

>> There's a response plan.

Imagine if all of your organization's processes were managed this way. Excellent indeed.

Embracing Leader Standard Work

Everyday Operational Excellence extends beyond what process operators do, and into what supervisors, managers and leaders do. *Leader Standard Work* is a common concept in organizations that have embraced Lean ways working.

Leader Standard Work ensures that key tasks for leadership and management are undertaken consistently. We've seen that standardization forms the basis for maintenance and improvement, and the same applies here. Where leaders apply Leader Standard Work, a continuous improvement culture is driven, and its importance is demonstrated from the very top of the organization.

Leader Standard Work can be undertaken by members of the senior leadership team, managers, and supervisors. The activities are consistent, but the areas of focus will of course differ. However, there should be an alignment between the processes and tasks carried out at every level and in every process and the objectives and goals set out in the organization's strategy, so it's clear how the outputs of every process contribute to the organization's overall success.

Standardized tasks typically include (but are not limited to) the following:

>> **Gemba walks:** Leaders (and managers and supervisors) are encouraged to go to the Gemba on a frequent and regular basis to observe processes, talk with people, listen to people, and support problem solving. These visits are not to be confused with audits or "inspections" as they provide opportunities to reinforce the continuous improvement culture, recognize good practice, and provide coaching.

>> **Daily review:** The application of Leader Standard Work involves working to a routine and establishing a cadence for management activities. Daily meetings are part of this, and there will also be a sequence of weekly and monthly meetings. Daily meetings are carried out at the start of the day or at the start of a shift, sometimes called huddles or daily standups, though we have heard them called very many other things including "morning prayers" and "fit-to-fly" meetings. The meetings should take no longer than 15 minutes and should follow a structured agenda. Members of the senior leadership team, managers, and supervisors will all engage with their teams to hold these meetings. The performance metrics being discussed will be different, but the structure of the meeting will be the same. The meetings should be done in front of the performance boards, whether they are done in person or virtually. The agenda might cover the items outlined below. These are the same agenda items that Agile practitioners use to structure their daily scrum meetings (as we discuss in Chapter 16).

- What was achieved yesterday

- What we will do today

- Problems, unusual requirements or obstacles to address

>> **Mentoring:** Mentoring systems should be in place to support learning and development, with a focus on the behaviors that support Continuous Improvement because there is more to Leader Standard Work than tasks and tools.

A template used to support Leader Standard Work is provided in Figure 18-2. This template is used to structure leadership and management activities to ensure that key aspects are being addressed. Note that it includes the location and the people who'll be involved. The reviews won't be carried out in a meeting room after a review of some data or management information; they'll be done where the work takes place and with the people that do the work.

FIGURE 18-2:
A template to
support Leader
Standard Work.

Standard Leadership Practices								
Job Role:				Dept:		Date:		
Focus Area	Location	Review of...	With...	To Ensure...	Indicator/ Proof of Review	Frequency		
						Mthly	Wkly	Dly

TIP

The ongoing application of Everyday Operational Excellence also serves to introduce and instill a common language of Lean Six Sigma principles, concepts and tools. In turn, this approach supports the ongoing identification of improvement opportunities that can be actioned either by managers and their teams, or through more formal DMAIC or DMADV projects.

Engaging the team

Owning and managing the process is part of the change in thinking and behaving that is an essential ingredient in the transformation of an organization. The people in the process, however, also need to feel able and be able to challenge and improve the process and the way in which they work. For that to happen, those people need to feel engaged and empowered.

In owning and working on the process, you need to ensure it really is *managed* — that you're genuinely working on the process with the people in the process. In order to make your team feel engaged, you need to actively involve those people in the daily team brief. Agreeing on ownership of different activities or elements of the activity board (see Chapter 13) is one way to help increase people's sense of participation.

The people in the process need to feel empowered; they need to be an integral part of the journey the organization is undertaking. The manager must thus work on the process with the people in the process to find ways of continuously improving the process.

Empowerment clearly isn't a new idea; indeed, the 1620 edition of the *Oxford English Dictionary* defines it as "to enable."

Our approach to empowerment centers on these vital elements from the perspective of the team member:

>> They feel competent. They're learning from experience and gaining new skills and abilities as their potential is developed.

>> They can see how their team's activities link to the goals of the organization. They understand that they're an integral part of a larger effort.

>> They enjoy their work and have fun — as everyone should!

With these ingredients in place, an individual team and the organization as a whole significantly increase their chances of success.

To lead and manage a strong and efficient team, you need to:

>> Develop people
- Coach and train people during new assignments
- Help people build on their skills

>> Build trust
- Promote an atmosphere of cooperation
- Trust people to do an effective job

>> Promote autonomy
- Encourage people to take the initiative
- Provide appropriate coaching and support when needed

>> Encourage openness
- Forgive mistakes made by others
- Admit to your own mistakes

>> Recognize accomplishments
- Celebrate successes
- Reward people for innovations

>> Shape direction
- Provide a vision of the future
- Tackle controversial activities

>> Demonstrate objectivity

- Use facts in decision making
- Respond to facts rather than unsubstantiated data

REMEMBER

A direct and very strong correlation exists between employee satisfaction and customer satisfaction.

Using the right methodology

Everyday Operational Excellence involves creating a situation whereby "this is the way we do things around here" and everybody knows it. The right projects are identified, prioritized, and actioned using the right methodology. Not every project will need to use the DMAIC or DMADV frameworks.

In fact, a project focus may not be necessary; maybe small tweaks to a process will suffice. The elements of a managed process are in place so that the everyday activities are carried out seamlessly using the principles, concepts, tools and techniques of Lean Six Sigma. People working in the process feel they're listened to and that they're able to challenge and help improve things.

Creating a culture of Continuous Improvement

For Everyday Operational Excellence to be a reality, managers need to be working on the process and staff must feel engaged and empowered. These factors help get the principles and concepts of Lean Six Sigma into the organization's DNA.

But Everyday Operational Excellence involves more than that, of course. To initiate a cultural transformation you need to consider which attitudes have to shift, and how significantly the average manager or employee needs to change their viewpoint. Maybe particular policies need to be changed, which may have implications for recruitment, appraisal, promotion or pay and reward structures.

REMEMBER

Most significantly, leaders and managers must thoroughly understand what the organization does, live its philosophy and teach it to others. They need to support people and the work they carry out, and take responsibility for the processes they operate. And they must demonstrate a genuine passion for Lean Six Sigma and its underlying principles and thinking.

Understanding Organizational Culture

Defining the concept of "culture" in organizations is difficult, yet most people have an idea of what the term means in their own organization. They know their organization's "unwritten rules" and can describe "the way things get done around here" a lot more vividly than can a written rulebook or set of documented policies.

At the core of most organizations is a set of values and beliefs that pervade everything and dictate more strongly than any management fad what people *think* should be done and *how* it should be done. These enduring beliefs create attitudes and behaviors that may undermine your Lean Six Sigma project if people consider your project to threaten them.

Alongside the formal declared change (the plan), another process is happening — often hidden in the shadows but still having a powerful impact. The best Lean Six Sigma practitioners recognize the hidden cultural and unwritten rules, and they manage change in the cultural process as keenly as they manage the work process being improved.

Many change initiatives fail because their proponents don't have enough awareness of the cultural factors involved. Many mergers and acquisitions fail to achieve the promised gains for this reason. Culture is complex, powerful, and based on events of the past. In any organization, rituals, stories, myths, heroes, and villains play important roles. Gerry Johnson, at Cranfield University in the UK, developed the idea of a *cultural web,* shown in Figure 18-3.

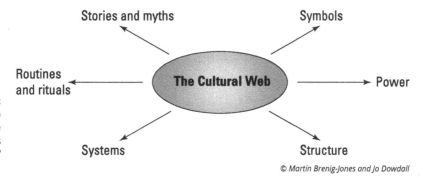

FIGURE 18-3:
The cultural web is essentially "the way we do things around here."

© *Martin Brenig-Jones and Jo Dowdall*

TIP

The stories we tell have an impact on the culture of an organization. Create some Lean Six Sigma success stories, share them, and encourage others to do the same.

Chapter **19**

Leading the Deployment and Selecting the Right Projects

This chapter is about leading the deployment of Lean Six Sigma in your organization. The key to successful deployment is the active involvement of leaders and managers, who must be seen to be leading and supporting the approach. Leadership doesn't just come from the top, though. In this chapter, we look at the different roles needed to create an effective deployment program. Selecting the right projects is also key. Later in the chapter, we look at what makes a suitable DMAIC project and how to prioritize the opportunities.

Considering Key Factors for Successful Deployment

Successful deployment involves:

- **Doing the right work:** Ensure your projects are focused on the right issues and linked to your business objectives.

- **Doing the work right:** Run your projects effectively, using good-quality people, utilizing the right Lean Six Sigma tools and methods, applying sound project-management techniques and ensuring rigorous governance through committed sponsorship, project reviews and tollgates reviews.

- **Creating the right environment:** Lean Six Sigma flourishes as the natural way of working in certain settings. Creating the right environment is about leadership, recognition, training and encouraging people to do the right things effectively, and ensuring the team's work is supported.

Figure 19-1 is a simple illustration of a successful deployment model.

- Doing the right work
  - Strategic alignment
  - Project selection
  - Managing by fact

- Doing the work right
  - Lean Six Sigma tools and methods
  - Programme management
  - Project management
  - Process management

- Creating the right environment
  - Leadership behavior
  - Effective sponsorship
  - Mentoring, coaching
  - Effective teamwork
  - Resourcing

© Martin Brenig-Jones and Jo Dowdall

FIGURE 19-1: Successful deployment.

Understanding Executive Sponsorship

Ideally, the executive sponsor for Lean Six Sigma is the most senior person in the organization, with a real interest in seeing it become more than simply a "quality" initiative. Indeed the reason that the approach has continued to win support from senior executives is because it creates tangible business benefits through delivering improvement and change.

The role of the executive sponsor is not to be confused with the role of a project sponsor. The executive sponsor's role is to provide strategic direction and support for the overall deployment program. Effective executive sponsors also recognize that Lean Six Sigma is critical to their own success.

An executive sponsor who really is passionate about Lean Six Sigma shouldn't underestimate the motivational effect they can have on those involved in implementing the approach. Here's a quick list of the things an executive sponsor should do:

>> Provide the drive and strategic direction for the program.

>> Articulate a clear vision of how they see the future and why this approach is so important.

>> Appoint someone to manage the deployment (a deployment program manager).

>> Provide the budget and resources for the teams as needed.

>> Agree on the scope of the program.

>> Make space on the leadership team meeting agenda to review progress and keep informed by getting involved.

>> Spread the message personally through a variety of communication channels and through their behavior and actions.

>> Take part in "showcases" and recognition events such as, for example, at certification and award ceremonies. Recognition is really key to success.

>> Act as a role model — and not get diverted off-track.

Active involvement is required, not passive acquiescence. As executive sponsors understand more about the principles and the tools and techniques of Lean Six Sigma, some great opportunities for their application in and around their own office and in the leadership and management processes in the organization will be identified.

Here are four simple Lean Six Sigma techniques that can be encouraged and applied directly by the senior executive team:

>> **Avoid jumping to solutions.** When confronted by challenging and complex business problems, is there a tendency to jump to solutions or expect the team to do so? "Managing by fact" means being informed by data. Clearly, if

the solution really is clear don't hold back, but all too often we see situations in which quick-fire decisions are made at senior level only to be regretted later at significant cost to the organization.

>> **Beware of the average.** Understand the danger of only seeing averages being reported, and the illusion this gives that targets are being met. Control charts and other visual methods (described in Chapter 8) provide a way to understand the performance of processes or value streams. They enable you to determine when to take action and when not to.

>> **Encourage the use of visual management.** As described in Chapter 13, simplifying regular reports by using visual management techniques can provide great opportunities for senior management. The approach helps everyone to clearly see what's going on.

>> **Review one of the management processes that supports the senior executive team.** For example, review the monthly reporting process by carrying out a value-add analysis. In one organization we worked with, a 70-page monthly progress report was produced, but most of the contents were never read, so a cut-down report proved to be much more useful and useable.

TIP

If you haven't yet secured commitment from the top team, you could consider running some pilot projects so that you can demonstrate the results and the potential. You may even find a convert, and as we know, converts can become the most passionate of advocates.

Considering Size and Sector

Very often at events and training courses, we will be approached by someone who'll say they like the sound of Lean Six Sigma but don't think it will apply to them because they're "not manufacturing," or that their organization is too big or too small for it. Our answer is always that the principles and tools of Lean Six Sigma are universal. Read all about them in Chapter 2 to prove it.

No matter what size or sector your organization is, it will be made up of a system of processes. And where there are processes, there are opportunities to make them better. The processes may not be documented, or even be very clearly defined, but activities are being undertaken and Lean Six Sigma can help you to tame them, manage and improve them, and make them excellent.

The processes will also have customers. Some organizations may not refer to them as such, but there will be people on the receiving end of your processes. Think of customers as those who receive the outputs of your process. A SIPOC might help you to set this out clearly (see Chapter 3 for details). Are those customers getting what they want from the processes? Do you really know what they want? Lean Six Sigma can help to make sure.

Figure 19-2 shows how you can start a Lean Six Sigma journey using a fairly basic toolset. As your Continuous Improvement maturity develops, process performance improves. You first tame your business processes and then improve them using the more advanced tools from the Lean Six Sigma toolset as you build experience and expertise.

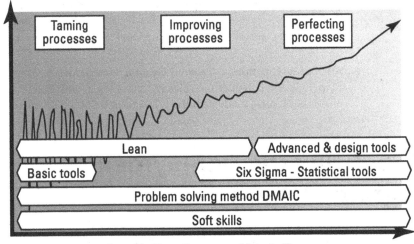

FIGURE 19-2:
Applying Lean Six Sigma to processes.

Anyone with a leadership role can start to apply the principles of Lean Six Sigma in their organization, no matter how small. They won't be able to do it entirely on their own, however. The deployment program manager is also key to making Lean Six Sigma happen. The role of managers is also crucial.

Recognizing the Important Role of Managers

Managers play a significant role in Lean Six Sigma, but they are often overlooked. They are sometimes referred to as "the meat in the sandwich," meaning they are supporting the leaders to deliver the organization's goals and managing and motivating their team members. They have responsibility for managing people *and* processes, and both of these are critical aspects of the Lean Six Sigma approach.

>> **On the people side,** they manage the team(s) of people that execute business processes; advocate and role-model the organization's ways of working (for example, its values or its 5S program, and so on); recruit, train, and support team members; communicate team, department, and organizational goals; appraise and give feedback to team members about performance; engage with managers and leaders across the organization; provide people resources for process-improvement activities.

>> **On the process side,** they report process performance; are responsible for ensuring process documentation and materials are up to date; support process improvements; are the first escalation point for decisions; identify the need for corrective actions; ensure quality standards are met.

All of these functions are absolutely vital "when the rubber hits the road." Be sure to include and consider the roles of managers in your Lean Six Sigma deployment effort, equipping them with the information and tools required to play their part.

Introducing the Deployment Program Manager

Deployment program managers do just would you would expect: They manage the deployment of Lean Six Sigma into the organization, working closely with the executive sponsor and the leadership team. They should be a respected member of the team who *wants* to take on the role. The ideal deployment program manager has the following characteristics:

>> Practical

>> Networker

>> Resource investigator

>> Planner

>> Team worker

>> Will find the time

>> Motivated

>> Good communicator

- » Open-minded

- » Curious

- » Has a continuous improvement mindset

We could go on to include a good sense of humor, charisma, dynamism, magician, miracle worker and many other characteristics, but let's be realistic! What is crucial is that the deployment program manager is capable of not only getting things up and running but also works well with people at all levels.

It's possible to start a Lean Six Sigma program without having a Lean Six Sigma expert already in place. If there is someone with the characteristics listed above, they will have the potential to learn about Lean Six Sigma as the program progresses. You don't have to bring someone in from outside in order to get started.

Look for a balance between technical (hard) and people (change management) skills. Even the best Black Belts or Master Black Belts (described in Chapter 2) should be able to offer this balance.

The Lean Six Sigma deployment program manager gets things up and running by:

- » Organizing senior executive workshop-style training.

- » Selecting and working with a suitable training/coaching provider.

- » Facilitating the program startup through an initial series of improvement projects.

- » Ensuring that progress is monitored and that initial projects stay on track and deliver tangible benefits.

- » Establishing governance (at the appropriate degree).

- » Ensuring the message is spread via different channels right across the organization.

- » Putting internal resources in place to support the program.

- » Organizing and running a steering group of senior deployment champions from across the organization.

- » Ensuring that employee participation is duly recognized as well as project successes.

- » Sharing best practice as it develops across the organization.

Clearly, no one size fits all. We're at pains to point out that Lean Six Sigma can drive improvement in organizations of every size and shape, in all sectors. So adapt the role of the deployment program manager to suit your own situation.

TIP

In very small organizations the senior executive sponsor and the deployment program manager roles can be combined (leadership and management) but, if you can work as a double act, then so much the better.

Starting Your Lean Six Sigma Program

Investing time in getting the start-up right is well worth it. How you go about launching your Lean Six Sigma program will affect its success.

Of course, you may be reading this book before you've even floated the idea of running a Lean Six Sigma program with your team. As a first step, therefore, you may need to think about how you'll win support, especially if people have had negative experiences with other initiatives in the past. To make your program successful, you need to introduce it gradually, in stages.

TIP

Consider visiting organizations that have successfully introduced this kind of approach. But bear in mind that it has taken decades for organizations like Toyota or Ricoh to embed this culture into their organizations and they'll be the first to say that they have further to go and more to do. You'll find that where there is a genuine Continuous Improvement culture, the approach is so deeply rooted in the values and principles, it pervades everything they do. The principles are more important than the tools and in best-practice organizations they are reflected in the behaviors of the leadership team.

You could consider starting with engaging the leadership team in a series of "kick off" events that combine elements of training, covering the basics of Lean Six Sigma, with how it can best be applied in the organization, through a series of targeted improvement initiatives. Most importantly, these sessions need to highlight the role of the senior team and how its members will affect the success of the Lean Six Sigma program throughout the organization.

You need to select processes that can be improved by the Lean Six Sigma approach. A positive impact early on will smooth the path for integrating the approach throughout the whole organization.

To ensure the success of your Lean Six Sigma startup, you need to:

>> Raise awareness and engage senior executives.

>> Identify advocates and champions.

>> Develop a network across the organization.

- ≫ Develop expertise.

- ≫ Deploy Lean Six Sigma tools and techniques through relevant and well-scoped projects.

- ≫ Support business unit adoption/roll-out.

- ≫ Encourage everyday use of the Lean Six Sigma tools.

- ≫ Establish and monitor measures of success, which could include things like a healthy pipeline of candidate projects, project benefits, involvement, engagement, and certifications.

- ≫ Generate, communicate, and celebrate successes.

Understanding What Project Sponsors Do

We've looked at how leadership and management are needed at the overall *deployment* level and the sponsorship that is needed at program level. At the *project* level, every improvement initiative should also have a sponsor (or "champion") who's prepared to devote the time and support needed to help the project team overcome any roadblocks on its journey.

The project sponsor is involved in selecting the project and the team members for it. As the project progresses, they support the project by:

- ≫ Providing strategic direction for the team.

- ≫ Developing the improvement charter (see Chapter 2), ensuring the scope of the project is appropriate and not too big.

- ≫ Keeping informed about the project's progress and taking an active involvement in project reviews.

- ≫ Providing financial and other resources for the project team.

- ≫ Helping to ensure the business benefits are realized in practice.

- ≫ Being prepared to stop a project if necessary.

- ≫ Helping to get buy-in for the project across the organization.

- ≫ Ensuring appropriate reward and recognition for the project team in the light of its success.

- ≫ Acting as the "Voice of the Business" to keep the project lead (or "belt") informed of changes that might impact on the project.

Driving Strategy Deployment with Lean Six Sigma

In recent years more organizations have recognized the advantages of using Lean Six Sigma as a method for deploying strategy across their organizations. Strategy deployment is now viewed as such a major area of development that it's covered in our book *Lean Six Sigma Transformation For Dummies* (Wiley). In a nutshell, strategy deployment looks at how organizations can build on their use of Lean Six Sigma to instigate operational improvements that create a more holistic approach across the entire organization to drive change and turn strategy into action in a coordinated and focused way.

Olympic rowers know only too well that unless team members row in time and in the same direction they'll never achieve gold. Organizations are no different, though often we see that although everyone is working hard, they're not all focused on working on the right things. Getting everyone working together in alignment is something that will take time and effort, and demands clear direction from the top.

TIP

Remember that a mountain is made up of tiny grains of earth. Break the strategy down into actionable steps in a way that ensures the scope of the tactical actions is agreed and clearly linked to the strategic objectives and goals.

Strategy deployment is an important subject. It's outside the scope of this book but builds on the foundations set here. For now, let's focus on the application of Lean Six Sigma to improve operational processes and launching a Lean Six Sigma program from scratch.

Generating a List of Candidate Improvement Projects

You need to choose a selection of projects for launching your Lean Six Sigma program, but where do you start? As Figure 19-3 demonstrates, so many opportunities seem to be available and a number of problems and issues need addressing!

In fact, selecting the initial projects, along with selecting the right people to work on them, is a practical way of getting the leadership team involved early on in a Lean Six Sigma program. A well facilitated project selection workshop is an effective way to kick-start the approach. It gets the senior team working on things that they really care about and using some of the Lean Six Sigma tools in action (for example, a paired comparison, as described in Chapter 4).

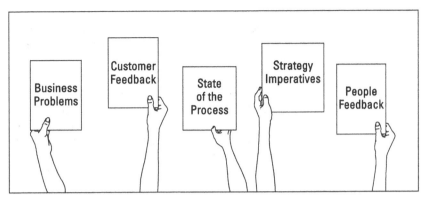

FIGURE 19-3:
So many options
to choose from!

© Martin Brenig-Jones and Jo Dowdall

We advise running a short (say, two- to three-hour) briefing session a couple of weeks before the project selection workshop to demystify Lean Six Sigma and get everyone considering potential candidates in terms of both processes and people. This way everyone will have had a chance to consult with their own teams, if necessary, and to come armed with their list of candidates before the project selection workshop.

Figure 19-4 describes project selection as a simple three-step process. After you have a long list of candidates, you then need to assess them and reduce the number to a short list of projects that are suited to the approach.

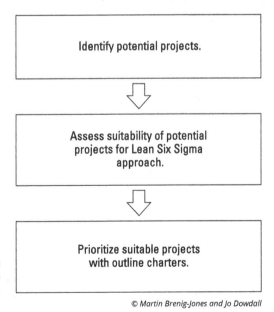

FIGURE 19-4:
Three steps to
project selection.

© Martin Brenig-Jones and Jo Dowdall

It may seem obvious, but your first step is to identify your top-level processes, recognize who the customers are, and ensure that you understand their requirements.

You could carry out a series of initial process "health checks" across the organization, reviewing performance measures and using high-level process maps. These are likely to be a combination of SIPOC diagrams and Value Stream Maps (which we cover in Chapters 3 and 5). These health checks will also help you to start identifying waste and non-value-adding activities. Improvement opportunities may already be obvious, but you may need to collect some data to help quantify and validate them. Typical measures include those to assess activity or unit time, cycle or lead time, error rates and work in progress. You can also start to use control charts to understand the different types of variation in these processes (as described in Chapter 8) as well as looking at process capability. These measures will help you understand how well you're doing in relation to customer requirements, highlight bottlenecks and delays, and enable you to focus on reducing rework activity and bring your processes under better control.

In determining which problem to tackle first, you may want to start simply. Consider carrying out some waste walks to spot opportunities for improvement (see Chapter 10 for details). Another technique that works well is for everyone in the team to consider this question: "What are the top ten things we would like to fix in this organization?" You probably already know which process problems need tackling, but go for bite-sized opportunities to start with, rather than biting off more than you can chew. Process activities that seem ripe for improvement could be exhibiting the following symptoms:

>> High correction rates and rework levels

>> Long processing times

>> Too many steps in which things go back and forth

>> Excessive delays between steps

>> Excessive checking

>> High levels of work in progress or inventory

>> Processes for which no standard way of doing the work exists

>> Late deliveries to customers

>> High levels of customer complaints

Potential projects will come from many different sources. Top-down or bottom-up approaches are both fine, but as you develop more of a culture of Continuous Improvement you'll find that more ideas will come from the people who do the work: the process operators (shown in Figure 19-5). Improvement ideas have to be taken seriously, evaluated, and acted on quickly. Many of these suggestions may be "just-do-it" tasks, but some will be good candidates for the Lean Six Sigma approach.

Management Driven
Projects are identified through a link with strategic business goals.

Operator Driven
Projects are identified through association with current process issues.

© Martin Brenig-Jones and Jo Dowdall

FIGURE 19-5: Identifying where suggestions come from.

WARNING

You need to balance strategy and business plans with problems seen in everyday process operations. Generating improvement ideas won't be difficult, but you can't do everything! Each suggestion needs to be assessed to see whether it's suitable for the Lean Six Sigma approach.

Deciding Whether Lean Six Sigma Is the Right Approach

When starting up a Lean Six Sigma program, we suggest you focus initially on process improvement opportunities using the DMAIC (Define, Measure, Analyze, Improve, and Control) approach rather than major process re-design or new product development using DfSS (Design for Six Sigma, which is covered in Chapter 14). Getting some basic experience in using Lean Six Sigma for improvement before using it for design is recommended. Build your knowledge base gradually and save the more advanced tools for when the Lean Six Sigma program is well established within your organization.

Remember the rule of "not jumping to solutions." Taking a more measured approach isn't easy if you and your team are conditioned to jump into action and if progress is measured by activity rather than finding the root causes of problems.

In some cases, the solution *is* clear right at the start and, if this really is the case, don't use DMAIC. Just get on and do it! Lean Six Sigma isn't suitable for everything. However, if the solution isn't clear, if you haven't got the facts and data, or you aren't sure what's causing the problem, then jumping to the solution too quickly can be very costly. You can probably think of examples of "jumping to the solution" without the full facts or any real root-cause analysis being carried out. Starting a Lean Six Sigma DMAIC project will present a challenge for some managers because it will require them to admit they don't have all the answers. That's okay!

In assessing your candidate list of improvement ideas, think about whether the solution is clear. If it is, then you won't need to use the DMAIC method. Use a good project management approach to implement the changes needed.

Answering these three questions may help:

>> Does a gap exist between current and required performance?

>> Is the cause of the problem already understood?

>> Is the solution already apparent?

If the answers are yes, no, and no, then the project is likely to be suitable for Lean Six Sigma DMAIC.

Prioritizing projects

Your team is likely to have only a limited amount of resources to deploy on running DMAIC improvement projects, so you need to be selective.

Involving the senior team in a project selection workshop (covered earlier in this chapter) is a good way to engage them, and if you've already run an executive awareness session beforehand, they'll arrive with several improvement ideas. Now you need to filter these and agree on your first set of improvement projects and who's going to lead them.

If you have lots of ideas, you could use a simple voting technique to reduce your long list to a more manageable number before going on to use a more detailed criteria-based approach. A simple voting approach is effective for a first-round reduction. Don't throw away anything that's on the list though, as these ideas can be added to a project "hopper" for future consideration. Remember that this isn't a once-only task; you'll also set up a project selection process to continue after you've selected the first group of projects. After all, you want to see Continuous Improvement, not a one-hit wonder!

Figure 19-6 outlines a list of criteria you could use to sift potential projects. This can of course be adapted to suit your own organization.

Criteria for Success	Rating	
Clear link to a real business need	Yes	No
Measurable cost or performance benefits	Yes	No
Customer requirements well understood or input from the customer can be obtained	Yes	No
Customer satisfaction will be positively impacted	Yes	No
Strong support/sponsorship in place	Yes	No
Scope is clear and reasonably narrow	Yes	No
Historical and current data is accessible	Yes	No
Achievable in 3-6 months	Yes	No
Not capital intensive	Yes	No
Resource is available	Yes	No
Clear ownership for delivery	Yes	No
Project is doable – the problem lies within the organization's control	Yes	No
Now is the right time to do this project	Yes	No
Process won't be changed by another initiative during the timeframe of the project	Yes	No
Can't afford not to do this project	Yes	No

FIGURE 19-6: A list of criteria for assessing project viability.

© Martin Brenig-Jones and Jo Dowdall

In Chapter 12, we look at using a criteria-based assessment to decide which solutions could be applied to a process problem. This technique can also be used to prioritize potential improvement projects. The criteria you use to rate the potential projects need to be carefully considered. They may include cost, the impact on particular strategic goals, and acceptance. The list isn't fixed; do adapt it to meet your own priorities and organizational needs.

If you like, you can keep things simple and use a 3 × 3 matrix, as shown in Figure 19-7, with each potential project mapped against benefit and effort, or cost. This matrix allows you to identify visually the most "desirable" projects, as well as those that may be potential quick wins. Quick wins can be taken down a slightly different route using a Rapid Improvement approach, which we cover in Chapter 17.

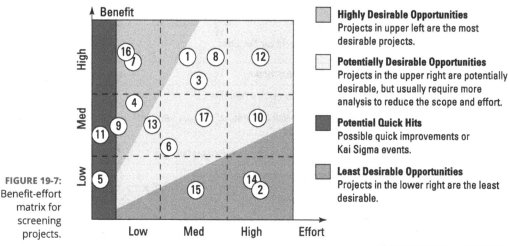

© Martin Brenig-Jones and Jo Dowdall

FIGURE 19-7: Benefit-effort matrix for screening projects.

Deciding on which approach fits which project

At a project level, it's important to distinguish between those problems that can be tackled using a rapid improvement approach and those that need to be approached in a more formal way, using DMAIC over perhaps three to four months.

Start simply, securing commitment and ongoing support. As you make progress in your deployment, you can increasingly link your activities to the organization's business plans and strategic objectives. You might look to policy deployment as the next stage, especially if you're aiming for breakthrough results. You can use cause and effect analysis to distinguish which processes need which approach. For example, Figure 19-8 uses Ys to refer to effects and Xs to denote causes. The organization as a whole has to achieve its top-level business goals (the big Ys in Figure 19-8), which are "caused" by the organizational processes performing well and delivering their outputs. The process Ys are in turn "caused" by the in-process variables being in control. This approach will affect the way you manage the whole organization. Significant benefits will surface at the top by focusing improvement resources on those Xs that will have the biggest positive impact all the way up the chain.

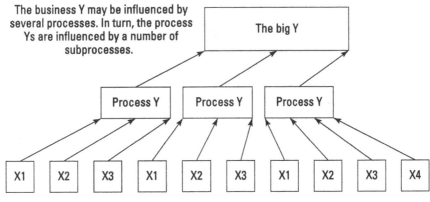

The business Y may be influenced by several processes. In turn, the process Ys are influenced by a number of subprocesses.

The big Y

Process Y   Process Y   Process Y

X1 X2 X3 X1 X2 X3 X1 X2 X3 X4

We need to understand the various linkages and the variables that drive the big Ys. And we need to determine Project Ys too!

© Martin Brenig-Jones and Jo Dowdall

FIGURE 19-8: Being business wise with the business Ys.

Now consider the startup of a typical DMAIC project, which is likely to run over three to four months.

Setting Up a DMAIC Project

At the senior team level, you first need to gain agreement on a number of basic details:

>> **Who will take on the role of project sponsor?** This person will represent the voice of the organization and ensure that the project is kept on track and steered in the right direction. The project sponsor will need specific training, reflecting a balance between the leadership aspects of the role and a good grounding in Lean Six Sigma (to a minimum of Yellow Belt level; Chapter 2 explains the martial arts analogy).

>> **Who will take the project lead?** If you're just starting up, we recommend that the project leader is selected for Green Belt training and that the project is used as an example to bear in mind during the training. If you don't have internal experts available (Black Belts or Master Black Belts), we suggest you use a training organization to provide project coaching to the Green Belt trainees as they work through their projects.

After these two roles have been assigned, the project sponsor and the project leader can get started on the project's Define phase, focusing initially on the project charter (see Chapter 2). They also need to appoint project team members. Process operators should be involved in the project as they're the people who know the process best. They'll also be much more inclined to adopt improvements if they've been involved in developing them. From here onwards, the project will move through the DMAIC phases described in Chapter 2.

REMEMBER

Don't forget the key factors in a successful Lean Six Sigma deployment: Doing the right work, doing the work right, and creating the right environment.

Chapter **20**

Putting It All Together: Checklists to Support Your DMAIC Project

This checklist chapter is a little different from the usual *For Dummies* format. It provides a series of lists to support you in your process improvement journey, as well as some helpful tips and reminders. The main deliverables of the DMAIC phases have been outlined, as well as guidance for completing a tollgate review at the end of each phase. This will help to make improvements in a systematic and effective way.

By following the DMAIC process and working in line with the Lean Six Sigma principles (outlined in Chapter 2), you will solve your process problem and make a measurable and sustainable difference. Think of the tools and techniques as enablers to help you along the way. You're unlikely to need every single tool included in this book, but by trying out the tools and techniques, you'll get to know which works best in which situation. If you are working towards achieving certification for a Lean Six Sigma "belt" (also covered in Chapter 2), pay attention to the specific requirements of your certification body.

REMEMBER

Different problems may need different approaches and, indeed, some problems may not need DMAIC. If you know what's causing the problem, or you have identified a solution that will address a known cause, just do it! That said, some of the tools in this book will help you to "just do it well."

We recommend that the project lead and project sponsor carry out a tollgate review at the end of each DMAIC phase, at least. The reviews will allow the project lead and project sponsor to do the following:

>> Monitor the progress of the team.

>> Identify whether additional resources are required.

>> Make decisions and/or help overcome sensitive issues.

>> Ensure coordination among all teams.

>> Understand and discuss any issues, risks. and opportunities from across the business that will impact on the improvement work being undertaken.

>> Keep the momentum going.

Now let's look at each DMAIC phase in turn.

Defining the Project

The Define phase provides focus and clarity, and it starts with a clear definition of the problem that is going to be solved with Lean Six Sigma. We advise that the scope of work is outlined carefully and managed so that it doesn't grow too big. Here, the process that sits behind the problem will be defined, and its customers and their needs identified. You can read all about these aspects in detail in Chapters 2 to 4.

Delivering the Define phase

Items to address in the Define phase of your Lean Six Sigma project:

>> Development of a project charter (like the one shared in Chapter 2) to capture the initial outline of this piece of improvement work. It will need to be updated as you progress through the phases and learn more about the work to be done, but should address the following elements:

   • A business case

   • A problem statement

- A goal statement

- The project scope

- High-level milestones

- Agreed upon roles and responsibilities

- The CTQs, or at least a plan to agree to them (This element may need to be carried over into the Measure phase.)

>> An "elevator speech" or key message about your project. Whether you're in the elevator, in the coffee queue or waiting for a meeting or video call to start, having a clear and simple project pitch on hand is very useful when it comes to communicating, influencing and building acceptance for your project.

>> An outline of the high-level process that sits behind the problem you're trying to solve. The SIPOC diagram (covered in Chapter 3) is the perfect tool for capturing the high-level steps of the process, as well as its suppliers, inputs, outputs, and major process steps.

>> An understanding of who the process customers are and what matters most to them about the process you're working on. These requirements need to be defined in a measurable way as CTQs (see Chapter 4).

>> A project Sponsor, who is committed to supporting the project. (Read more about their role in Chapter 19.)

>> A small improvement team.

>> A stakeholder analysis, so that you can be sure you are engaging with and communicating with stakeholders appropriately throughout your project.

>> A risk assessment for the project, to help you plan and manage the work in the best possible way.

Getting through the Define phase tollgate

Some key questions to be answered in the first tollgate review meeting:

>> Are we focusing on the right problem, and on the right aspect of the problem?

>> Is the purpose of this piece of work clear and is there common agreement between the team (and stakeholders)?

>> Are the right people working in the right roles on the project? Are sufficient resources allocated? Does everyone understand their roles and responsibilities?

>> Has the team identified all the customers of the process? How will customers be affected by successful completion? What research has been done to understand customer needs?

>> Does the team understand how this improvement work will contribute to the success of the organization?

>> What else happening in the business will impact on this piece of work?

>> How often is the team meeting? How much work is being done by each team member outside of workshops? How is the team monitoring its progress?

If there any issues or concerns arising from the tollgate that need to be tackled before the Define phase is completed, agree on an action plan and address them before you move on.

Moving into the Measure Phase

The Measure phase is about understanding how the work gets done and understanding how well the work gets done. Here, the detailed steps of the process will be identified, and measurement will be undertaken. To support fact-based decision making, relevant, accurate, and reliable data is needed, which will allow for a clear understanding of how well the customer needs (CTQs) are being met. Data will also be collected from inputs and in-process variables so that "cause and effect" can be understood. Chapters 5 through 8 explain these aspects of your Lean Six Sigma project in detail.

Making good on Measure phase deliverables

Items to address in the Measure phase of your project:

>> A clear understanding of the current process. This can be obtained from going to the Gemba, or Process Stapling (that is, understanding how the process works from the perspective of the thing going through the process).

>> A visual representation of the process in the form of a flowchart, deployment process chart, Value Stream Map, or spaghetti map (see Chapter 5). Making the process visual helps you to understand it and challenge it.

>> A data collection plan, so that you can obtain accurate and reliable data that will help you understand process performance. Use the five-step data collection process to guide you, which is covered in Chapter 7. Remember that the data you collect should be representative, so check out the guidance provided on sampling to make sure.

>> An understanding (or "baseline") of how the process is currently performing in relation to the CTQs. You could calculate the sigma value of your process using the guidance in Chapter 1.

>> An understanding of patterns in process performance. You could create a run chart to identify how the process performs over time, or use a control chart (see Chapter 8) to understand more about the variation at play.

>> Data on input and in-process variables (Xs) that you can analyze to understand which factors are driving the output results you're seeing. The data will need to be appropriately segmented. For example, if you want to find out whether performance differs on certain days of the week, data needs to be collected by day of the week.

>> Updates to the project charter as required. For example the scope may have been tightened now you know more about the process.

>> Ongoing stakeholder management and communication activities.

Getting through the Measure phase tollgate

Some key questions to be answered in the Measure phase tollgate review meeting:

>> How did you develop a detailed understanding of the current process? Do you have a process map? Were the right experts involved in creating it?

>> Have you been to see the process being carried out?

>> What measures were used to understand performance? Where and how was the data obtained?

>> Has a balance of measures (output, input and in-process) been considered?

>> How well are CTQs being met?

>> Who is involved, and who else needs to be involved at this stage?

>> Have any quick wins been identified?

If there any issues or concerns arising from the tollgate review that need to be sorted out before the Measure phase is completed, agree on an action plan and address these before you move on. The knowledge gained and the data collected in this phase is an essential input to the Analyze phase.

Analyzing to Identify Root Causes

Identifying and removing the root causes of a problem will prevent it happening again. The Analyze phase is about identifying and verifying the possible causes. A number of different types of analysis can be undertaken, using process tools and data tools. These tools are outlined in Chapters 8 through 11.

Acing the Analyze phase

Items to address in the Analyze phase of your Lean Six Sigma Project:

>> A refocus or sharpening up of the problem statement, based on what has been learned in the Measure phase. For example, the initial problem statement may have stated that the process takes too long. You might now have identified that rework associated with a particular process step is consuming most of that time. Now you can focus on this aspect of the process to figure out why this rework is needed.

>> Identification of the potential causes of the process problem, based on what has been learned in the Measure phase and using data and observations from the process to validate them. The fishbone technique can be used to help you capture these. You can dig below the surface with the Five Whys technique.

>> An identification or analysis of waste (such as waiting time or cost of rework) in the process. Can you use data to quantify this waste?

>> An understanding of process flow (see Chapter 11). You may have identified constraints in the process, or you may have observed the impact of batching or of the layout and organization of the process. Ask why things happen to identify actionable causes.

>> A visual display of the data to understand patterns. Remember that a picture paints a thousand words.

>> Use of statistical tools such as hypothesis testing to tell you whether the difference seen in data sets is statistically significant, or regression analysis to measure the relationship between variables.

>> Confirmation of potential causes you can get to work on.

>> Ongoing stakeholder management and communication activities.

Getting through the Analyze phase tollgate

Some key questions to be answered in the Analyze phase tollgate review meeting:

>> Have you identified the possible causes and what are they? How have you confirmed or verified the causes?

>> Have you challenged the process steps for "value-add"? What waste did you identify?

>> Can the root causes you identified be addressed? Is prioritisation required?

>> Do the analyses dig down deep enough? Or do they dig too deep? (Make sure the causes are actionable.)

>> Do any aspects of leadership/management have an impact on the process? For example, are there checks and controls within the process?

>> Who is involved and who needs to be working on the team now?

Quantifying the Opportunity

In addition to the tollgate reviews conducted with the project sponsor at the end of each phase, the Lean Six Sigma improvement journey should include *benefit reviews* at specific stages.

These benefit reviews provide an opportunity to take stock of the financials associated with your process improvement. This first review looks at *quantifying the opportunity*.

The primary focus of the first benefit review is to understand the extent of non-value-adding activities and waste, and the potential for improvement. When you completed the Measure phase, you were able to understand the current situation and level of performance. Having completed the Analyze phase, your level of understanding should have increased significantly. You'll know why performance is at the level it is, and you should understand the costs involved in the process, both overall and at the individual process steps level. You'll have identified the waste and the non-value-adding steps, including the rework loops, and understood their impact on your ability to meet the CTQs.

To quantify the opportunity, you need to calculate the benefits and saving that would occur if all this waste and non-value-adding work were eliminated, making sure you document your assumptions. You may feel the opportunity is too small to bother about, or so large that it justifies widening the scope of the project or developing a phased approach with a number of smaller but targeted projects. Either way, this is the time to review and agree on your project goals, sensibly estimating what's possible for your project and updating the improvement charter, communication plan and storyboard as necessary. (See our ten tips for storyboard development in Chapter 21).

TIP

Work with colleagues in the Finance department or the Program Management Office to make sure you are reporting benefits using conventions that are consistent across the organization.

Identifying and Planning the Improvements

The Improve phase is where most people want to start! Now that you have identified the root cause of the problem, you can begin to generate improvement ideas to help solve it. You can then review and prioritize the ideas generated. The chosen solution(s) will then be tested or piloted, with measurement to ascertain its impact on the problem. Results and learnings should then be considered, and an implementation plan developed. Guidance on these aspects of your projects is provided in Chapters 12 and 13.

All DMAIC phases should include focus on managing change and building acceptance, but now that the solution and the nature of the change is known, involvement, engagement, and communication with stakeholders is especially important as you work to make it happen. Chapter 6 addresses managing change.

Executing the Improve phase

Items to address in the Improve phase of your Lean Six Sigma Project:

>> Generation of ideas and solutions, making sure they genuinely address the root cause that will solve the problem. Engage people and use tools to promote creativity and different thinking. Heed the advice of Einstein here: "We cannot solve our problems with the same thinking we used when we created them."

- » Prioritization that is systematic and transparent, allowing stakeholders to understand how the decisions have been made, using, for example, the criteria-based checklist (Chapter 12), the paired comparison (Chapter 4), or a benefit/effort matrix like the one included in Chapter 19.

- » A documented rationale for the chosen solution(s) and how it or they will address the root causes.

- » A new version of the process, documented in flowchart or deployment flowchart format. This will ensure all necessary detail is considered and will provide clarity on roles and responsibilities when the improvements are implemented.

- » A risk assessment or impact assessment to ensure any risks or knock-on effects of the change are identified and addressed. The FMEA tool (covered in Chapter 13) provides a useful framework. Prevention and error proofing should also be considered.

- » A suitable approach for managing the test or pilot of your solution(s), which includes clearly defined success criteria and details of the measures to be taken. Post pilot, there should be a full review of the results and learnings.

- » An outline of cost/benefit analysis and assumptions behind the assessment.

- » A detailed plan for implementing the new process, which takes learnings from the pilot into account.

- » Ongoing stakeholder management and communication activities.

Getting through the Improve phase tollgate

Some key questions to be answered in the Improve phase tollgate review meeting:

- » What are the possible solutions? How would they address the root cause? Are they "breakthrough" enough?

- » What criteria were used to prioritize solutions?

- » Are the solutions viable?

- » Who has been informed or consulted with? Have you identified all stakeholders who need to know about this?

- » What actions are being taken to build acceptance?

- » What are the risks associated with the solution(s) and what can be done to mitigate the risks?

- » Is a test or pilot required? How will this be managed? How will the results be measured?

>> How will the solution(s) be implemented? Is there a plan in place?

>> How will Change Management aspects be addressed?

As always, if there are any issues or concerns arising from the tollgate that need to be tackled before the Improve phase is completed, agree on an action plan and address these before you move on. This tollgate is an especially important one, as it determines if and when the solution(s) will be implemented.

Confirming the Customer and Business Benefits

The second of the benefit reviews looks to confirm the deliverables from the project, and secure authority for the solution to be fully implemented. As with *quantify the opportunity* (covered in the first review), the review also provides an opportunity to look at the project more generally, and key questions include the following:

>> How are things going?

>> Are you on course?

>> What have you learned? And forgotten?

>> What's gone well and why?

>> Can the solution be applied elsewhere?

>> What conclusions can be drawn?

The main focus is to confirm the deliverables. In completing the Improve phase, you should feel confident that the chosen solution will address the root cause(s) and ensure you meet the project goals. Given that management by fact is a key principle of Lean Six Sigma, you should have appropriate measurement data and evidence from the pilot that your solution will deliver.

A range of different benefits could result from your project:

>> Reduced errors and waste

>> Faster cycle time

>> Improved customer satisfaction

>> Reduced cost

WARNING

In assessing how well these match the project objectives, do remember that quantifying some benefits (for example, benefits of enhanced employee or customer satisfaction) may be difficult. When it comes to projecting when the benefits are likely to emerge, don't lose sight of the fact that a time gap will probably exist between the cause and effect, especially where customer perception data is concerned.

As well as looking at the benefits, this review also looks to confirm any costs associated with the solution and its implementation. Again, your piloting activity should have helped you pull this information together, provided you have treated it as though it were a full-scale implementation. Use guidelines from your organization to help you assess and present the benefits and costs, and make sure you have documented the assumptions behind your benefits assessment.

This review has some key outputs that include the following:

>> Confirmation that the project is on track

>> Confidence in the solution and implementation plan

>> A confirmed benefit analysis complete with documented assumptions

>> An updated improvement charter

The project sponsor needs to address the following issues:

>> Are you confident that your benefit statement can be justified?

>> Have you documented your assumptions?

>> Do you feel that expenses associated with implementing the required changes can now be reliably forecast and controlled?

>> Given the lessons learned from the pilot, do you need to review your team membership for the final implementation?

Implementing the Solutions and Controlling the Process

The Control phase has two parts. The first looks to implement the solution; the second takes stock of what's been achieved. After all your hard work, you need to implement the solution in a way that ensures you make the gain you expected — and hold it!

The handover process and a control plan are vital features of the Control phase. You can read about these in Chapter 18. Getting the right measures in place is a crucial element of the control plan, and you need to be satisfied that the data collection plan has been effectively deployed. In assessing the benefits, you have the opportunity to determine the accuracy of your earlier benefit analysis, though remember it may take a while for the change to have an effect.

Completing the Control phase

Items to address in the Control phase of your Lean Six Sigma Project:

>> Implementation of the solution / deployment of the standardized process.

>> A handover to the appropriate manager or process owner, with all roles and responsibilities clearly defined.

>> Updated process documentation that has been incorporated into the organization's management system.

>> Delivery of training to process operators, and communication to stakeholders.

>> An approach for ongoing data collection so that performance can be monitored and the process managed.

>> Evidence of the success of the improvement project, including actual costs and benefits or at the very least an estimate of when these will be available.

>> Documentation of the lessons learned. These may include learnings on technical aspects of Lean Six Sigma and learnings about managing change. All projects have lessons, so always make the time to define them and learn from them.

>> Recommendations or ideas for further improvement opportunities.

>> Thanks and recognition to the team members for their contribution to the project's success.

>> A revised elevator speech about what has been achieved.

Getting through the Control phase tollgate

Some key questions to be answered in the Control phase tollgate review meeting:

>> Have the changes to the process been standardized? Has documentation been updated? Is it clear who will now own this and be responsible for updating it?

>> Have all the people who do this work been trained?

>> Have roles and responsibilities for the improved process been defined, agreed to, and communicated?

>> How do results match expectations?

>> How will ongoing results be monitored? How will any additional opportunities for improvement be handled?

>> Were there any unforeseen effects of the change and what is their impact?

>> What can we do to recognize the team for their work on this?

>> How well did the plan work?

>> What lessons learned have been identified?

>> Could learnings or aspects of the solution(s) be replicated elsewhere in the organization?

Conducting the Final Benefit Review

This is the formal post-implementation review. The questions are very similar to those posed at the end of the Control phase, but take a wider business perspective. They are as follows:

>> How satisfied are you that the problem has been solved?

- How well have the objectives been met?
- What is the data telling you?
- Which root causes still need to be addressed?
- What other residual issues does the business need to resolve?

>> What benefits have been realized or are in the pipeline?

- How do the benefits compare to what was predicted?
- Do your customers feel an improvement has occurred? How do you know?
- Are the costs in line with predictions?
- Have any other benefits resulted from the project?

>> Can you apply any lessons, ideas or best practices developed during this project elsewhere in the business?

- What have you learned?

- Where else in the business might these lessons be helpful?

- Do similar problems exist in another area and could this solution be applied there?

>> What should you and your improvement team do next?

- Has the next project been identified?

- What should the organization do to suitably recognize your team's efforts and success?

TIP

Develop some key messages (a new elevator speech) to summarize the benefits of your project. Share it widely and be proud of your achievements.

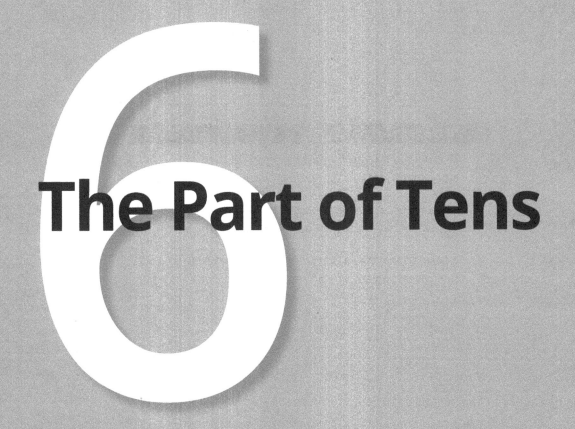

The Part of Tens

Chapter **21**

Ten Tips for Best-Practice Project Storyboards

C reating a storyboard for your Lean Six Sigma project is an excellent way to communicate about the project, method and results to the wider organization. It allows you to tell the story of the improvement project from beginning to end, pass on your learnings, challenges, 'Aha!' moments and any aspects of your solution that could be of benefit elsewhere in the organization. Storyboards are used as evidence for certification (e.g. Green Belt or Black Belt) and also support project tollgate reviews.

Use a combination of slides, words, images and videos to tell your story, and share, share, share! The storyboard doesn't have to be high-tech — it's not about PowerPoint wizardry. Photographs of your flipcharts, or screenshots of your team's work on an online collaboration tool, with some supporting narrative will do. Storyboarding is a straightforward technique: It's just about telling a story!

What follows are our top tips for developing an excellent storyboard.

Keep It Brief

Where Lean Six Sigma practitioners are using their storyboards for certification we recommend that it consists of around 15 to 25 PowerPoint slides (having the storyboard in PowerPoint form makes it easy to share and easy to format). Too much information can overload the audience, so avoid anything that takes too long to read or talk through. You can of course, keep other more detailed versions, to share with different audiences.

Make It Visual

A picture paints a thousand words! Photos of flipcharts, photos of Process Stapling activities, and screenshots of your process map and they work brilliantly in storyboards. A "before and after" visual can also be very effective, for example in a 5S project or where spaghetti mapping has been used to track the movement in a process. A photograph of the project team is a good addition too. But remember, you must also . . .

Make It Flow

Just as a good story includes a narrative flow, so should a good storyboard. Storytellers achieve flow by connecting one sentence with another, helping us moving seamlessly from one idea to the next. Often when reviewing storyboards, we see some great looking and well executed "tools and techniques," but without any narrative to join them together, the storyboard feels like a collection of tools, not a story.

When you mapped the process, what were your key observations? And what did you go on to do about that? When you measured process performance what did you learn? Adding this sort of information to your storyboard helps connect the elements together and gives a much greater insight into the improvement journey.

Weave the Story Together with a Golden Thread

A *golden thread* is used by storytellers to link various parts of a story together. It's a central theme or key focus that the reader is reminded of at key points, and it gets nicely tied off at the end. This technique is used by writers from Charles Dickens to Stephen King and all the best TED Talkers you've seen. CTQs provide the golden thread for Lean Six Sigma practitioners.

CTQs are the Critical to Quality requirements of the customer. In other words, they're the things that matter most to them about the process in question. These should feature in every phase of the DMAIC project. In the Define phase, we identify the CTQs and these establish the focus of the improvement work to follow. We then measure CTQ performance in the Measure phase (along with some measurement of in-process and input variables to enable an understanding of cause and effect). In the Analyze phase, we identify what's causing the CTQ results and in the Improve phase we see how the causes can be addressed with appropriate and focused solutions. Finally, in the Control phase, we see the solutions being implemented in order improve CTQ performance, and we see what CTQ performance looks like as a result of the intervention. The CTQs will therefore be an integral part of the project Story.

Keep It Up to Date as You Go Along

Keeping the storyboard up to date as you work through the project promotes reflection and helps to consolidate learning. What has gone well? It's important to recognize those things and celebrate them. What could be better? Capture lessons learned as you go, and that can happen at the end of each project phase or at other points in the project. (For example, what did the team learn about Process Stapling? Or about data collection?) Taking time to reflect on progress and consolidate the storyboard stimulates ideas.

An up-to-date storyboard supports effective and efficient tollgate review meetings with the project sponsor, as well as discussion in between tollgates. It also facilitates communication with other stakeholders, including your team, your manager and your coach.

Finally, keeping the storyboard up to date saves you from the fate of having to document everything at the end of the project, when the details might be difficult to recall and the task seems massive. Your future self will thank you for keeping the storyboard up to date.

Don't Forget the "Happily Ever After" Part

Remember, a good story ties the golden thread up into a satisfying conclusion, and so should yours. Include details about the results achieved and the benefits attained. Remember to include information on all of the different types of benefit too, such as, for example, environmental benefits, compliance or reputational benefits, "feel good" benefits, as well as the "harder" (but easier to measure) benefits of time savings and cost savings.

Keep It Simple

The storyboard is clearly an important and valuable document — but it shouldn't be a complicated one. Too many acronyms and too much jargon can make the story difficult to read or understand, so keep it simple, and add a short glossary if it's really needed.

Abraham Lincoln's Gettysburg Address took only two minutes to deliver and used 246 words, most of them one or two syllables. The speaker before Lincoln spoke for two hours and used 13,607 words, yet hardly ever gets a mention! Simplicity makes for memorable messages.

On the same note, remember that the improvement project you're writing about is likely to have a "change" focus (therefore a people focus) as well as a technical focus. Content on activities such as stakeholder management, communication, and influencing is as important as the other tools and techniques — arguably more so.

Develop a One-Page Summary

As you and your organization go on to deliver more projects, you're likely to amass a lot of storyboards, and you might even develop a library! Consider creating a one-pager to capture key information about the projects so that you have an at-a-glance summary at your fingertips. Be sure to include all of the benefits delivered by the project.

Reflect on the Lessons Learned

Every project has its lessons. Take the time to reflect on your lessons learned and capture them in your project storyboard. They could include what went well, what didn't go well, and what could be done differently in the next project. Real learning happens when you start to "do" Lean Six Sigma.

Share, Share, Share!

Of course, the storyboard is a means to an end, and that is to tell your story. It has huge value beyond project management or "belt" certification. Tell stakeholders! Tell colleagues! Tell people at the coffee queue! Tell people at the end of a Zoom meeting! Distil some key messages from your storyboard and use them whenever you can to raise awareness, build support, and celebrate successes. We can shape the culture we want through the stories we tell.

Chapter **22**

Ten Pitfalls to Avoid

This chapter describes things that can go wrong with Lean Six Sigma so you can avoid the common pitfalls. Our experience (over 25 years!) of observing many different organizations has allowed us to build a bank of knowledge of what works and what doesn't. Read on and see whether these pitfalls are ones that are likely to affect you, and plan your approach wisely.

Jumping to Solutions

Many people seem hard-wired to jump straight to a solution when presented with a problem. In action movies, everything works out in the end and the hero makes the right decisions in a split second and lives on for another day (or film). Unfortunately, business life isn't quite the same: knee-jerk solutions can be costly and can fail to address the root cause of the problem.

Shooting from the hip — or, in business, the all too common "shooting from the lip" — without collecting and analyzing the facts and data isn't the best approach to solving complex business problems.

Lean Six Sigma involves understanding what the problem is and then going through several steps to gain a better understanding of it (Define, Measure), working down to the root causes (Analyze), looking at the various solution options and then choosing the most appropriate (Improve), and implementing the solution and holding the gains (Control).

Although this approach sounds straightforward and sensible, for many business executives, who people look to for instant answers, it's counter-intuitive.

Leaders and managers in your organization don't need to know everything about Lean Six Sigma, but an understanding of the principles is extremely beneficial, and encourages a pause between stimulus and response so that the problem and the causes can be understood before action is taken.

Coming Down with Analysis Paralysis

Getting the balance right is important. During the Analyze phase of a Lean Six Sigma project you may be tempted to get further and further into root cause analysis and lose sight of the primary reason for the improvement project, which is to make a difference and see positive changes in your business. Your team may get bogged down in the sheer volume of analysis options that can be carried out as they make more discoveries.

Knowing when to end the analysis and start the Improve phase can be difficult. Try regarding this decision as a judicial case and weigh up the balance of evidence for and against the "defendants" — the causes of the problem in your Lean Six Sigma project.

You're probably ready to move to the Improve stage if you answer yes to the following question:

> "Are we sure that we understand enough about the process, problem and causes to develop effective solutions?"

And no to this one:

> "Is the value of additional data and analysis worth the extra cost in time, resources and momentum?"

The project sponsor has a key role in ensuring that you keep the business interests at the forefront when answering these questions and in steering the team ahead on the business track.

REMEMBER

Achieving Six Sigma — 3.4 defects per 1 million opportunities — may be an aspiration, but you are highly unlikely to achieve it in one project. (Refer to Chapter 1 for calculating Process Sigma values.) Moving from 2 Sigma to 3 Sigma and then onto 4 Sigma in your Lean Six Sigma projects is entirely normal. You'll also find that it takes a lot more effort as you climb further up the Process Sigma scale.

Small bite-sized projects move your performance in the right direction, so be prepared to accept just a small increase in the Process Sigma value of your processes.

Falling into Common Project Traps

Want to know how to ensure project failure? Try a negative brainstorming technique: it's a great icebreaker at the start of a project and is certain to get your team bouncing with ideas. Instead of brainstorming ideas to make the project a success, you brainstorm the opposite: "How can we ensure project disaster?" You'll be amazed at the number of suggestions the team comes up with! Then you can turn these negative thoughts into positive ones. You'll end up with a really positive set of suggestions based on practical experience of what really can make projects fail and how to avoid these pitfalls.

For starters, we discuss some common project traps here.

Methodology madness problems include the following:

>> Not using a structured and planned approach

>> Predetermining your solution

>> Providing poorly managed handovers

>> Allowing the Control phase to be weak, thus failing to hold the gain

Scope scandals are as follows:

>> Running too many projects at the same time

>> Undertaking too large a project

>> Having a goal that isn't measurable or is too vague

>> Ignoring "outside-in" customer focus

>> Failing to link the goal to a real business need

>> Allowing the project scope to keep growing

Team turmoil to keep an eye on:

>> Creating a team with the wrong mix of skills or functional representation (for example, not getting the finance or HR departments in when needed)

- » Offering inadequate training
- » Making a poor choice of team leader
- » Failing to agree on the time requirements of the team
- » Having no shared vision of success

Problems related to lack of support include these:

- » Using unsupportive key stakeholders
- » Having no active project sponsor or champion
- » Running competing projects or projects with conflicting objectives
- » Allowing poor leadership behavior
- » Failing to allow enough time to run the project systematically

Stifling the Program Before You've Started

Chances are, some people in your organization don't share your vision and are all too keen to stamp on your program before you get it off the ground. Here are a few comments we've heard people say when stifling a Lean Six Sigma program:

- » "This is just common sense."
- » "Our place is different."
- » "It costs too much."
- » "We're all too busy to do that."
- » "Let's get back to reality."
- » "Why change? It's still okay."
- » "We're not ready for this yet."
- » "It's a good thought but highly impractical."
- » "Not that crazy idea again!"
- » "We've always done it this way."
- » "We're no worse than our competitors!"

Chapter 6 covers the people aspects of Lean Six Sigma. What can you do to build acceptance?

Ignoring Change Management

Many traditional Lean Six Sigma training courses cover the "hard stuff," such as the statistical techniques, the DMAIC methodology, and an extensive array of tools and techniques, but they don't deal with the people side. You need to focus on the people side if you're going to build acceptance for change.

Sometimes Lean Six Sigma practitioners try to run projects that focus on statistical tools and blind people with newly learned expressions, and then they're disappointed when their stakeholders don't accept the idea.

REMEMBER

$$E = Q \times A$$

The *quality* (Q) of the solution that comes from the use of the "hard" tools and the *acceptance* (A) of the solution that comes from the "soft" tools are equally important. You need both quality and acceptance to win support and achieve an *effective* (E) outcome. See Chapter 6 for more insight into this issue.

From our experience the people side of projects is often the most difficult.

Getting Complacent

Underestimating the amount of energy you need to make your Lean Six Sigma program a success is a major pitfall. Complacency sets in surprisingly quickly if you don't drive and lead your program with a sense of urgency. You need an active Lean Six Sigma deployment program manager, with support from a senior executive, to keep your program alive, relevant and on the business agenda.

Organizational changes are frequent in many businesses. We've seen Lean Six Sigma programs wither when a deployment program manager is diverted to internal organizational politics. Ensuring that the senior executive team is actively involved is important. Institutionalizing the whole approach is key, so that Lean Six Sigma becomes part of the "way we do things around here."

Thinking That You're Already Doing It

A quick skim through the Lean Six Sigma literature or rapid overview of your processes may lead you to believe that your organization is "already doing it." Many managers think that they already solve problems using a systematic problem-solving process, but often they don't think about or test solution options properly before putting them into action.

You may think, "We already use process flowcharts." Many organizations do use this technique, but often without first understanding the true requirements of the process from the customer's perspective. Unless you adopt Lean Six Sigma in a structured way, you won't be able to fully utilize the power of process-mapping techniques to really get under the surface of how your existing processes work.

Genuine senior management buy-in for this kind of "peripheral" process-mapping activity is also unusual. Isolated cases do exist in organizations as part of a cottage industry of enthusiasts who are doing their best but operating outside the scope of a serious senior management-led initiative. A well-designed Lean Six Sigma program builds on existing knowledge and legitimizes improvement work into a framework that involves everyone and introduces a common set of tools across the organization.

Believing the Myths

A whole series of myths has developed around the use of Lean Six Sigma. For Lean Six Sigma to work in practice, you need to dispel the following ideas:

>> **Lean Six Sigma is all we need.** No. Lean Six Sigma can, and should, be integrated with other approaches.

>> **Lean Six Sigma is just for manufacturing or production improvement.** No. All processes can be improved. Lean Six Sigma is used successfully in transaction and service processes.

>> **Lean Six Sigma is just about statistical tools and measures.** No. Lean Six Sigma actually involves cultural change.

>> **Lean Six Sigma is just about individuals and experts.** No. To work best, Lean Six Sigma involves everyone in a team effort, including senior executives.

Doing the Wrong Things Right

Most of us want to do the right things right. Process analysis is a great tool to show us what we're doing in practice and help us answer the questions "Why?" and "Are we doing this step correctly?"

According to systems theorist, Russ Ackoff:

The righter you do the wrong thing, the wronger you become; if you make a mistake doing the wrong things and correct it, you become wronger; if you make a mistake doing the right thing and correct it, you become righter. Therefore it is better to do the right thing wrong than the wrong thing right.

In fact, you have four options:

1. **Doing the right thing right. Most people want to do this.**

    Serving great food and providing top-notch service in a stylish restaurant is an example.

2. **Doing the right thing wrong. Apply the tools to fix the problem.**

    Imagine great service and a beautiful restaurant but really bad food. Listen to the voice of the customer, recognize that the poor quality of the food is the key driver of customer dissatisfaction and tackle the root causes of the problem. That is, you analyze the process, discover the critical factors underlying the causes of the problem and solve those. Often problems can be resolved simply; in this case, maybe by using less salt.

3. **Doing the wrong thing right. This is non-value-adding.**

    To continue the example, you concentrate on making the restaurant look even better but still serve awful food. That is, you don't find out what the real customer requirements are, jump to the wrong solution and spend unnecessary money.

4. **Doing the wrong thing wrong. Working to get this right is pointless.**

    For example, spending lots of money restyling the restaurant when customers actually liked the earlier style.

The ultimate danger is kicking off a Lean Six Sigma project to fix the situation in option 4 above — and still ending up doing the wrong thing!

Overtraining

Clearly, getting trained up in Lean Six Sigma is important and a well thought out training plan needs to form part of the overall deployment program. But training works best when it's delivered "just in time" and at the right level.

An organization just starting to use Lean Six Sigma will be full of opportunities for process improvement that can be tackled using the tools learned on a good Green Belt course. Ideally, this six-day training can be split into three smaller modules of two days each, wrapped around a real project being carried out to ensure the training is delivered at the right level and at the right time to fit into the life of the project.

Avoid the pitfall of believing that Black Belt training must be "better" than Green Belt training and therefore sending people on a full Black Belt course, complete with advanced statistical training, before starting any projects. Start simply, develop the basic skills, provide expert coaching support to the Green Belts, run initial projects quickly to deliver tangible benefits to the organization, and then select the right candidates to be trained in the Lean Six Sigma advanced tools when needed.

Training people at an advanced level too soon is a waste of money and will probably deter people from using the approach.

Chapter **23**

Ten (Plus One) Places to Go for Help

P lenty of help, guidance, and knowledge are available to support you in using Lean Six Sigma. In this chapter, we show you where to find all the advice and resources you need.

Your Colleagues

A well-managed Lean Six Sigma program relies on teamwork and support being available for everyone involved across the organization through an internal network. Support can be offered through a spectrum of different colored "belts"; for example, Black Belts supporting Green Belts. (See Chapter 2 for more on how the martial arts relate to Lean Six Sigma.) Ideally, Black Belts will be able to call on support from Master Black Belts who are professional experts in Lean Six Sigma. If you haven't got these "in house," this support may be outsourced to a specialist.

The "belt" terminology isn't mandatory. Many organizations just use terms such as "practitioner" and "expert" instead of Green Belt and Black Belt.

Being able to access this kind of support network is important. You probably already know that a big difference exists between using a tool in a training environment and operating in the real world, where your first port of call for help is usually your own colleagues.

Your Sponsor

Every project deserves a good sponsor, or "champion" (described in detail in Chapter 19). When things get tough, as most projects do from time to time, your project sponsor is a good source of help. Your sponsor supports your project team, helps unblock project barriers and assists you when you need buy-in at a more senior level in your organization.

Other Organizations

Every year, the number of organizations deploying Lean Six Sigma increases. Over time, the combination of tools and techniques may have changed, but the essentials of using a systematic method, focusing on understanding customer requirements and improving processes are well tried and tested. Visiting some other organizations and learning from their experiences is well worthwhile. You may not be able to look deep inside your competitors' businesses, but you can discover lots by visiting similar-sized companies in different sectors. Industry and government special interest groups are a good source of help and often arrange visits for groups to observe companies at work. If you have the chance to visit a Toyota or Ricoh plant, for example, in just a few hours you'll learn a lot about the cultural approach that forms the basis for continuous improvement and Lean thinking in general.

The Internet

Lots of sites are aimed at Lean Six Sigma devotees. Just for fun, here's a snippet of trivia: if you search the web using the expression "Six Sigma Pink Floyd," you discover that Roger Waters set up a band in 1964 called Sigma 6 before forming Pink Floyd a year later. That was 20 years before Motorola came up with the idea of Six Sigma. Progressive rock indeed!

Following are some of our favorite websites with extensive articles and features devoted to Lean Six Sigma:

>> `www.agile.business.org`: The Agile Business Consortium site includes access to the latest research into business agility, case studies, and other resources.

>> `www.asq.org`: The site for the American Society for Quality, offering very comprehensive online resources and publications.

>> `www.bqf.org.uk`: The BQF exists to enable excellence in UK organizations. The site contains information on training and provides access to a variety of interesting events and online workshops.

>> `www.catalystconsulting.co.uk`: The authors' own website, regularly updated with new articles, access to an extensive online learning resource area (Business Improvement Zone) and some free to use statistical tools.

>> `www.efqm.org`: Full of useful material and case studies.

>> `www.goldratt.com`: This website focuses on the theory of constraints, an approach for managing and reducing process bottlenecks.

>> `www.isssp.com`: Dedicated to Lean Six Sigma, with plenty of articles.

>> `www.isixsigma.com`: The number one (US-focused) Six Sigma website, with bulletin boards, job ads, and links. For addicts only.

>> `www.leanenterprise.org.uk`: LERC was formed in 1994, bringing together the benchmarking and Lean production work of Daniel Jones (together with James Womack of MIT) and the work of Peter Hines on supplier development and materials management.

>> `www.leanproduction.com`: A useful website providing lots of information about Lean, Kaizen, and the theory of constraints.

>> `www.nist.gov/baldrige`: This website provides information about the Baldrige Model and award.

>> `www.processexcellencenetwork.com`: The Process Excellence Network, a division of IQPC, provides access to a wide range of content for Process Excellence practitioners.

>> `www.qfdi.org`: The site for the Quality Function Deployment (QFD) Institute. QFD is an approach to really understanding customer requirements and linking them to processes, products, and services. QFD is often used when Lean Six Sigma companies want to design new products and services. QFD is an additional tool used in Design for Six Sigma (DfSS).

>> `www.quality.org`: The website for the Chartered Quality Institute (CQI).

- >> `www.qualitydigest.com`: A useful online magazine on quality.

- >> `www.shingoprize.org`: This website provides information about the Shingo Model and award.

Social Media

Here's a resource that continues to grow and provide a wealth of information. Put your keywords into a search engine, for example "statistical process control," and you'll find all sorts of sites to look at and videos to watch.

Maybe you can follow someone on Twitter too, or perhaps you can start something yourself!

LinkedIn is an excellent source of information related to Lean Six Sigma transformations. You can access several Lean Six Sigma groups to network with practitioners and champions.

Networks and Associations

You can find all sorts of networks and associations relating to Lean Six Sigma. Some networks offer online and offline services to encourage collaboration and knowledge exchange between members, and they often hold regular members' meetings.

National and regional quality associations such as the American Society for Quality (ASQ), the European Foundation for Quality Management (EFQM) and the British Quality Foundation (BQF) provide opportunities to share good, and not so good, practice through meetings, visits to businesses, conferences, workshops and online resources, although these aren't dedicated purely to Lean Six Sigma. The CQI provides an extensive quality-focused knowledge library to members offering insights into the approaches used in different organizations.

Conferences

Lean Six Sigma conferences are a regular feature of the conference calendar these days, both online and in person. They provide a range of speakers, smaller workshops, opportunities for networking, and informal discussions regarding every aspect of Lean Six Sigma. Whether you're just starting out or want to keep up with the latest thinking and new developments, conferences and webinars are a great source of information.

Books

You can find a wealth of books on the individual aspects of Lean and Six Sigma, and a few on Lean Six Sigma. Here are some of our favorites:

>> *Practitioner's Guide to Statistics and Lean Six Sigma for Process Improvements* by Mike J. Harry, Prem S. Mann, Ofelia C. De Hodgins, Richard L. Hulbert and Christopher J. Lacke (John Wiley & Sons, Inc.): An 800-page excellent book covering all aspects of Lean Six Sigma in detail. A great reference book for the serious practitioner.

>> *Lean Six Sigma for Leaders* by Martin Brenig-Jones and Jo Dowdall: A practical guide for leaders highlighting that there's more to Lean Six Sigma than process improvement projects. It includes some fascinating case studies.

>> *Implementing Six Sigma* by Forrest Breyfogle III (Wiley-Interscience): A comprehensive reference textbook.

>> *Integrated Enterprise Excellence*, Vols. I, II and III by Forrest Breyfogle III (Bridgeway Books): You can't get better than this if you want to become a serious aficionado.

>> *Making Six Sigma Last* by George Eckes (John Wiley & Sons, Inc.): Cultural aspects of making it happen and succeed.

>> *Quantitative Approaches in Business Studies*, 8th edition, by Clare Morris (FT/Prentice Hall): An academic textbook offering a good foundation in statistical methods in business.

>> *SPC in the Office* by Mal Owen and John Morgan (Greenfield): Full of useful case studies about using control charts in the office.

>> *The Lean Six Sigma Improvement Journey* by John Morgan: Light-hearted coverage of each tool (of which there are many), with the aid of color-coded illustrations, available on the UK Amazon site.

>> *The Six Sigma Revolution* by George Eckes (John Wiley & Sons, Inc.): The principles of Six Sigma.

>> *The Six Sigma Way*, 2nd edition, by Peter Pande, Robert Neuman and Roland Cavanagh (McGraw-Hill): Good general overview and how-to.

- *The Six Sigma Way Team Fieldbook* by Peter Pande, Robert Neuman and Roland Cavanagh (McGraw-Hill): Practical implementation guide.

- *The Machine That Changed the World* by James Womack, Daniel Jones and Daniel Roos (Simon & Schuster): Latest re-issue of the classic text on Lean business.

- *The Toyota Way: 14 Management Principles from the World's Greatest Manufacturer*, Jeffrey Liker (McGraw-Hill): The management principles behind the Toyota approach. Very readable and helpful.

- *Lean Six Sigma and Minitab: The Complete Toolbox Guide for Business Improvement* (4th edition): This Minitab-based guide provides practical instructions and many screenshots.

- Our book, *Lean Six Sigma for Business Transformation For Dummies* (John Wiley & Sons, Inc.) devoted to linking transformational strategy to action through the use of Lean Six Sigma in a systematic manner.

Periodicals

Several journals are devoted to Lean and Six Sigma and related areas including:

- *International Journal of Six Sigma and Competitive Advantage:* Stays at the forefront of Six Sigma developments.

- *Business Process Management Journal:* Insights into driving efficiency through a process approach, including process improvement and change management.

- *Quality World:* The magazine of the Chartered Quality Institute in the UK, with regular features on Lean Six Sigma.

Software

You can certainly start down the Lean Six Sigma road without having to invest in specialist software, but as your journey proceeds you may want to enhance your toolkit with statistical and other software. In this section, we mention a few of our essentials.

Process mapping is best done on brown paper, or through an online collaborative working tool (see below). If you decide to use software for process flowcharting, consider Visio, IBM Blueworks, or iGrafx.

Statistical analysis

Most everyday mortals use only a fraction of the full capability of their spreadsheet program such as Excel or Numbers. These programs are good at statistical analysis, but because they weren't designed specifically for this purpose, producing even the most basic Pareto chart without help from a kind soul who's produced a template for this purpose is surprisingly challenging. You can access some simple tools via the Catalyst Consulting website.

You can also find several plug-ins for your spreadsheet program to help you perform Pareto analysis, and slice and dice your data quickly and easily without having to design your own template.

Microsoft provides a neat data analysis "Toolpak" for Excel, which has been extended with the latest versions. For more complex statistical analysis, try the Excel plug-in SigmaXL, which lets you produce a variety of displays including SIPOCs, cause and effect diagrams, failure mode and effects analysis, and several types of control chart, as well as a comprehensive range of statistical tools.

Most Black Belts and Master Black Belts favor Minitab Statistical Software. This package has been around for many years and is also a favorite of universities and colleges teaching statistics. Minitab is a very comprehensive statistical analysis package designed for serious statistical analysis. Don't try it at home without some serious training as part of an Advanced Green Belt or full Black Belt course.

JMP Statistical Discovery Software is another package which can be used in the world of Lean Six Sigma. It links statistics to a highly visual graphic representation, allowing you to visually explore the relationships between process inputs and outputs, and then to identify the key process variables.

Simulation

For more advanced statistical and predictive modeling, take a look at Crystal Ball from Oracle. This software is good for forecasting, simulation, and evaluating optimization options. An alternative software-modeling tool is SIMUL8, which can be used for planning, design, and optimization of manufacturing or transactional service systems. These models allow testing of scenarios in a virtual environment and are often concerned with cost, time and inventory.

Deployment management

For large-scale deployments, consider forming a project library and use tracking software to help you and your colleagues across the organization manage and report on projects. A number of software systems are designed specifically for this purpose, and they are well worth investigating as your deployment grows across the organization.

Online collaboration tools

We have been working with some fantastic apps that allow the tools and techniques of Lean Six Sigma to be used "virtually" when it hasn't been possible to use them face to face. These tools include Mural, Miro, Stormboard, and Jamboard. In some ways in fact, working virtually has led to more engagement! For example, with these apps, everyone can contribute to a process mapping session, so there's no single scribe who is responsible for writing the process steps down onto a sticky note. Everyone can join in!

Training and Consulting Companies

A wide range of specialist training and consulting companies provide services for clients in the Lean Six Sigma arena. In your quest for training, you'll find a few global players and lots of smaller specialists and one-person bands.

TIP

When you choose a supplier, try to use the quality × acceptance equation that we describe in Chapter 6. You want your trainer to have excellent technical skills, but also consider how well they'd work with your organization. Will your organization's culture accept the trainer? Will the trainer instill confidence and provide all the services you require?

In our experience, few organizations bother to check suppliers' references. But unlike choosing a partner or spouse, in business asking previous clients how well the partnership worked is fine! Working over a long period with a training and consulting company is a bit like a marriage: Shared values are a good foundation for belief, integrity, respect, trust, and honesty.

Index

benefit reviews, 38–39, 303–304, 306–307, 309–310

benefit-effort matrix for screening projects, 294

bias
  in customer interviews, 63
  in qualitative research, 61
  in voice of customer information, 65

bimodal distribution on histograms, 150–151

Black Belts, 42

books, as help resource, 331–332

bots, 216

bottlenecks, 28, 91, 179, 189. *See also* theory of constraints

brain
  communicating with, 103
  impact of change on, 98

brainstorming, 155–156, 194, 321

brainwriting, 195–196

Brown, Paul, 61

buffer, building, 182–183

business benefits, confirming in benefits review, 306–307

Business Black Belts, 42

business process robotics, 216

C

candidate improvement projects, generating list of, 288–291

capability indices, 145–149

capacity CTQs, 68

Carlzon, Jan, 94–95

Catalyst Consulting website, 333

CATS (Change as Three Steps) model, 102–103

cause and effect, 116, 159, 294–295

cause and effect (fishbone) diagram, 154–155

cell manufacturing (autonomous working), 185–187

certification processes, 42

chain, identifying weakest link in, 180

champion, project, 287, 295–296, 307, 320, 328

Change as Three Steps (CATS) model, 102–103

change management
  assumption busting, 105–108
  coping with change, 101–103

elements of change model, 106–107

gaining acceptance for change, 98–99

ignoring, as pitfall to avoid, 323

impact of change, 98

and Improve phase, 304

overview, 22–23

status quo, sizing up, 99–101

understanding people, 97–98

vision, creating, 103–105

change phase, iceberg model, 102–103

changeover time, 87

chaos state of process, 144, 145

characteristics and measures room, QFD, 226

Cheat Sheet, explained, 3

check sheets, 128–129

checklists to support projects
  Analyze phase, 302–303
  benefit reviews, 303–304, 306–307, 309–310
  Control phase, 307–309
  Define phase, 298–300
  Improve phase, 304–306
  Measure phase, 300–302
  overview, 297–298

Chi-Square test, 163

Cho, Fujio, 9, 10

circles, in process mapping, 80

clear scope, importance of, 34

collaboration tools, online, 334

collaborative work, in Agile, 249

colleagues, as help resources, 327–328

collecting data
  confirming root causes, 158–159
  deciding what to measure, 113
  developing plan for
    clear operational definitions, creating, 116–117
    collecting data, 128–130
    identifying ways to improve approach, 130–131
    measures, agreeing on, 114–116
    overview, 114
    sampling plan, developing, 120–128
    validating measurement system, 118–120
  importance of good data, 112
  managing by fact, 29, 111–113

O

observation of customers, 64–65

observations in Value Stream Maps, 93

Observe step, Design Thinking, 239–240

Ohno, Taiichi, 9, 84, 167, 171, 216

on the brink state, of process, 144, 145

one piece flow (single piece flow), 11–12, 28, 184

1-10-100 rule, 207

1.5 sigma shift, 21–22

one-dimensionals (satisfiers), in Kano model, 56–57

one-page summary, of storyboard, 316

online collaboration tools, 334

operational definitions, 116–117, 130

operational excellence. *See also* process management

  creating culture of continuous improvement, 276

  engaging team, 274–276

  Leader Standard Work, 272–274

  overview, 269, 272

  right methodology, using, 276

opportunities

  assessing, 171

  quantifying, 38, 303–304

  in Value Stream Maps, 93

Oracle Crystal Ball, 333

Orange Belts, 42

organizational culture, 277

organizations, as help resources, 328

organizing workplace

  5S method, 209

  overview, 208

  red-tag exercises, 210

  visual management, 210–212

output measures, in data collection plan, 114, 116, 117

outputs, in SIPOCs, 50, 52

outside-in thinking, 58, 70, 71

overprocessing, 175–176

overproduction, 12, 172, 175, 183

overtraining, 325–326

P

paired comparisons, 70, 199

Pareto, Vilfredo, 59

Pareto charts, 151–152

Pareto Principle (80:20 rule), 59, 151

Patagonia, 177

Patton, George, 97

peaks and troughs, avoiding, 213–215

PEMME (People, Equipment, Method, Materials and Environment), 45–46

people

  assumption busting, 105–108

  coping with change, 101–103

  elements of change model, 106–107

  gaining acceptance for change, 98–99

  impact of change on, 98

  involving and equipping in process, 29

  in Lean thinking, 10

  manager role related to, 284

  in processes, 45

  skills waste, 176–177

  status quo, sizing up, 99–101

  swim lane charts, 81–82

  understanding, 97–98

  vision, creating, 103–105

People, Equipment, Method, Materials and Environment (PEMME), 45–46

perfect flow, 189

performance, measuring using customer-focused measures, 70–71

performance benchmarking, 228

periodicals, as help resource, 332

persona map, 239

pictures, generating ideas with, 195

Piggly Wiggly, 8

pilot design, in DMADV, 222

piloting ideas, 201

pinchpoints. *See* theory of constraints

pitfalls to avoid

  analysis paralysis, 320–321

  believing myths, 324

process operators, 291, 296
process owners, 57, 269, 270
process performance review meetings, 211–212
process sampling, 122–123
Process Sigma values, 18–22
Process Stapling, 28, 74–76, 168–169
process suboptimization, 175, 180
process variables, 159
processes. *See also* projects, Lean Six Sigma
  applying Lean Six Sigma to, 282–283
  and appropriateness of Lean Six Sigma, 291–295
  basics of, 45–46
  capability indices, 145–149
  capability of in DMADV/DfSS, 220
  cause and effect analysis, 294–295
  drawing picture of, 49–53
  error proofing, 206–208
  examining state of, in control charts, 143–145
  Failure Mode and Effects Analysis, 206
  generating list of candidate projects, 290–291
  greener, 177
  identifying internal and external customers, 47–48
  leveling work, 213–215
  manager role related to, 284
  matching voice of customer to, 115
  overview, 45
  pinpointing elements of, 46–47
  Robotic Process Automation, 216
  in SIPOCs, 50, 51
  stable, 134, 139
  standardizing, 270–271
  value-add/non-value-add analysis, 169–171
  voice of the process, 115, 139
processing time, measuring for process mapping, 83–84
processing time (unit time/activity time)
  measuring for process mapping, 83
  in value-add/non-value-add analysis, 169–170
product backlog, in Agile, 250
product families, identifying, 187–188
Product Owner, 252
production cycle, managing

batches, problems related to, 184–185
  push versus pull production, 183–184
  single piece flow, moving to, 184
Project Charter, 298–299
project leader, 295–296
Project Management, 24–25
project sponsors (champions), 287, 295–296, 307, 320, 328
projects, Lean Six Sigma
  checklists to support
    Analyze phase, 302–303
    benefit reviews, 303–304, 306–307, 309–310
    Control phase, 307–309
    Define phase, 298–300
    Improve phase, 304–306
    Measure phase, 300–302
    overview, 297–298
  common traps to avoid, 321–322
  deciding on appropriateness of, 291–295
  deciding on which approach fits, 294–295
  generating list of candidates, 288–291
  prioritizing, 292–294
  setting up, 295–296
  storyboards for, tips for creating, 313–317
proportion defective, 127
Prototype step, Design Thinking, 243–244
psychological safety, in Agile, 249
Pugh Matrix (controlled convergence), 232–234
pull production, 12, 28, 182, 183–184
push production, 182, 183–184
Put to other uses step, SCAMPER method, 243
p-value, hypothesis tests, 164

Q

qualitative benchmarking, 229
qualitative research, 61
Quality Function Deployment (QFD)
  characteristics and measures, 226
  competitive benchmarking, 227–229
  competitive comparison, 225–226, 227
  correlation, 229–230
  customer needs, 225–226

W

X

Y

About the Authors

Martin Brenig-Jones is Chief Executive of Catalyst Consulting Ltd. Prior to joining Catalyst, Martin was Head of Quality at the global telecommunications company, BT, one of the world's leading communications services companies, where he had responsibility for quality and business excellence across the group. Martin has also been a member of the General Committee of Lloyd's Register, on LRQA's technical committee, and served on the executive board of the British Quality Foundation prior to moving into business consulting. He has been a senior assessor for the UK Excellence Award and the European Quality Award. During the last 20 years, Martin has focused on the application of Lean Six Sigma to help organizations of all sizes and sectors to improve their operations. He has trained and coached more than a thousand people in Lean Six Sigma and business-improvement techniques working mainly across Europe and occasionally in the United States, Asia, and Africa. He has worked with organizations in a diverse range of sectors including IT, transport, computer manufacturing, local government, police, health, aerospace, rail, telecoms, and financial services.

Martin studied electronic engineering at the University of Liverpool and has a postgraduate diploma in management. He is a member of the Institute of Engineering and Technology, and in his earlier career, he worked in telecommunications, software, and systems development. Martin is a keen photographer and videographer, and although now living in England, he is a Welshman at heart and continues to support the Welsh Rugby team as well as being a Liverpool FC fan.

Jo Dowdall is a Consulting Partner at Catalyst Consulting, where she delivers training, coaching, and consulting services to a host of clients, across a range of sizes, sectors and countries. Jo has worked in Continuous Improvement for over 20 years and loves making business improvement relatable and accessible.

Jo's Continuous Improvement career started in Quality. She admits falling into this by accident rather than design — being recommended to apply for a Quality Coordinator role after applying for and failing to get the job of an HR Coordinator. This was a positive move for Jo, both because she discovered her passion for Quality and business improvement, and because she would have made a lousy HR Coordinator.

In her next role Jo led a regional Excellence Awards program. She was responsible for developing the assessment framework, training assessors, supporting organizations through the process, and undertaking lots of assessments.

Jo is also an experienced Lean Six Sigma practitioner, having learned firsthand what to do (and what not to do) to deliver sustainable process improvements as well as build acceptance for change. She has a postgraduate diploma in Quality.

Jo loves writing books and articles about Lean Six Sigma and improvement. She writes poetry too, and once attempted a poem about the Improve phase of a DMAIC project. That was a one-off.

Authors' Acknowledgments

From Martin:

First, I must say a massive thank you to Jo Dowdall, who has stepped into some big shoes taking on the role as coauthor on this particular book. Jo has done an outstanding job and given the book a total refresh. She always has a smile and has such positive motivational energy. It has been a pleasure to work with you, Jo, on our second book together after *LSS for Leaders*. What's next?

I must also thank everyone at Catalyst. What an inspirational supportive and brilliant team! If there were a book called *Lean Six Sigma for Experts*, they would have to be the authors because their knowledge, experience, and expertise go deeper than you can imagine. True experts and a privilege to work with every one of them.

I would also like to thank my clients who come from a very wide range of interesting sectors from organizations across the world and who have given me the experience that I have tried to distill into this book.

I also want to thank my four brilliant children, Jo, Laurence, Alex, and Oliver, and now their own growing families. They have always been so patient with the bod who is always seeing "process improvement opportunities," particularly annoying when on holiday. Mind you I am starting to notice some of my traits in them. Keep it up kids.

Finally, I want to thank Di, the greatest wife, friend, mother, and teacher in the world who lives with someone who spends far too much time doing what some people call "work" but which I find hard to distinguish from pleasure and leisure.

From Jo:

Thanks so much Martin for involving me in the development of this book. You are such fun to work with that sometimes I forget you are the boss! Thank you for your encouragement. Thanks too to my excellent Catalyst colleagues for their support. In particular, thank you Moore Allison, Mark Jones, and James Dwan for your guidance and specialist input to the chapters on Measurement and Analysis, DfSS, Design Thinking, and Agile.

Our dearly missed friend, colleague, and mentor John Morgan played a huge role in developing the previous editions of *Lean Six Sigma For Dummies*. I could never fill his shoes but am grateful for the opportunity to contribute to the 4th edition. Thank you, John.

I'd also like to thank Elizabeth Stilwell at Wiley for smoothly and expertly guiding us through the process for writing this book. Huge thanks are also due to Tim Gallan for his editing skills and patience. Thank you, Tim. And also thanks to Jim Alloway for his technical review.

Most of all, I'd like to thank my family for their patience, love, and support. Working on the book during the global pandemic could have been horrendous. I am so lucky to have been "locked down" with the most nurturing, loving, and fun people I know. Thank you Ant. Thank you Buck.

Publisher's Acknowledgments

Acquisitions Editor: Elizabeth Stilwell

Development Editor: Tim Gallan

Technical Reviewer: Jim Alloway

Production Editor: Tamilmani Varadharaj

Cover Image: © GaudiLab/Shutterstock